Share Trading, Fraud and the Crash of 1929

A Biography of Clarence Hatry

This is the first comprehensive biography of Clarence Charles Hatry, 1888–1965, an enigmatic and charismatic public figure. Hatry was the son of Jewish immigrant parents who became a company promoter and whose companies collapsed in 1929, leading to a crash on the London stock exchange. He was brought down by a desperate fraud. At his trial three months later, the judge said that he could not imagine a worse crime.

Analysing transactions in detail, the book reveals Hatry's brilliance as a manipulator and a world-class networker and persuader. It also demonstrates his vain belief in his ability to overcome any risks and his insecurity that led him to surround himself with sycophants who would not challenge his ideas. It shows how others used Hatry to make money, and, as he destroyed himself, as a scapegoat who distracted from the City's failings. Despite his deepest ambitions, he remained an outsider.

Until now there has been no full biography of Clarence Hatry, which may be attributable to the lack of records, as his business papers are believed all to have been destroyed. This comprehensive biography is based on examination of the memoirs of Hatry's contemporaries, the archives and records which they and their companies preserved, and press reports of Hatry's activities.

Marking the 90th anniversary of Hatry's collapse, this book will be important reading for academics and researchers looking to gain a greater understanding of the context of the 1929 crash, or of financial crises generally.

Chris Swinson is a Visiting Fellow at Durham University Business School and a former President of the Institute of Chartered Accountants in England and Wales. Chris spent a large part of his professional career investigating frauds and their consequences.

Financial History
Edited by **Farley Grubb** and **Anne L. Murphy**

The Globalization of Merchant Banking before 1850
The Case of Huth & Co.
Manuel Llorca-Jaña

Monetary Statecraft in Brazil
1808–2014
Kurt Mettenheim

Banking Modern America
Studies in Regulatory History
Edited by Jesse Stiller

Money, Politics and Power
Banking and Public Finance in Wartime England, 1694–96
Richard A. Kleer

Regulation of the London Stock Exchange
Share Trading, Fraud and Reform 1914–1945
Chris Swinson

Monetary Plurality in Local, Regional and Global Economies
Edited by Georgina M. Gómez

Share Trading, Fraud and the Crash of 1929
A Biography of Clarence Hatry
Chris Swinson

The Origins of Modern Banking in Spain
Monetary Plurality and Local Monopolies
Edited by Carles Sudrià and Yolanda Blasco-Martel

For more information about this series, please visit www.routledge.com/series/FINHIS

Share Trading, Fraud and the Crash of 1929

A Biography of Clarence Hatry

Chris Swinson

Routledge
Taylor & Francis Group
LONDON AND NEW YORK

First published 2019
by Routledge
2 Park Square, Milton Park, Abingdon, Oxon OX14 4RN

and by Routledge
605 Third Avenue, New York, NY 10017

First issued in paperback 2020

Routledge is an imprint of the Taylor & Francis Group, an informa business

British Library Cataloguing-in-Publication Data
A catalogue record for this book is available from the British Library

Library of Congress Cataloging-in-Publication Data
A catalog record has been requested for this book

ISBN 13: 978-0-367-73100-7 (pbk)
ISBN 13: 978-0-367-13500-3 (hbk)
ISBN 13: 978-0-429-02682-9 (ebk)

Typeset in Bembo
by Swales & Willis, Exeter, Devon, UK

For
Timothy, Elly and Imogen

'Clarence Hatry was a clever outsider, whose moneymaking alchemy – mixing genuinely productive innovations with tax avoidance and sailing legally close to the wind – attracted many City insiders and business vendors. In 1921 it made a peerage seem attainable. His final resort to fraud in 1929 brought a lengthy prison sentence, yet still left him with loyal sympathisers. Dr Swinson is the shrewd, engaged and balanced biographer that such a complex larger-than-life character requires: this will be the definitive study'.

– *Leslie Hannah*, Professor Emeritus of Business History,
London School of Economics, UK

'Chris Swinson's deep research has produced a biography of Clarence Hatry that is not only authoritative in its unravelling of corporate misdeeds; it is also an elegant study of Hatry's social milieu and a light-and-shade portrait of a fascinating fraudster'.

– *Martin Vander Weyer*, Business Editor, *The Spectator*

'A well-written page turner about a larger-than-life company promoter whose life story certainly beats fiction hands down'.

– *Janette Rutterford*, Professor of
Financial Management, Open University, UK

Contents

Abbreviations

AAMC	Associated Automatic Machine Corporation Limited
AIL	Agricultural Industries Limited
BAC	British Automatic Company Limited
BST	British Shareholders Trust Limited
C&GS	Corporation & General Securities Limited
CIPFA	Chartered Institute of Public Finance and Accountancy
DUA	Dundee University Archive
IMTA	Institute of Municipal Treasurers and Accountants
JIL	Jute Industries Limited
LBA	Lloyds Bank Archives
LMA	London Metropolitan Archive
LML	Leyland Motors Limited
LSX	London Stock Exchange
NLA	National Library of Australia
PFS	PFS Limited (Profit from Steel)
PPC	Photomaton Parent Corporation Limited
TNA	The National Archives
VMH	VMH Limited (Violet Marguerite Hatry)

People

Name	*Description*
Allibone, Abraham Cory	Town clerk of the Borough of Wakefield.
Andrews, Emily	Coventry Patmore's first wife.
Astor, Colonel J.J.	Sold house at St Margaret's Bay near Dover to Hatry, 1946.
Avory, Sir Horace	Judge at Clarence Hatry's trial.
Baldwin, Stanley	Conservative politician and prime minister.
Balfour, Jabez	Company promoter.
Barclay, Theodore	Associate of Gerard Lee Bevan. Senior partner, Sheppards & Company, stockbrokers.
Barr, Captain Charlie	Captain of the racing yacht *Westward*.
Beardsley, Aubrey	Campaigner against the top hat.
Bearsted, Lord	Chairman, M. Samuel & Company, merchant bankers.
Beecham, Sir Joseph	Pharmaceutical manufacturer. Associate of James White.
Beecham, Sir Thomas	Associate of James White.
Beerbohm, Max	Author and campaigner against the top hat.
Benenson, Grigori	Property dealer in New York.
Bevan, Gerard Lee	Senior partner, Ellis & Company, stockbrokers. Director of City Equitable Fire Insurance Company.
Bevan, Sophie	Wife of Gerard Lee Bevan.
Binder, Bernhard	Chartered Accountant. Chairman of British Shareholders Trust.
Bingham, Capt. the Hon.	Heir to Lord Clanmorris, director of Hatry's companies.
Birkett K.C., Norman	Barrister who represented Clarence Hatry at trial.
Blackwell, Sir Ernley	Principal legal adviser, Home Office.
Bliss, Superintendent	Metropolitan Police. Led inquiry into transaction involving Hatchards, 1956.
Bodkin, Sir Archibald	Director of Public Prosecutions, 1929.

(*Continued*)

(Cont.)

Name	*Description*
Burnett, Sir David	Former Lord Mayor of London. Director of City Equitable Fire Insurance Company.
Chamberlain, Neville	Conservative politician and prime minister. Proposed by Hatry as chairman of United Steel.
Clausen, Sir George	Landscape painter, resident in Haverstock Hill area.
Clifford-Turner, Harry	Partner in Clifford-Turner & Company, solicitors.
Cochrane, Alexander S.	New York carpet manufacturer. Commissioned the yacht *Westward.*
Collins, Arthur	Past president, Institute of Municipal Treasurers and Accountants. Founder, Municipal Loans Bureau.
Connolly, Sir James	Australian politician. Arranged introductions for Hatry to Australian authorities intending to raise money in London by loan issues.
Crane, J.R.	Director of Rich & Cowan, publishers of Hatry's book *Light Out of Darkness.*
Cripps, Frederick	Brother of Stafford Cripps. Associate of Grigori Benenson.
Crisp, Sir Frank	Partner, Ashurst Morris Crisp, solicitors. Legal adviser to the Liberal Party.
Crisp, Sir John	Partner, Ashurst Morris Crisp, solicitors.
Danby, Thomas	Portrait painter, resident in Haverstock Hill area.
Daniels, Edmund	Managing director of Austin Friars Trust.
Davies, T.B.	Acquired from Hatry the racing yacht *Westward.*
Dawson, Sir Douglas	Equerry to the King. Director of City and Equitable Fire Insurance and Hatry's companies.
Debenham, Ernest	Chairman, Debenhams.
Debenham, Piers	Son of Ernest Debenham. Director of Debenhams.
De Reuter, Baron Julius	Sold Reuters Bank to Clarence Hatry.
D'Erlanger, Baron Emile	Financier.
Dixon, John	Secretary and director, Austin Friars Trust Limited.
Dollman, Mr	Duped Clarence Hatry with bill of exchange fraud, 1909.
Du Cros, Sir Arthur	Conservative MP for Hastings. Chairman Dunlop Rubber Company and Parent Trust & Finance.
Duguid, Charles	Former City editor, *Daily Mail.* Head of New Issues Department, Commercial Bank of London, 1920.
Duncan, Stanley	Chartered Accountant. Partner in Price, Waterhouse & Company.
Edgar, Edward Mackay	Partner, Sperling & Company. Associate of Clarence Hatry.
Edgley, Cyril	General manager of Argosy and Sundial Libraries when acquired by Hatchards.

(*Continued*)

(Cont.)

Name	*Description*
Eiser, Johann (John)	Clarence Hatry's uncle.
Eiser, Lucy (née Katzenstein)	Clarence Hatry's aunt.
Ferguson, Ronald	Clarence Hatry's maternal grandfather.
Fleming, Robert	Founded a group of investment trusts. Advised the Cox Brothers Limited on the flotation by Hatry of Jute Industries Limited.
Forte, Charles	Developed chain of coffee shops.
Furness, Viscount	Inherited a controlling interest in Furness with shipping group.
Game, Phillip	Partner in Ashurst Morris Crisp, solicitors. Misapplied clients' funds to invest in Hatchards.
Garnsey, Sir Gilbert	Chartered Accountant. Partner in Price, Waterhouse & Company.
Gaze, Ronald	Managing director of Marshalls Provincial Stores.
Gialdini, John	Director of Austin Friars Trust.
Greenfield, George	Wartime friend of Cecil Hatry. Managed T. Werner Laurie, publishers, for Hatry.
Grenside, Henry	Director of City Equitable Fire Insurance Company.
Gray, James	Manager, Threadneedle Street branch of Lloyds Bank Limited.
Grew, Major	Governor, Maidenhead prison.
Guest, Captain Frederick	Liberal Party chief whip, 1920.
Guy, John	Managing director, Parent Trust & Finance.
Haass, Eugene Otto	Partner in Bank of British Commerce, 1909.
Haig-Thomas, Peter	Nephew of David Thomas, Lord Rhondda. Associate of Gerard Lee Bevan. Director of Hatry's companies.
Hassid, M.A.	Disaffected shareholder in Hatchards Group.
Hatry, Adolphus	Clarence Hatry's paternal grandfather.
Hatry, Cecil	Clarence Hatry's son.
Hatry, Diana	Clarence Hatry's daughter.
Hatry, Eric	Clarence Hatry's brother.
Hatry, Gerald	Clarence Hatry's brother.
Hatry, Henriette (née Katzenstein)	Clarence Hatry's mother.
Hatry, Jacques Martin	French general whose name was assumed by Clarence Hatry's family.
Hatry, Johanna (née Escalès)	Clarence Hatry's paternal grandmother.
Hatry, Julius	Clarence Hatry's father.
Hatry, Violet Marguerite	Clarence Hatry's wife.

(*Continued*)

(Cont.)

Name	*Description*
Hatry, Wilfred	Clarence Hatry's brother.
Hemming, Bernard	London agent for Massing Frères, silk mill in Sarreguemines.
Henderson, Ian	Disaffected shareholder in Hatchards Group.
Hewart, Gordon	Lord Chief Justice, 1938.
Hicks Beach, Sir Michael (later Earl St Aldwyn)	Conservative politician, chairman Capital Issues Committee 1915–1916.
Hilton, Robert S.	Managing director, United Steel Companies Limited.
Hoare, Sir Samuel	Conservative politician. Home secretary, 1938.
Hobhouse, Sir Charles	Former Liberal politician. Chairman, Commercial Bank of London
Horne, Henry	Company promoter. Founder of 'Red Triangle' group of cement companies.
Isler, Charles Fritz	Partner in Bank of British Commerce, 1909.
Jersey, Earl of	Investor in Hatchards; supported Hatry's acquisition.
Johnson, J.R.	Arthur Collins' successor as city treasurer of Birmingham.
Jones, Walter Benton	Chairman, United Steel Companies Limited.
Josepho, Anatol	Inventor of Photomaton machine.
Jowitt, Sir William	Attorney general, 1930. Prosecuted Hatry in 1930.
Kahn, Otto	Partner in London office of Kuhn Loeb.
Kettle, Russell	Chartered Accountant. Partner in Deloitte, Plender Griffiths & Company.
King, Revd C. Seymour	Chaplain, Maidenhead prison.
Kinloch, Sir David	Father of Richard Norton's fiancée.
Kylsant, Lord	Chairman of Royal Mail Steamship Group.
Lansbury, George	Former leader of the Labour Party. Supported the campaign for Hatry's early release from prison.
Lawson, Nigel	City editor of the *Sunday Telegraph*. Revealed Hatry's involvement in John Wallace & Sons.
Leith, Gordon	Partner in London office of Kuhn Loeb.
Lewis, Rosa	Proprietor of the Cavendish Hotel.
Lidbury, Charles	General manager, Westminster Bank.
Locker-Lampson, Commander Oliver	Conservative politician. Supported campaign for Hatry's early release from prison.
Logan, Bruce	Insurance broker, partner of Clarence Hatry and Deighton Patmore.
Lorang, Claud	Company promoter.
Lyon, Laurance	Conservative MP for Hastings. Used Hatry's services in abortive attempt to acquire *The Globe* newspaper.

(*Continued*)

(Cont.)

Name	*Description*
Mansell, Edward George	General manager of City Equitable and Fire Insurance Company.
March, Earl of	Son of Duke of Richmond, director of some of Hatry's companies.
Maxwell, Sir Alexander	Deputy secretary, Home Office, 1938.
Milligan, Moir	Director of City Equitable Fire Insurance Company.
Montagu, Lord Charles	Stockbroker and mentor of Frederick Szarvasy.
Moore, Sir Thomas	Conservative MP. Supported the campaign for Hatry's early release from prison.
Morgenthau, Henry	Leader of syndicate which acquired from Anatol Josepho rights to the Photomaton machine.
Norman, Montagu	Governor of the Bank of London.
Norton, Richard (later Lord Grantly)	Before 1914, borrowed money with Clarence Hatry's assistance. Later a merchant banker. Partner in London office of Kuhn Loeb.
Norton, Winifred	Before 1914, borrowed money with Clarence Hatry's assistance. Sister of Richard Norton.
O'Hagan, Osborne	Company promoter. Director of Blue Circle Cement group.
Oliver, Frederick	Director, Debenhams.
Passmore, Stanley	Partner, J.D. Langton & Passmore, solicitors. Chairman, Marshalls Provincial Stores.
Patmore, Brigit	Wife of Deighton Patmore.
Patmore, Coventry	Deighton Patmore's grandfather.
Patmore, Deighton	Insurance broker, partner of Clarence Hatry and Bruce Logan.
Pearson, Sir Weetman (later Lord Cowdray)	Owner of Mexican Eagle Oil Company.
Pease, J.W. Beaumont	Chairman of Lloyds Bank Limited, 1929.
Pelham Clinton, Henry	Son of Duke of Newcastle, director of Hatry's companies.
Petruisot, Jeanne	Mistress of Gerard Lee Bevan.
Phillips, John (later Lord St Davids)	Associate of David Lloyd George. Founder of group of Old Broad Street investment trusts.
Phillips, Owen (later Lord Kylsant)	Chairman of Royal Mail Steamship Group.
Pope, Fred	Director of Debenhams. Manager of the provincial department stores in Debenhams.
Powys, Atherton	Partner in Pollock & Company, solicitors. Managed Hatry's personal affairs during his imprisonment.

(*Continued*)

(Cont.)

Name	*Description*
Rackham, Arthur	Illustrator, resident in Haverstock Hill area.
Rees, Prison Officer	Prison officer at Maidenhead prison.
Ribblesdale, Lord	Resident of Cavendish Hotel, director of Hatry's companies.
Richmond, Frederick	Chairman, Debenhams.
Roger, Sir Alexander	Former chairman, Commercial Bank of London.
St Davids, Viscount	Associate of David Lloyd George. Founder of group of Old Broad Street investment trusts.
Seafield, Countess of	Investor in the Hatchards Group.
Selfridge, Gordon	Founder, Selfridge Department Store, London.
Simon, Sir John	Conservative politician. Home secretary, 1937.
Slater, John	Acquired from Hatry a controlling interest in Amalgamated Industrials Limited 1920.
Spens, J. Ivan	Director of United Steel.
Steinhart, Henry	Partner of Johann Eiser.
Stenhouse, Hugh	Chairman of Stenhouse Holdings. Acquired Hatry's shares in John Wallace & Sons, 1963.
Stubbings, Inspector George	Head of fraud section, City of London Police.
Szarvasy, Frederick	Company promoter and, later, a company doctor. Founder of British Foreign & Colonial Corporation.
Tabor, Albert	Director, Austin Friars Trust Limited.
Tidey, Daniel	Developer of properties in Belsize Park.
Tollemache, Miles de Orellane	First husband of Diana Hatry, Clarence Hatry's daughter.
Treweek, Ernest	Securities clerk, Commercial Bank of London.
Truscott, Alderman Sir George	Former Lord Mayor of London. Magistrate at Hatry's initial pre-trial hearings.
Vernier, Léon	Alias of Gerard Lee Bevan.
Warwick, Frances Countess of	Mistress of King Edward VII.
Webber, Major Leonard	Estate manager of the Nocton estate.
Weinfeld, Bernard	Immigration agent. Cooperated with Hatry in scheme for insuring immigrants.
Wheeler, Sir Arthur	Company promoter.
White, James	Company promoter.
Wilde, Oscar	Campaigner against the top hat.
Winchester, Marquess of	Chairman of Corporate & General Securities. Director of Hatry's companies.
Wolfson, Isaac	Acquired Godfrey & Company, music shops, from the Hatchards Group.

(*Continued*)

(Cont.)

Name	*Description*
Workman, Robert	London shipbroker. Owner of Workman Clark, Belfast, shipbuilder.
Wright, Maurice	Chartered Accountant. Director of Debenhams.
Younger, Sir George	Conservative Party chief whip, 1920.

Acknowledgements

As an articled clerk, I spent most of 1974 at Pinners Hall, Austin Friars, working on the receivership of Triumph Investment Trust, one of the casualties of the secondary banking crisis. In the course of my work, I discovered that 45 years earlier Pinners Hall had seen another crisis: the collapse of Clarence Hatry's companies and the stock exchange crash that followed. That was my first encounter with Clarence Hatry.

This book's gestation has taken so long partly because I was for many years distracted by other activities but also because of Hatry's elusiveness. In tracking him down I have relied upon the services of many libraries and archives without which the project would have been impossible. I am especially grateful for the help and support of:

- the Guildhall Library which houses the London Stock Exchange Archive,
- the Dundee University Archive which houses the Jute Industries Archive,
- the London Library which houses a splendid collection of London street and telephone directories,
- the National Archives with their many surprises (such as Hatry's medical records while in prison),
- the British Library with its peerless collection of obscure periodicals.

My research was enriched by the help of Didier Hemmert of the Archives Municipales, Sarreguemines, who found for me traces of the Hatry family on both sides of the border between France and Germany. On a visit to Sarreguemines in 2017, Didier Hammert with Hubert Girard and their wives not only made Christine and me most welcome but also helped us to understand the challenges faced by people living in places where the national association changed regularly as borders moved. We will long remember the first sight of Hubert at Metz station wearing a top hat in recognition of the Hatry family's trade, and our visits to cemeteries to locate the graves of members of the Hatry family which Didier had identified for us.

Completion of this project has benefited from my doctoral research supervised by Ranald Michie and David McCollum-Oldroyd. With their encouragement and insight my understanding and confidence were to develop inestimably. Only gradually am I learning how much I benefited from their wisdom.

Following my doctoral research, completion of this book has been greatly assisted by the welcome and support of the Durham University Business School. I have also benefited from the welcome of the London School of Economics Sociology Department.

I owe much to friends who have helped and supported me in this project by reading drafts, offering insights, suggesting lines of enquiry, or, on occasion, just listening: Dinah Bisdee, Rob Bryer, Shona Butterfield, Roy Chandler, Toby Dennis, Chris Fusaro, Sarah Ferguson, Susan Gompels, Teresa Graham, Bridget Hutter, Julia Irvine, Rob Laking, Hugh Murphy, Michael Oliver, David Prince, Janette Rutterford, (the late) Bill Tiplady, Martin Vander Weyer, Peter Walton and (the late) Eddie Weiss. I do not know how to repay them all.

This book is dedicated to my granddaughter Imogen, my daughter-in-law Elly and my son Timothy, who read drafts of chapters on the long coach journeys returning to Scotland from Glasgow Warriors fixtures in Wales. I hope they believe the effort was worthwhile.

Throughout this endeavour, Christine, my wife, has been with me. She was there in 1974 when I first encountered Hatry. She was there when I walked the streets of the City to locate his various offices. She was there (uncomplaining) when on a visit to Hampstead to buy her an outfit for our son's wedding I insisted that we should view Julius Hatry's house in Belsize Park which was nearby. She was there as we tracked down the Hatry family in Sarreguemines and Zweibrucken. She is here as I complete this. What a star!

To all of them, I am more grateful than I can say.

CS

1 Growing up in London

On 16 June 1871, Berliners were called to the streets to welcome the newly proclaimed Kaiser and his victorious army. Following tradition, the army's parade climaxed in front of the Brandenburger Tor which had been decorated for the occasion 'by an abundance of green garlands'. As it marched along the Unter den Linden, the parade passed between captured French cannon and beneath a series of triumphal arches bearing paintings celebrating the recent war against France described lyrically by the Prussian correspondent of *The Times*:

> Germania, standing erect in a gold chariot, rushes into battle. She is always the same blue-eyed virgin of mild maidenly type ... But her sons, crowding around the sentimental mother, are fierce and stalwart men. While they are cutting their way through death and flame the German eagle in the sky swoops down on her Napoleonic colleague.[1]

Forty-two thousand men took part in the parade which took three and a half hours to pass.

Five hundred and fifty miles away in Paris there was little to celebrate. A year earlier, the Emperor Napoleon III had declared war on Germany to pre-empt a German threat to France and to prevent the unification of Germany. Two months later, with unimagined speed, the German armies had defeated the disorganised French at Sedan, imprisoned Napoleon himself and laid siege to Paris. After a few short months, the French government was obliged to capitulate, which involved acceptance of a humiliating peace treaty and led to civil war as the rest of France fought to subdue the Paris Commune.[2]

In the months of fighting, the centre of Paris had been sorely damaged. Although some buildings such as Notre-Dame, Sainte Chapelle and the Louvre survived, many, such as the Hotel de Ville, the Tuileries Palace and the memorial in the Place Vendôme, had been destroyed. Almost everything living, even the rats, had been eaten. To survive the cold of winter, almost all wood had been taken for burning. Whereas the lime trees still flourished along the Unter den Linden, the Champs-Élysées were treeless.[3]

With time, physical scars could be made good, but the psychological scars were more durable.[4] To secure peace, France was obliged to accept the cession to Germany of the north-eastern *départements* of Alsace and Lorraine, including the bastion towns of Metz and Strasbourg. France was also obliged to pay reparations of five billion francs and to suffer occupation by German troops until the full amount had been paid. The bitterness caused by the peace terms imposed by the German victors was deepened by the German high command's choice of the Hall of Mirrors at the Palace of Versailles as the venue for the declaration of the new German Reich and of the King of Prussia as Kaiser. The degrading terms of the peace would long be resented by the French who were humiliated by Bismarck's knowing use of the glorious setting of Versailles.[5]

Eager to protest against this national humiliation, Parisians chose to boycott the products of German businesses: especially those which had become German through the cession of Alsace and Lorraine. The boycotts were enthusiastically supported by the many merchants and manufacturers whose businesses had been interrupted by the war; none more so than the Parisian hatters.

In Zweibrücken, on the German side of the border with Lorraine, a young man called Julius Hatry followed these developments closely. This small town had seen such upheavals before. In recent centuries it had switched on a number of occasions from one country to another. Each successive change is reflected in the town cemetery which hosts a memorial to Napoleon's Grande Armée, which in 1812 had marched through Zweibrücken on its way to Moscow, as well as the iron-cross marked graves of German soldiers who invaded Lorraine in 1870.

Julius's family had long been established in Zweibrücken and taken the name Hatry at the beginning of the nineteenth century when, for a period of about 20 years, the town found itself within French territory and named Deux-Ponts. A Napoleonic decree had required Jewish families to adopt conventional family surnames and, in place of the name they had been using, 'of Oppenheim', they had chosen 'Hatry' after General Jacques Martin Hatry, an Alsatian who had been commander in chief of the French army which conquered the fortress of Luxembourg in 1795.[6] Choice of such a name must have been intended as a sign of commitment to France but was to prove an embarrassment.

When, a few years later, the territory was returned to German rule following the Congress of Vienna, the Hatry family found that it faced not only the anti-Semitism prevalent in the area[7] but the disadvantage of bearing a name that proclaimed a preference for French rule. Maintaining this identity confirmed the family's separateness and ensured that they were treated as outsiders.

Apart from one or two graves in the Jewish section of the town's cemetery and in nearby Jewish cemeteries, no evidence can now be traced of the Hatry family's life in Zweibrücken. The synagogue which was close to the dyeworks was rased to the ground in the course of Kristallnacht in 1938 and the last vestiges of the family dyeworks by the river in the centre of town must have been destroyed in the blanket bombing raids of 1945. The family business seems to have been successful, however, supporting the family for many generations. This settled existence was to be undermined by the Parisians' boycott of German businesses.

The success of the family's dyeworks was closely linked to the success of the silk mills of Lorraine, whose fabric they dyed. There were several substantial mills in Sarreguemines, which was close to Zweibrücken, and which, as a result of the peace treaty in 1871, had become a part of Germany. These mills specialised in the production of silk velvet and silk plush, which was similar to velvet but had a longer nap. These fabrics were used in the manufacture of silk top hats: a fashion which had originated in Germany but had been adopted in Paris and London.

In 1870, Sarreguemines had been overwhelmed by the advance of the German army and sales of silk had been suspended. After the fighting ceased, what might have been just a temporary interruption threatened to become permanent through the Parisian hatters' boycott of what henceforth was to be regarded as German fabric.

For the Hatry family, this called in question the future health of the family's dyeworks. For Julius, it had an even closer significance. Julius Hatry's father, Adolphus, had married the daughter of a Sarreguemines family which owned Escalès Frères, a silk velvet mill whose business was also threatened by the Parisian hatters' boycott. Adolphus and Julius thus found themselves in the midst of two families whose livelihoods were threatened by the Parisian hatters on whom they had previously relied.

Like the other silk mills in Sarreguemines, Escalès Frères had to find other markets for its products. Before 1860, it had been impracticable to sell silk velvet to hatters in London as the application of tariffs made it too expensive. However, a new Anglo-French commercial treaty signed in April 1860 had led to the removal of tariffs so that sales in London had become possible. One or two of the larger mills in Sarreguemines had tried to exploit this opportunity by appointing agents in London. Massing Frères, for example, had appointed Bernard Hemming who set himself up in Nelson Square off Blackfriars Road in Southwark. The upshot was that in 1871, at the age of 24, Julius Hatry was sent by his family to London to sell the products of Gebrüder Escalès (as the mill was known after 1871) to the hatters of London.[8]

It is difficult for the millennial generation to appreciate the attitude to dress in the late nineteenth century or the importance that was attached to headwear. Dress codes have become more relaxed. Hat wearing is not so common. Top hats are still worn, but rarely and as a way of signifying that an event is exceptional. Few own their own top hats, preferring to hire a hat as necessary. Even when a top hat is worn, it will rarely be a silk top hat. Manufacture of silk top hats had ceased by the beginning of the 1914–1918 war and did not restart afterwards, so silk hats are now increasingly rare and valuable.

In contrast, the world to which Julius Hatry was introduced in 1871 was one of strict dress codes. Dress in late Victorian and Edwardian England signified rank and, especially among the middle and upper classes, was regarded as a barometer of respectability. No office boy would go without a hat. Poor dress was seen as a sign of degeneracy. Some took the question of clothing to almost extreme lengths, changing clothes several times a day (especially when in London) to match the rules understood to apply to each function they attended.

The ultimate arbiter from the time he set up his court at Marlborough House in 1860 until his death in 1910 was Edward VII. What the Prince of Wales said about dress had the force of iron law. When a junior Guards officer arrived at the Marlborough Club wearing a top hat and not a tailcoat, the prince, after staring at him with disgust, said: 'I suppose, my young friend, you are going to a costume ball'. When a private secretary, Fritz Ponsonby, visited an exhibition in a morning coat, the prince said: 'I thought everyone must know that a short jacket is always worn with a silk hat at a private view in the morning'. When the Marquess of Salisbury, as prime minister, attended Buckingham Palace in privy councillor's tunic with the trousers of an elder brother of Trinity House, rather than knee-breeches and buckled shoes, the prince expressed astonishment that the marquess had not noticed the error.[9]

This obsession with clothing now seems ridiculous, but it was humoured by the sycophants who hoped to win the approval of the prince. For his part, he observed his own rules and expected that those who sought his company should do likewise, believing that through this an impression of dignity and grandeur would be conveyed to anyone outside the charmed circle. Dressing any differently would signify membership of a lower class.

Although other classes were not directly exposed to the Prince of Wales' displeasure, they also adopted a rigid approach to dress codes. In the 1870s, the professional classes were beginning to discard the frock coat in favour of the morning coat which by 1900 had become normal wear. For anyone on business in London or other major cities this would be worn with a black silk top hat. The middle classes tended to wear the lounge suit, which in time would completely replace the morning coat. These attitudes suffused life not only in the major cities but in most towns and throughout society. H.G. Wells was later to recall how, on becoming an apprentice draper in Southsea in 1881, his change in status was marked by the acquisition of a morning coat and a top hat and how each subsequent advancement was marked by acquisition of top hats of increasingly superior quality. He remarked that the top hat:

> was the symbol of complete practical submission to a whole world of social conventions. It was a symbol of being a member of the club or at least of wanting to be. Many aspirants yearned to be asked to make that submission, because it indicated they had advanced.[10]

Adherence was not universal. Some stood out against convention, such as Oscar Wilde, Max Beerbohm and Aubrey Beardsley who were well-known dandies. Yet their refusal to follow convention was self-consciously intended as a sign of their nonconformity and tended to confirm rather than deny the strength of that convention.

This was the world to which Julius Hatry moved in 1871 and on which the demand for his family's products would depend.

He faced a considerable challenge. There is no evidence in trade directories or the hatters' trade press of Gebrüder Escalès having an office in London or even advertising for sales before 1870. Julius faced an urgent need to find new customers in what was for him (and Gebrüder Escalès) a new environment using a language that was not his mother tongue. Although he had to do this far from the support network his family would have provided in Zweibrücken, he had the advantage that others of the Sarreguemines silk mills had appointed agents in London and he evidently looked to them for assistance.[11] Quite apart from the difficulties of his position, the move to London was an opportunity. If he could establish his family's business and achieve acceptance in London society, he would enable his family to escape their uncomfortable experience as Jewish outsiders in Zweibrücken. This perhaps explains why alone among the families owning silk mills in Sarreguemines, the Hatry family did not appoint an agent in London but sent a member of the family. It was also a tangible demonstration of Gebrüder Escalès' commitment to London at a time when it was relatively easy for German immigrants to defraud creditors by disappearing after trading for a short time on credit they had never intended to repay.[12] To integrate into London society, Julius was prepared to accept sacrifices. Not least, he decided that he should leave his Jewishness behind and adopted instead the observances of the Anglican church.[13]

Julius was not without advantages, however.

Hats were sold either by a small number of specialist shops or by general outfitters who would provide all of the kit that a gentleman would require. Many of the specialist shops and a number of the chains of gentlemen's outfitters had their hat factories in Southwark, the historical centre of London's hat trade. Around the factories were grouped the dozens of independent suppliers of the materials required for hat manufacture: fabric, metal or leather. Just a few doors from Julius's new premises in Stamford Street, Charles Cooper & Company claimed to manufacture or import 'every description of hat, cap and helmet materials, mourning bands, irons, tools and sundries'. Concentration of the hatting trade in Southwark made at least a part of the market for Gebrüder Escalès' silk velvet easy to find. No doubt Julius was steered towards Southwark by the agents of the other Sarreguemines silk mills whose places of business were all located near Nelson Square, the centre of the hatting trade.[14]

Proximity to potential customers did not guarantee that Julius's silk would be welcomed, but here he benefited from a further advantage: the reputation of silk velvet from Lorraine. Top hats were made by forming a rigid base in calico which was then covered with shellac.[15] When the shellac was heated, the silk velvet cover would be applied so that it became stuck to the base as the shellac cooled. During this process, inferior silk would become discoloured and could not achieve the glossy black finish to which the hatters aspired and which was *de rigueur* in society. The main competition for silk from the mills in Lorraine came from the silk mills in Macclesfield, whose products were known to be more susceptible to discoloration than the Lorraine mills' products.[16]

Julius had one other advantage: although he was not accompanied by other members of his family, there were many French and German émigrés in London. By the end of the 1870s, each of the Sarreguemines silk mills had established a selling office in Southwark so that there already was a small group of agents with which Julius could identify. The Sarregueminois émigrés were not unique in resettling in London. The humiliation of the war with Germany was followed by years of repression as people sought revenge for the humiliation of the defeat and the embarrassment of the Paris Commune. In contrast, London society was liberal and offered protection as the British extradition treaty with France excluded extradition for political crimes. London became a safe haven for many willing to risk the channel crossing. Julius and his German and French friends had no need to feel isolated in London.[17]

Julius also sought the company of German émigrés, for there was a thin but constant stream of Jewish emigrants from the Rhineland wanting to escape an air of anti-Semitism. Julius's closest and most enduring friend was Johann Eiser, a member of a Frankfurt family involved in stockbroking who was eventually to become a member of the London Stock Exchange.

Whatever challenges Julius faced, he was able to find a demand for the velvet and plush produced by Gebrüder Escalès, which was augmented by selling silk plaits from a connection in Marostica, Italy.[18] Julius also grew in the estimation of other silk agents for whom he acted in civil litigation as an expert witness on the quality of silk velvet.[19] This not only supported the mill in Sarreguemines, but it also gave him the confidence to settle permanently in London, contemplating marriage and family life. As a prelude, in 1885 he applied to become naturalised as a British citizen, which ensured that whomever he married would also become a British citizen on marriage and that their children would also be British citizens. Julius's application was supported by the London agents of other Sarreguemines silk mills and by a stockbroker to whom he had been introduced by his close friend Johann Eiser. Fittingly, Julius and Johann's naturalisation certificates bear consecutive numbers in the Home Office register, suggesting that their applications were submitted together.[20]

The woman to whom Julius was to be married, Henriette Katzenstein, was a member of a Frankfurt family.[21] They were brought together through the hat trade as the Katzenstein family business specialised in selling leather fitments such as preservers and linings which were used in manufacturing hats.[22] Within a year of Julius's naturalisation, they had married in Frankfurt and Julius had stopped living above his shop in Southwark.

They set up home in Belsize Park: a good choice for established men of business who wished to start a family.

Until 1850, the area had been marked by substantial houses surrounded by large estates: a preserve of inherited wealth. As London's network of railways and buses had gradually spread towards Hampstead, so the land's development value had grown and with it the temptation to realise the value. So it was that, in company with the opening of Hampstead Heath station on what is now the North London line and the development of new bus routes along Haverstock Hill, the landowners began to sell their estates for development. New houses were built, creating the suburb which was to be known as Belsize Park. Daniel Tidey, the developer, aimed to bring the fashionable styles of Kensington and Bayswater to Belsize. He built classically styled eight–ten bedroomed semi-detached houses with large porticos and lavish stucco to attract the wealthy middle classes.

By the 1880s, Belsize Park was no longer as fashionable as it had been when first built, and its houses not quite so sought after, but it had become a comfortable community of barristers, merchants, stockbrokers and senior civil servants. The prosperous middle class had supplanted inherited wealth. Nearby, to the east of Haverstock Hill, there was a community of artists, including Sir George Clausen, the landscape painter; Thomas Danby, the portrait painter; and Arthur Rackham, the illustrator. For the well-established merchant or professional man, Belsize Park was a welcoming place to live.

In 1885, the year in which he married Henriette Katzenstein, Julius Hatry was just the sort of successful merchant for whom Belsize Park had been built. Not only did it offer Julius and Henriette the prospect of living among a congenial community, it offered good communications to Southwark: the location of the business he had created. Every few minutes, buses ran along Haverstock Hill, heading for Waterloo, a quarter of a mile from his premises at Stamford Street, and plans were being promoted for a new underground railway, now known as the Northern line, which would have stations at Chalk Farm and Belsize Park offering the prospect of fast connections to Waterloo and Southwark.

For the five years after 1885, Julius Hatry's personal and business lives proceeded happily. Julius was granted British citizenship in March 1886. Two sons were born: Gerald in August 1887 and Clarence in December 1888.[23] The business prospered to such an extent that Julius was able to take more prominent premises in the City, at 12/13 Cheapside, not far from the Mansion House.[24]

Three more sons were to be born: Wilfred in December 1890, Alan in February 1895 and Eric in May 1896, although Wilfred died of pneumonia when he was only 11 months old.[25] In 1897, Henriette Hatry's sister, Lucy, married Julius Hatry's close friend Johann Eiser and they set up home close to Belsize Park. By this time, Henriette's mother, Johanna, had moved to London on the death of her husband and lived with Henriette and Julius. Cementing the closeness of the two families, two or three years later, Julius became the godfather of the Eisers' son. The impression that the families' lives were happy is matched by evidence of growing social integration. In 1901, Julius became a freeman of the City of London and a member of the dyeworkers livery company[26] of which a number of prominent politicians such as Sir Michael Hicks Beach, the Conservative chancellor, were also members. At about the same time, he was able to buy the leasehold of the Belsize Park property. Julius Hatry thus achieved the social ambition of many immigrants: acceptance as a respected man of property, implying a secure future for his family.

But although the family grew, and became established, the 1890s brought commercial uncertainty.

The fashion for silk top hats had begun to wane. However good they looked when freshly brushed, silk hats were impractical. The slightest shower spoiled the appearance of the silk and a severe drenching ruined it. Often when retrieving a top hat from under a seat at the end of an evening at the theatre, a man would find that his feet had scuffed the hat and left it irreparably dented. Above all they were expensive: more expensive than other hats such as the derby or the homburg that were becoming more popular. Fashion was also assailed by campaigners such as Lord Ronald Gower, an associate of Oscar Wilde. In letters to newspapers he claimed that the top hat only survived in London because of snobbishness, and that if only the Prince of Wales would stop wearing them, everyone else would follow and the fashion would die. He also suggested that the fashion had already been deserted in the rest of Europe where silk top hats were only worn by bagmen and undertakers.[27]

The Prince of Wales did not forsake the top hat,[28] but demand fell even without his example. By continuing to compete against each other for smaller orders, the Lorraine mills succeeded only in driving down their prices and increasing customers' demands for cheap credit. Eventually, the mills decided to stop competing with each other by creating a single organisation through which they would all sell their products. The new organisation, the 'Comptoir for Black Hat Plushes,' came to life in 1896 representing Gebrüder Escalès,[29] Emile Huber & Company, Massing Frères, J.R. Martin, C.W. Oehme and S. Waschka Söhne. From 1 September 1896, the Comptoir traded from premises in the City at 4 and 5 Love Lane, originally the premises of the London agent of Emile Huber, the largest Sarreguemines silk mill. The building was near the current site of the City's police station in Wood Street and behind the Guildhall, but it no longer exists. In 1896, the short lane was full of the multi-occupancy buildings which abounded in the City at that time and provided accommodation for large numbers of small businesses.[30] The Comptoir was under the management of Julius Hatry, whom the *Hatters' Gazette* described as 'the right man in the right place'. Although Julius's management of the Comptoir was welcomed, the *Gazette* warned that if the effect of creating the Comptoir was to increase silk prices and thus the cost of silk hats, it would be counterproductive as making top hats dearer 'would be fatal' and the result would be 'seriously disastrous to the trade'. As stabilising the price of plush was the point of creating the Comptoir, the trade press's warning was a sign that the Comptoir might fail to stave off a further decline in demand and the financial consequences that would follow.[31]

The warning in the trade press was prescient. In spite of the Comptoir's elimination of competition between the Sarreguemines mills and Julius Hatry's persuasiveness and networking, demand from top hat manufacturers for silk plushes continued to fall.[32] Gradually the number of mills represented in London and competing for orders also fell,[33] but not by enough to offset the loss of demand. While these years were personally rewarding for Julius, he could not have been optimistic for the future of his business.

Then fate intervened. In 1906, after a period of declining health, Julius was found to have lung cancer from which he died at his home in Belsize Park in the presence of his family on 11 May 1907.[34] He left all his possessions including his business to his wife, Henriette.[35] In the final months of his life, Julius would not have been able to manage the business so other members of the family had taken over the responsibility. Henriette never played a part in developing and managing the business so there was little choice but for the two oldest sons, Gerald and Clarence, to become silk merchants.[36] For Clarence in particular this must have come as an unwelcome shock. In 1906 he was still only 17 and was attending St Paul's School in the expectation of spending the next three years of his life at university.[37] These plans came to nothing.

Creating a new business in the 1870s had been a serious challenge for Clarence's father, but the challenge for the sons in 1907 was greater. Gerald and Clarence were young and can have had no detailed knowledge of the silk trade, let alone the network of customers and contacts that Julius had been so successful in creating. Moreover, whereas the market for silk velvet and plush had been buoyant in the 1870s, by 1907 it was failing. At a time of declining demand and increasing competition for orders, holding together the network that Julius had created would have been difficult for experienced people. For the two young brothers it proved impossible. Initially the two brothers worked together, with Gerald managing the Cheapside premises and Clarence managing the warehouse at Old Change near St Paul's. After a year or two, however, Gerald withdrew[38] and Clarence assumed sole responsibility for management.[39]

Nothing he attempted, such as reducing costs by vacating the Love Lane premises, was able to revive the profitability of the silk business, so he tried to create other sources of income. A perfume and oil importing business was started in Basinghall Street close to the old premises in Love Lane.[40] This came to nothing. Calling himself an electrical engineer, he incorporated a new company, Clarence Engineering Limited, which was granted a patent for an electrical bell system for summoning servants. In the manner of latter day telephone switchboards, Hatry's invention incorporated a board with moveable shutters which were similar to those used later in telephone switchboards and were supposed to indicate in which of a building's rooms a bell push had been operated. Unfortunately, the system proved unreliable. Bell pushes might be operated without any shutters moving to tell servants where the call had come from, or on other occasions all the shutters would fall at once.[41] Apart from managing to sell the patent rights for 20 pounds, the company also came to nothing.[42]

Eventually, in 1909, the silk business was so short of money that Hatry was driven to borrow money and this proved his undoing. He managed to borrow money from a small organisation called the Bank of British Commerce against his mother's lease of 48 Belsize Park.[43] While the name of the lender may have sounded impressive, it was no more than a partnership of two individuals called Eugene Otto Haass and Charles Fritz Isler who knew of the Hatry family by way of a connection in Sarreguemines. The Haass family had resided there for many years and in 1869/1870 had been involved in one of the street committees which organised the town's defence against the Prussian invasion.[44] They were also involved in manufacturing silk. In 1908, Messrs Isler and Haass set up their banking business at Cross Keys House, Moorgate, and were introduced to Hatry by a Mr Dollman of Basinghall Street, where Hatry had set up his perfume and oil business. Dollman persuaded Clarence Hatry to raise money by way of issuing two bills of exchange. One bill was for the amount that Hatry required. The other was for an amount that Dollman wished to raise and which he promised to pay Hatry before the bill had to be paid. At the time, this was a well-known ruse by which confidence men would obtain money from the unwary. So well-known was the ruse that it had been described by Anthony Trollope in *Framley Parsonage*[45] as the means by which a country parson, Revd Robarts, was deprived of money and became financially embarrassed.

Clarence Hatry realised quickly that he was being conned by Dollman and tried to cancel the arrangement. He was able to recover one of the bills, but Dollman had already discounted the second bill so it could not be recovered. To add to the problem, the British Bank of Commerce became insolvent because Messrs Haass and Isler had extracted any cash it received. Thus when the time for honouring the bill came around and Hatry could not pay, he faced the receivers for the so-called bank, who showed no mercy. Clarence and his mother were served with winding up petitions. Both Clarence and his mother were declared bankrupt, although Clarence was granted an immediate discharge on the grounds he owed his misfortune to the accident of his father's untimely death.[46]

Henriette's furniture was sold to meet a part of the debt due. The lease of 48 Belsize Park was forfeit. Henriette was left without a home, and with her younger sons moved to live with her sister, Lucy, and her husband, Johann.[47]

For the Comptoir, this marked the end of the business. Its management was taken over by Emile Huber & Company, the largest of the Sarreguemines mills, and shortly afterwards, it was sold to one of its major customers. The premises in the City were vacated and the business was transferred to premises in Southwark, close to Julius Hatry's original location in Southwark Street.[48] By this stage, there was almost no demand for silk top hats and manufacturers were ceasing production. The inevitable consequence was that the silk mills in Sarreguemines were forced to close even before the onset of the 1914–1918 war.

The slow death of the Comptoir marked the ultimate failure of all Julius's efforts to establish a new business. For his son Clarence it was a disaster. His father's death had brought to an end any chance of going to university; now bankruptcy endangered hopes of future commercial success. What was worse, he knew that the bankruptcy had been brought about because he had not seen through a common and well-known artifice for duping the unwary. In addition to the destruction of his own hopes, the failure had led to his mother's bankruptcy and the loss of the house to which she had moved on her marriage to Julius and in which she had lived for 25 years. It had been a visible sign of the social position they had achieved. Reflecting that he could not have halted the decline in the market for silk top hats may have provided some consolation, but the final collapse owed much to Hatry's naivety in bills of exchange dealings. He thus had a personal responsibility for his mother's bankruptcy and was shamed by it.

These experiences were to define Clarence Hatry's response to adversity throughout his life. The financial insecurity which his father had moved to London to avoid and which he had himself experienced in 1910 must have been intolerable, for he never ceased in his attempts to make money. But his search for social acceptance was even more important.

By moving to London, Julius Hatry seized an opportunity to establish his family in a milieu that would permit their social integration, achieving some success partly through his personal skills but also through his willingness to make sacrifices. Even though he might not have been able to prevent the collapse of his late father's business, Clarence Hatry knew that he had contributed to the manner of the business's demise and that this had brought into question the social position his father had achieved.

This knowledge was to prove a weakness throughout his career: a weakness that became evident to others when he tried too hard to be accepted. It was a weakness that others could exploit when he assumed too readily his acceptance as an equal. It led to his greatest mistakes, which all occurred when he was confronted with an overt denial of his status.

Notes

1 *The Times*, 17 June 1871, page 10.
2 Horne, 1965, pages 314–315.
3 Horne, 1965, pages 418–420, 460–461, 464.
4 Horne, 1965, pages 508–509.
5 Horne, 1965, pages 314–315.
6 Archives Municipales, Sarreguemines.
7 Panayi, 2000, pages 39–50.

8 It was not uncommon for families to send their sons to other countries in this way (Panayi, 1995, page 71).
9 Rose, 1975, cited by Heffer, 2017, page 24.
10 Wells, 1934, volume I, pages 284–285.
11 This is evidenced by the fact that several of the other mills' agents supported Julius Hatry's application for naturalisation in 1885. TNA files HO 144/164/A42253; HO 334/13/4501.
12 Reuschel, 1895. Davies, 2018, pages 232–238.
13 Abandoning Jewishness was not to be straightforward. As late as 1928, more than 50 years later, in a reference provided to Morgans in New York, Morgan Grenfell was to comment of Julius's son, Clarence: 'He is a Jew'. Cited in Kynaston, 1999, page 140.
14 London street directories.
15 For an illustrated description of top hat manufacture and the attachment of the silk cover see *Hatters' Gazette*, 1 June 1899, page 309 et seq.
16 'A deplorable fact connected with the material used … is the necessity that exists of importing it … It cannot be produced in this country'. This was believed to stem from the continental mastery of the practice of 'weighting': the mixing of cotton fibre with silk fibre in the making of velvet. The English mills and dyers had not mastered this practice. *Hatters' Gazette*, 1 February 1896, page 90.
17 There were several institutions in London which existed to support immigrants (Panayi, 1995, page 145).
18 Advertisement, *Hatters' Gazette*, 1 April 1884, page 369.
19 Report of proceedings brought by Massing Frères against Hermann Marx. *Hatters' Gazette*, 1 August 1883, page 401.
20 TNA files HO 144/969/B32605; HO 334/13/4502.
21 Marriage certificate.
22 The Katzenstein family business is described in the London street directories of 1885 and 1886. It appears that at the time of the marriage, the Katzenstein family opened a place of business in the East End of London, although the entry was not repeated after one year.
23 Birth certificates.
24 London street directories.
25 Birth and death certificates.
26 Registration of freeman's status.
27 The campaign against the top hat was first reported in 1884 (*Hatters' Gazette*, 1 July 1884). Its editorial pronounced that the *Gazette* would continue to defend the top hat against newspaper onslaughts and the subsequent progress of the campaign can be tracked in its columns until in 1899 it was reporting that 'the days when the chimney pot will be as extinct as the proverbial dodo is only a question of time' (*Hatters' Gazette*, 1 September 1899, page 474).
28 Although the Prince of Wales was reported to be wearing soft felt hats more frequently (*Hatters' Gazette*, 1 September 1899, page 473).
29 Alone among the Sarreguemines mills, Gebrüder Escalès continued to advertise separately from the Comptoir: selling plushes of all colours for ladies' hats (i.e. not simply black plushes for top hats) (*Hatters' Gazette*, 1 January 1902).
30 London street directories.
31 *Hatters' Gazette*, 1895.
32 In January 1899, it was reported that there were only about 400 men employed in the manufacture of top hats, whereas 40 years earlier about 1,200 men had been employed (*Hatters' Gazette*, 2 January 1899, page 24).
33 London street directories.
34 Death certificate.

35 Probated will.
36 Evidence given by Henriette Hatry in her public examination at the time she was declared bankrupt (TNA file B9/717).
37 Greenfield, 1995, page 46.
38 A newspaper report suggested that Gerald left the country after a creditor brought a civil action concerning a bill of exchange (*Sunday Times*, 17 July 1910, page 16).
39 London street directories.
40 London street directories.
41 Greenfield, 1995, page 46.
42 Clarence Engineering Limited (TNA files BT 31/12,908/104,848; BT 34/2,281/104,848).
43 Hatry had used a bill of exchange to borrow money on at least one other occasion. In July 1910, Mr Albert Harkness sued Hatry's mother for £210 due on a bill of exchange, Mr Harkness's father had been given the bill by Clarence and Gerald Hatry against the payment of four months' salary for his assistance in finding capital for the family business. With the encouragement of the judge, the parties reached a settlement and the hearing did not proceed. It was stated that the disagreement had arisen because of the way in which the matter had been handled by Gerald Hatry, who was reported to have left the country (*Sunday Times*, 17 July 1910, page 16).
44 Archives Municipales, Sarreguemines. *Confluence*.
45 Trollope, 1881.
46 Bankruptcy hearings, TNA files B 9/717 and B 9/563. Insolvency of British Bank of Commerce, TNA file B 9/559–562.
47 Census returns 1911.
48 London street directories. *Hatters' Gazette*.

References

Primary works: newspapers and periodicals

Confluence, Sarreguemines, France.
Hatters' Gazette.
Sunday Times.
The Times.

Primary works: contemporary books

Reuschel, R. (1895), *The Knights of Industry: Revelations about Foreign Long-Firms in London*. (The Author, London).
Trollope, A. (1881), *Framley Parsonage*. (Smith Elder, London).
Wells, H.G. (1934), *Experiment in Autobiography (Two Volumes)*. (Faber & Faber, London).

Secondary works

Davies, D. (2018), *Lying for Money*. (Profile Books, London).
Greenfield, G. (1995), *A Smattering of Monsters: A Kind of Memoir*. (Little Brown, London).
Heffer, S. (2017), *The Age of Decadence: Britain 1880 to 1914*. (Random House Books, London).

Horne, A. (1965), *The Fall of Paris: The Siege and the Commune 1870–71.* (MacMillan, London).

Kynaston, D. (1999), *The City of London: Volume III: Illusions of Gold 1914–1945.* (Chatto & Windus, London).

Panayi, P. (1995), *German Immigrants in Britain during the Nineteenth Century 1815–1964.* (Berg Publishers, Oxford).

Panayi, P. (2000), *Ethnic Minorities in Nineteenth and Twentieth Century Germany: Jews, Gypsies, Poles Turks and Others.* (Pearson Education, Harlow).

Rose, K. (1975), *The Later Cecils.* (Weidenfeld & Nicolson, London).

2 Clarence finds his feet

In 1910, Hatry's financial position was desperate, but he had identified a way out: the London Stock Exchange.

Before the 1914–1918 war, the stock exchange was not the gentlemanly club that some imagine: it more resembled the Wild West.[1] Periodically it was consumed by passionate trading in which fortunes could be made or lost as investors became desperate either not to miss out on a 'good thing' or to avoid being left holding a stock that had begun to look like a turkey. Trading on the exchange's floor was the preserve of its members, but they were surrounded by a community of people who could not trade on the exchange's floor but hoped to profit in some way from its trading. None became more notorious than the company promoters.

Promoters existed to fill a gap: between the owners of businesses needing to raise money and the members of the stock exchange who could meet their needs. While selling a company's shares might raise money, many business owners were ignorant of the ways of the stock exchange and as a result were nervous of using its services. By the same token, members of the exchange had little reason to appreciate the concerns and interests of owners. The result was that many business owners were intimidated by the exchange's reputation and fearful of the consequences of allowing new shareholders to share control of the company. There were old established City houses which would sponsor new issues of shares but they generally preferred to concentrate on larger issues for overseas governments or big companies which, being larger, were more profitable to manage. Issues for smaller domestic companies were left to be managed by stockbrokers and company promoters.[2]

Promotion involved a number of skills. Initially, someone had to spot that a business could raise money by selling its shares and persuade its owners that this would be a worthwhile project. Then the company had to be prepared for a public offer: ensuring that the amount and terms of its share capital would be attractive to potential investors and that its formal constitution was appropriate for a publicly held company. If directors were well known and regarded as respectable, investors might be more confident than if the directors had no public reputation. Company promoters would often recommend the introduction of directors who they believed would justify confidence among potential investors.[3]

A prospectus then had to be prepared describing the prospects of the company and its shares in terms that would persuade investors to buy – a task that was often given to specialist writers or journalists with a talent for convincing description.[4] All of this work required a knowledge not only of company law but also of the rules of the stock exchange as, when completed, the prospectus had to be submitted to the exchange's committee. Without the committee's formal approval, shares could not be dealt on the floor of the exchange.[5]

Finally, it was the promoter's role to make the offer known to prospective investors by all the means possible, which not only involved persuading stockbrokers to recommend an investment to their clients but also seeking positive newspaper coverage of an offer and perhaps mailing the prospectus directly to potential investors.[6]

The process of offering shares to the public for trading on the stock exchange, known as flotation, was riddled with opportunities for exploitation. Business owners might have an unrealistic view of their company's value and under- or over-value their shares. Prospective investors would often have little basis for assessing a company's prospects for future profit. From time to time, promoters could and did take advantage of these patches of ignorance. Prospectuses would present an unduly optimistic view of a proposition. Newspapers could be persuaded to reinforce that false optimism editorially in return for paid advertising. Company promoters became notorious through selling shares to ignorant investors at wild prices or making a large profit for themselves at the former owners' expense.[7]

For newspapers, company promoters provided a seemingly inexhaustible supply of scandalous stories as they often became notorious for their wealth or their dramatic collapses. For novelists, promoters could be painted as memorably grotesque characters such as Mr Merdle in Dickens' *Little Dorrit* or Augustus Melmotte in Trollope's morality tale, *The Way We Live Now*.[8]

Hatry came to know of this enthralling community by way of his uncle, John (formerly Johann) Eiser.

When he became a naturalised British citizen in 1885, John Eiser was working as a stockbroker's clerk. Five or six years later, he became a member of the exchange, trading in partnership with Henry Steinhart, an American who had also become a naturalised British citizen, but whose mother, a German, was known to Eiser through family connections in Frankfurt. In 1901, John Eiser's partnership with Steinhart was brought to an end, after which Eiser had established J.G. Eiser & Company, which by 1910 specialised in arbitrage trading with stockbrokers in Germany to exploit differences in the prices of shares quoted in both Frankfurt and London.[9]

Although Hatry first learned of the stock exchange through John Eiser, he could not use the connection to become a part of the community which encircled the exchange. As a result, Hatry lacked the sort of influential sponsor who proved so useful to intending promoters such as Frederick Szarvasy.

The son of Alexander Szarvasy, a Hungarian banker, he had come to England in 1901 and worked for Montagu Oppenheimer (later Montagu Stanley), a firm of stockbrokers. He decided to concentrate on new issues and, with support from Lord Charles Montagu, acquired Cornhill Contract Corporation, which had experience of managing new issues such as Chesterfield Tube Company. In the post-war boom of 1919, under the name British Foreign and Colonial Corporation Limited, he was to be responsible for eight issues.[10]

To seek his fortune in the exchange's community, Hatry needed to find a way into the community of financial traders and an opportunity to show he could make money.

Chance meetings in Brighton, where Hatry was recovering from rheumatic fever,[11] provided the opportunity he needed.

While walking on Brighton pier in 1909, he met Violet Marguerite Ferguson who he always called Dolly. He later recalled that she had been selling picture postcards. They fell for each other and were married on 28 June at Brighton Register Office.[12]

Almost nothing is known of Dolly Ferguson's origins. The marriage certificate records that her father, Ronald Ferguson, had independent means, but there are no other official records of such a person.[13] As other information shown on the certificate is incorrect, such as the ages of Violet and Clarence Hatry, it is possible that information about her father was also incorrect. Certainly, the only record of a birth of a Violet Ferguson at an appropriate time suggests that she was illegitimate. Her mother lived in Rotherhithe in south London at an address which was visited by public inspectors as it was believed to be insanitary.[14]

The marriage would last until death and provided Hatry with a new purpose. Mindful of the shame he had brought upon his mother, he sought to ensure that Violet and his family were always financially secure. There was a sound business purpose in this. The life of a company promoter was risky. By transferring his profits and assets to his wife, Hatry ensured that they would be protected from his creditors by the Married Women's Property Act, so that whatever temporary business setbacks might occur, his wife's funds always provided a reserve with which he could begin again.[15] On a number of occasions, Violet provided cash or transferred investments from the investment companies that Hatry later created for her, PFS Limited or VMH Limited.[16] On other occasions, Violet gave back jewellery so that it could be sold.[17]

The marriage did not, however, provide a way into the community that surrounded the stock exchange. That came by way of a second chance meeting: with Deighton Patmore who was a somewhat improbable insurance broker in a small way of business in Leicester Square.

Patmore's father and grandfather had both been poets, although his grandfather, Coventry Patmore, had been the better known as a result of the public reception of his long narrative poem, *The Angel in the House.*

This poem, completed in 1863, was an idealised account of his courtship of his first wife, Emily Andrews, whom he regarded as the perfect woman. Although feminists of the period derided the poem, and it was later to be satirised by Virginia Woolf, for many readers it represented the Victorian feminine ideal and was remembered fondly. Although not himself a poet, with his wife, Brigit, Deighton Patmore sought the company of poets and artists at the salon they maintained at their house in Kensington, and were both known to the community of writers and poets who lived on the west side of Haverstock Hill, close to Hatry's parents' house in Belsize Park.

Deighton Patmore gave the impression that he would have preferred to live as a poet and regretted that he had not inherited the talents of his grandfather and father. In short, he was a reluctant insurance broker who lacked the skill and perhaps the energy to make the most of his business. He specialised in providing services to employers seeking protection against the recent Workmen's Compensation Act, which had extended employees' rights to compensation by reducing the burden of proving that an injury had been sustained 'on the job'. From his office in Leicester Square, Patmore managed a trade association which would promise to defend employers when they faced claims under the Act and would back up the promise of defence by selling an insurance policy.[18]

When he met Hatry, Patmore was reflecting on a business problem. He had been approached by young men who were short of money but expected to receive substantial sums by inheritance, either on reaching a particular age or on the death of their parents. To finance their carefree lives, they hoped to borrow against their expected inheritance, covering the possibility that they might not survive to inherit by buying life insurance. While the banks and insurance companies would entertain this type of business, they required applicants to provide the names of two referees. Many applicants would not do this, preferring to hide from their friends and family the fact that they were borrowing money and the means they were using. Without a solution for this problem, Patmore could not arrange the loans or the parallel life insurance and thus potential commission income was lost.

Hatry suggested a straightforward solution: that the applicants should be asked to sign each other's forms. However contrived this solution may sound, it was accepted by banks and insurance companies, and opened the way for Patmore to earn commissions for arranging the loans and insurance.[19]

This was a turning point. Having demonstrated that he could make money by finding solutions for business problems, Hatry was invited to join Patmore's business to help exploit the idea, and began to build a network of relationships with the young people who found in Patmore and Hatry the answer to their financial prayers. This network was to provide Hatry's way in to the circle surrounding the stock exchange.

The world of high society was in its heyday as Vita Sackville-West described in her novel, *The Edwardians*:

> society … is composed of people who are both dissolute and prudent. They want to have their fun, and they want to keep their position. They glitter on the surface, but underneath the surface they are stupid – too stupid to recognize their own motives. They know only a limited number of things about themselves; that they need plenty of money, and that they must be seen in the right places, associated with the right people.[20]

To support their networking, Patmore and Hatry asked Bruce Logan to join them in partnership.[21] While Patmore's contribution to the partnership lay in his insurance connections, and Hatry's contribution was his flair for business ideas and networking, Logan's contribution lay in his social connections. He was a noted oar, being a member of the Thames Rowing Club crew that won the Stewards' Challenge Cup at Henley in 1911, winning the Silver Goblets at Henley in 1912 and a silver medal in the coxed four at the Olympics in 1912. Logan helped create a reputation among the *jeunesse dorée* that Patmore, Logan and Hatry Limited were the 'go to' people if money had to be borrowed. One typical borrower, Richard Norton, later Lord Grantley, who was introduced by his sister Winifred, recalled his first meeting with Hatry:

> I remember clearly my first sight of him, with his clever eyes and refined face. He was very Judaic in looks, and though quite young at the time – not more than a few years older than I was – he had already lost most of his hair, which increased his attractively intellectual appearance, and was not unbecoming. He had a very gentle voice and manners, and I took an instant liking to him … Over the next two or three years I raised, with Hatry as intermediary, very large sums of money from various sources. He never took a penny more than the modest commission to which he was entitled, although I had not the faintest idea what was going on, and was quite content to ask no questions providing he went on handing me £1,000 cheques from time to time, to fling away on my amusements in London. In fact he used to urge me to stop borrowing: and would lecture me, with the kindness of an elder brother, on the desirability of trying to get some work and earn some money.
>
> But I was in no mood for this. I had tasted the London of 1912, tempting fare for an idle and unambitious young man. I would thank Hatry, while his gentle grey eyes would look at me reproachfully, and, taking the cheque he had just extracted for me from a long-suffering lender of money, I would be off to lunch at the Ritz with the lady of my choice.[22]

By 1914, Richard Norton had borrowed £45,000 (more than £2 million in 2018 pounds) in this way.[23]

The supply of Richard Nortons was sufficient for the new partnership's business to prosper, so that within a short time, the three partners were sharing an annual profit of £20,000 (considerably in excess of £1 million in 2018 pounds). By this time Hatry had become the leader of the insurance broking partnership and took responsibility for its management. One of his most important decisions was to move the partnership from Leicester Square to a more prestigious address: 180 Piccadilly. Standing on a corner of Piccadilly just across Duke Street from Fortnum & Mason, on a site for many years occupied by the Swiss Railways offices but now occupied by hedge funds and private equity partnerships, this building was next door to Fortnum & Mason and midway between the Ritz and the Cavendish Hotel.

For the young people described by Vita Sackville-West, this hotel was a centre for fashionable life, overseen by its chatelaine, Rosa Lewis. Starting as a kitchen maid, she had established herself as a cook whom families could invite into their houses to cater for dinners, balls or country house parties. She employed a large number of kitchen girls as trainees who were all dressed alike in high-laced boots and chef's hats because, as she used to say, she could rely upon women to work harder than men. Conscious of maintaining her reputation, she would be in Covent Garden at 5 a.m. to buy the best vegetables and would then use her own kitchen to prepare as many of the dinner dishes as possible in advance. In the afternoon, Rosa and her entourage would descend on the relevant kitchen and the resident staff would bow out. In this way she would prepare the elaborate menus which had come to be expected of her. By 1897, when she was 30, Rosa Lewis had become the most successful and socially acceptable caterer of the time, hailed by Escoffier as the Queen of Cooks, sought after by hostesses such as Lady Randolph Churchill and befriended by King Edward VII when he was the Prince of Wales.

In 1902, allegedly with the help of the King, she acquired the Cavendish Hotel and set out to create the somewhat dubious ambience of the country houses she knew well. Heavily formal, country house parties combined social gloss with secret liaisons. Meals would be enormous and as elaborate as the dress that guests would be expected to wear. The organisation and precision required to stage the meals was matched by the care with which bedrooms would be allocated and promiscuity facilitated.[24]

The hotel was extended by buying neighbouring houses and was converted to a series of suites. There were no bars or lounges. Visitors were expected either to be guests of residents in their suites or were invited into Mrs Lewis's own suite where her hospitality, not least in the form of champagne, was legendary, as was the somewhat vague way in which bills would be calculated. Those who Mrs Lewis thought could afford to pay often found that they were making a contribution to those who she thought could not afford to pay. In Martin Vander Weyer's memorable phrase, the hotel became renowned as a haven of 'discreet, upper-crust misbehaviours': a reputation encouraged by holding dinners in the Elinor Glyn room, named after the popular romantic novelist whose books described outrageous country house weekends. Under Rosa Lewis's tutelage, the hotel became a favoured haunt not only of the affluent young, but also of soldiers, businessmen and politicians, notably Liberal politicians such as David Lloyd George, then chancellor of the exchequer, and Herbert Asquith, the prime minister. In 1915, it was at the Cavendish Hotel that Kitchener took his last dinner in London before leaving to travel to Scapa Flow for his fateful crossing to Russia.[25] It was precisely the place where a young broker such as Hatry could expect to meet people with political and commercial influence who might further his career.

A glance at the names of the directors of companies which Hatry was to form in the next few years shows just how successful he was in capitalising on the networking opportunities offered by the Cavendish Hotel. They included the Earl of March, son of the Duke of Richmond; Henry Pelham Clinton, son of the Duke of Newcastle; and Captain the Honourable Arthur Bingham, heir to Lord Clanmorris. From an earlier generation, they included Lord Ribblesdale, who is believed to have been the model used by G.B. Shaw for the character Henry Higgins in Pygmalion and is now chiefly remembered as the subject for a powerful portrait by John Singer Sargent which hangs in the National Gallery and is known as *The Ancestor*, the nickname given to Lord Ribblesdale by King Edward VII. Ribblesdale had been one of Mrs Lewis's regular country house clients in the 1890s and became a semi-permanent resident of the Cavendish Hotel after the death of his wife Charlotte in 1911. In the 1880s and 1890s, he had served as a whip in Liberal governments but had not subsequently held political appointments. He was however a consistent supporter of the Liberal Party who attracted to the hotel not only politicians but also their advisers such as Lord St Davids, who managed a group of investment trusts and was a close associate of Lloyd George, eventually serving as treasurer of his private political fund, and Sir Frank Crisp, senior partner of Ashurst Morris Crisp, the legal adviser to the Liberal Party and the doyen of company lawyers. Both Lord St Davids and Sir Frank Crisp were close associates of Osborne O'Hagan, the renowned and successful company promoter who when in London lived in Albany, opposite Hatry's office at 180 Piccadilly.

All of them represented opportunities for Hatry to gain connexions and influence, although the business which resulted was not always conventional or uncontroversial. In 1914, Hatry and Logan allowed someone they knew to deposit documents in the safe in their office.[26] The person concerned was holding the documents on behalf of Frances, Countess of Warwick, who in 1914 needed to raise money to pay off a debt of £16,000 which she owed to Arthur du Cros, the Tory member of parliament (MP) for Hastings and the head of the Dunlop Rubber Company. Unbeknown to Hatry and Logan, the documents deposited in their safe were letters which the countess had exchanged with King Edward VII when she was his mistress. She hoped that a threat to publish the letters would persuade the Royal Family to buy them so that she could pay off her loan.

Soon afterwards, both Hatry and Logan began to suspect that they were being followed by stolid-looking men wearing bowler hats. As Hatry later recalled:

> I became almost attached to my unsolicited attendant. On one occasion, after crossing a busy street and finding that he had been cut off by the traffic, I paused to allow him time to catch up with me. My conscience was clear and if someone was foolish enough to employ an ex-policeman (for such he obviously was) to keep track of my movements, there was no reason for me to get angry with the dutiful employee.[27]

In time, Hatry and Logan were approached by a partner of Messrs Russell, the King's solicitors, with an injunction requiring them not to part with the documents in their possession or permit them to be published. At this point, not having previously read them, Hatry and Logan began to appreciate the true nature of the countess's letters:

> They were the kind of intimate, careless notes that old friends drop each other, what in the modern jargon might be called 'off the record' letters. They apparently contained slighting references to the Kaiser ... uncomplimentary remarks about certain Cabinet Ministers and smoking room stories that the King [Edward VII] had heard late at night when the port had circulated freely.[28]

The Royal Family's desire to keep such letters private would have been understandable at any time but became a paramount concern in the atmosphere of July 1914 when war with Germany was becoming unavoidable. After some weeks, a settlement was reached in which the countess sold the letters to du Cros, who then destroyed them.

In the aftermath, du Cros was to receive a baronetcy. For Hatry himself there may have been another consequence:

> This anecdote had an odd sequel some seven or eight years later. A colleague on one of my company boards, Sir Douglas Dawson, who had been an Equerry to the King, told me that when my name was put forward for a certain honour, His Majesty was scrutinising the Letters Patent before signing them. He turned to his Equerry and said, 'Hatry? Hatry? Isn't that the little so-and-so we had trouble with over my father's letters?'[29]

This story appears unlikely. Laurance Lyon MP remembered that Hatry attempted to secure an honour in 1920 and blamed Hatry's failure on his impetuous hamfistedness.[30] If Lyon's memory is correct, it is unlikely that Letters Patent were ever presented to the King for signature. For whatever reason, Hatry never received any of the honours which he undoubtedly coveted and this anecdote, told to an author some decades later, shows Hatry in his vanity unwilling to admit to his own mistakes, preferring to blame other people's prejudices.

By the onset of war in 1914, Patmore, Logan and Hatry Limited had made substantial amounts of money and had gained in reputation, connexions and influence. The money enabled Hatry to begin experimenting as a promoter of companies.

The years immediately before the onset of the 1914–1918 war saw a remarkable wave of emigration from Eastern Europe to the United States of America.[31] Partly a reaction to the local wars and atrocities in the Balkans and Russia, the scale of the migration was similar to the scale of the exodus from Syria, Iraq and Afghanistan in the twenty-first century. In the peak year, 1907, the US Immigration Service processed 1,004,756 migrants applying for entry. Even though the numbers then declined, in 1913, 829,000 people travelled to New York, many of them carried by British shipping lines. Just as in the twenty-first century, the emigration was assisted by agents who arranged passages for all who wanted to make the long, complicated journey and were prepared to take the risk that they would be denied entry on arrival on the grounds of contagious disease, criminal background or insanity. In practice, the risk was relatively small because the immigration inspection station at Ellis Island only rejected about 2% of applications. Nonetheless many would understandably have been troubled by this risk. Travelling to the United States was not inexpensive and for many emigrants would have seriously depleted their resources to the point where paying for a return passage on rejection at Ellis Island would not have been possible.

As the son of two immigrants himself, Hatry had an affinity with the immigrant community and made the acquaintance of Bernard Weinfeld, one of the many agents who arranged passages for emigrants. In discussions with him, Hatry recognised that the possibility of rejection at Ellis Island was an insurable risk which might offer the prospect of profit. Using Patmore's insurance connexions, Hatry persuaded the Provident Clerks and General Guarantee and Accident Company Limited to underwrite an insurance policy which would cover the cost of a return passage for any insured migrant who was rejected on arrival at Ellis Island. He then arranged for the policy to be sold throughout Eastern Europe by local agents recruited by Weinfeld. By October 1913, there were 27 local agents based mainly in Austria but also in Poland, Russia and Germany.[32] The scheme was immediately successful – and profitable. Although some migrants were rejected on arrival at Ellis Island, the number of rejections was small, and the cost of arranging return passages was covered by the insurance company. After payment of the insurance company's premium (one shilling per policy), the balance of the premium received from migrants (ten shillings and sixpence per policy) was profit.

Initially, Hatry and Weinfeld kept this business as a private matter between themselves, but in mid-1913, Hatry saw an opportunity of making a capital profit by transferring the business (and Bernard Weinfeld's company, Ocean Express Limited) to a company set up by Patmore, Logan and Hatry Limited. So the Union Emigrants Association Limited came into being and its 23,000 £1 preference shares were sold. As it was a private company, the number of its shareholders was limited to 50 and there was no public offer: the shares presumably being passed to friends and connexions of the insurance broking business. The demand for shares exceeded supply, and after a month or two, a further company, Union Emigrants Association (Italy) Limited was incorporated and granted sole rights to market the migrant insurance policy in the kingdom of Italy. A further 18,000 £1 preference shares were sold by this new company.[33]

By 1914, Clarence Hatry's life had been transformed. He had married Violet Ferguson and two children had been born to them: Cecil in 1910 and Diana in September 1914. His family was settled in a flat in Iverna Court, South Kensington, where Diana was born.

Rather than being shackled to the remains of the moribund silk business, he had built a loan broking business which had already produced a considerable income for its partners. For the first time, he had promoted a company – and made a profit in the process. Even more importantly, he had proved that he could devise solutions for business problems and had begun to build a network of contacts. Perhaps most impressively, that network included not only the impoverished children of the rich who came to him for loans, but also the politicians and their advisers who frequented the Cavendish Hotel.

He was still only 26.

Notes

1 Braggion and Moore, 2013.
2 Michie, 1999, page 108 et seq.
3 Armstrong, 1990, page 126. For a comprehensive description and analysis of the promoters' practices before the 1914–1918 war see: Nye, 2012.
4 Armstrong, 1990, page 116.
5 LSX Rule 151(1) and Appendix 36 to the Rules. In considering admission to dealing, the LSX applied more restrictive criteria to securities which were admitted to the Official List as opposed to securities which were admitted to the Supplementary List. This distinction served as a signal to alert potential investors that securities admitted to the Official List were likely to carry a lower degree of risk. Burhop et al., 2012.
6 Armstrong, 1990, page 124.
7 Lavington, 1921, page 183 et seq. Armstrong, 1990, page 128 et seq.
8 Dickens, 1855–7; Trollope, 1874.
9 LSX annual lists of members. TNA file.
10 *The Times*, 21 March 1919, page 20; 5 April 1919, page 20; 28 April 1919, page 19; 12 May 1919, page 21; 22 May 1919, page 23; 12 August 1919, page 16; and 6 November 1919, page 19.
11 *Sunday Telegraph*, 1 August 1965, page 4.
12 Marriage certificate.
13 For example, no birth certificate can be found in either the English or Scottish registers for an appropriate date, nor does there appear to be a marriage certificate for a Ronald Ferguson at an appropriate date.
14 Mariner's Buildings, Dartmouth Road, Rotherhithe (Report of the Medical Officer for Health, Rotherhithe, 1898, Wellcome Library online, downloaded 12 August 2018).

15 Holcombe, 1983, page 160. Greenfield, 1995, page 51.
16 The name of PFS Limited stood for 'Profit From Steel' which arose from the fact that Hatry's advice to his wife concentrated on investment in the steel companies which he had been attempting to reorganise before his trial. The name of VMH Limited stood for Violet Marguerite Hatry.
17 Greenfield, 1995, page 51.
18 London street directories.
19 Lang, 1966, page 201.
20 Sackville-West, 1930, page 165.
21 Lang, 1966, page 196.
22 Wood and Wood, 1954, pages 57–58.
23 Wood and Wood, 1954, page 94.
24 Harrison, 1962; Masters, 1977.
25 Lawton, 1925, page 129.
26 Pullar, 1975, page 295.
27 Lang, 1966, pages 205–206.
28 Lang, 1966, page 207.
29 Lang, 1966, pages 209–210.
30 Anonymous, 1927.
31 Zahra, 2016, page 4.
32 A list of the agents appears as an appendix to the agreement by which the company acquired the business from Hatry and Weinfeld (TNA file BT 31/21650/130554).
33 TNA file BT 31/22200/135157.

References

Primary works: unpublished

TNA: Board of Trade papers.

Primary works: newspapers and periodicals

Sunday Telegraph
The Times

Primary works: contemporary books and papers

Anonymous. (1927), *By the Waters of Babylon.* (Hutchinson, London).
Dickens, C. (1855–7), *Little Dorrit.* (Chapman & Hall, London).
Lavington, F. (1921), *The English Capital Market.* (Methuen, London).
Sackville-West, V. (1930), *The Edwardians.* (Hogarth Press, London).
Trollope, A. (1874), *The Way We Live Now.* (Chapman, London).

Secondary works

Armstrong, J. (1990), 'The Rise and Fall of the Company Promoter and the Financing of British Industry', in Van Helten, J.J. and Cassis, Y. (eds), *Capitalism in a Mature Economy: Financial Institutions, Capital Exports and British Industry, 1870–1939.* (Edward Elgar, Aldershot).
Braggion, F and Moore, L (2013), 'How Insiders Traded before Rules', *Business History*, volume 55(4), pages 562–582.

Burhop, C., Chambers, D., and Cheffins, B.R. (2012), 'Regulating IPOs: Evidence from Going Public in London and Berlin', *Legal Studies Research Paper Series*. University of Cambridge Faculty of Law, paper 2/2012.

Greenfield, G. (1995), *A Smattering of Monsters: A Kind of Memoir*. (Little Brown, London).

Harrison, M. (1962), *Rosa: Rosa Lewis of the Cavendish*. (Peter Davies, London).

Holcombe, L. (1983), *Wives and Property: Reform of the Married Women's Property Law in Nineteenth-Century England*. (Martin Robertson, Oxford).

Lang, T. (1966), *The Darling Daisy Affair*. (Atheneum, New York).

Lawton, M. (1925), *The Queen of Cooks – And Some Kings: The Story of Rosa Lewis*. (Boni and Liveright, New York).

Masters, A. (1977), *Rosa Lewis: An Exceptional Edwardian*. (Weidenfeld and Nicolson, London).

Michie, R.C. (1999), *The London Stock Exchange: A History*. (Oxford University Press, Oxford).

Nye, J.G.D. (2012), 'The Company Promoter in London 1877–1914'. Unpublished PhD thesis, University of London

Pullar, F. (1975), *Frank Harris*. (Hamish Hamilton, London).

Wood, M. and Wood, A. (1954), *Silver Spoon: The Memoirs of Lord Grantly*. (Hutchinson, London).

Zahra, T. (2016), *The Great Departure: Mass Migration from Eastern Europe and the Making of the Free World*. (W.W. Norton, New York).

3 1914

The coming of war

At 2300 hours on Tuesday 4 August 1914, Britain went to war. A few weeks earlier such an event had seemed improbable. Even after the assassination of the unpopular Archduke Franz Ferdinand and his wife Sophia in Sarajevo, on 28 July 1914, it had generally been assumed that any dispute could be resolved without fighting – let alone fighting that involved Britain. As the culmination of a crisis that had careered out of control, the declaration of war was a shock to which a rash of suicides and premature births testified. For many people, there was a sense that the coming of war brought with it a different world, marking the end of an old order with the assumption of new powers by the state. Although there was a common presumption that the new war would follow the precedent of the Franco-Prussian war of 1870 and be over quickly, no one knew quite what to expect.[1]

For the Hatry family, the coming of war brought a personal disaster.

As Hatry's associate, Osborne O'Hagan, a well-known company promoter, observed: 'the City was totally unprepared for the catastrophe which was to fall upon it'.[2] No one had appreciated that a rapid descent into war would lead to a breakdown in the system of payments and transfers between countries. As the crisis drew near to its climax at the beginning of August, each of the stock exchanges in Europe recorded large falls in share prices and either closed or deferred settlement. In London, stockbrokers who had sold shares to brokers in exchanges that had already closed found that they would not receive the money due to them which they in turn needed to pay the brokers from whom they had bought the shares. The inevitable result was that the brokers were declared insolvent.[3]

Clarence Hatry's uncle John Eiser was the senior partner of J.G. Eiser & Company, one of the largest broking firms specialising in trade with brokers in Germany.[4] On 29 July 1914, it found itself unable to meet its debts in London because it was could not collect its debts from German brokers. It was no comfort that other firms suffered the same difficulty. In company with a small number of others, the firm was hammered and all of its partners ceased to be members of the London Stock Exchange. Just two days later, the exchange bowed to the inevitable by closing and declaring a moratorium on payments, thus saving other firms from the same disaster. In time, John

Eiser's family had to find new accommodation. Most poignantly, John Eiser's sister-in-law, Henriette, Clarence's mother, who had moved into the Eisers' home after her own financial crisis, found herself without a home for the second time in four years.[5]

For Clarence this brought back memories of his mother's loss of her Belsize Park home and the importance of his making more money not just to secure his own family's future but also his mother's.

Hatry was able to concentrate upon the family's financial problems because his health was fragile after a bout of rheumatic fever in childhood which left him with a slight limp, so he was honourably absolved from military service. Although hampered by his physical disability, Hatry's absolution from military service was to prove an opportunity. While commercial life in the City continued throughout the war, it was hampered by the numbers of men who were to serve in the armed forces and by the restrictions which the government insisted that the stock exchange should impose on its members.[6] Some firms, such as Clare & Company, a stockbroking firm which specialised in new issues, were obliged to cease operations for the duration of the war, only reopening in 1919 when its principals returned from their wartime service.[7] This was an opportunity for Hatry who was not a member of the exchange and was prepared to operate off-market beyond the reach of the exchange's rules.

Unfortunately, for a while, the coming of war disrupted his business activities. As young men went to war, their demand for loans to enjoy life in London disappeared, and with it the chance for Patmore, Logan and Hatry Limited to earn commissions. The tide of emigration from Eastern Europe to the USA stopped almost immediately, and with it the chance for Union Emigrants Association Limited to sell insurance to migrants. Within a short while, the company had closed and Bernard Weinfeld, the immigration agent who was Clarence Hatry's associate, had himself emigrated finally to New York.[8] Most frustratingly, Hatry's newest venture, the Planet Insurance Company, was stymied by the closure of the stock exchange.

It had become common practice for insurance companies to manage their risks by buying reinsurance from specialist reinsurance companies: a trade in which German and Austrian businesses predominated. Remarkably, no new reinsurance companies had been founded in Britain during the second half of the nineteenth century, although a few had been created between 1900 and 1910. During this same period, more than 40 had been founded on the mainland of Europe, with German companies surpassing the others. By 1914, German companies such as Münchener Rückverisherungs-Gesellschaft (known in London as Munich Re) accounted for as much as 60% of the market. With a number of supporters, Hatry proposed to challenge the German reinsurers by creating a British competitor. To this end, early in 1914, his syndicate acquired a small insurance company, the Planet Insurance Company Limited, and set about re-registering it as a public company and restructuring its capital in readiness for a public offer of shares to raise the additional capital which would be required. This is as far as the plan had reached by the onset of war in the summer of 1914.[9]

In this form, the plan was scotched by the war. The closure of the stock exchange caused the public issue to be delayed and although the exchange reopened in January 1915, new issues were to be tightly controlled. Although the government's rhetoric had implied that some new issues might be permitted, the market soon realised that in practice this was unlikely to happen.

As one door closed, another opened.

On the coming of war, proclamations immediately prohibited trading with the enemy, terminating all arrangements by which British insurance companies had arranged reinsurance with German and Austrian companies and prohibiting any new arrangements with such companies.[10] On its own, this would have created an instant demand for reinsurance capacity to enable British insurance companies to continue trading, but the position was made more serious because the coming of war heightened the risk of claims against insurance companies. Shipping companies became concerned about losing vessels through enemy action and property owners feared enemy action by air, although the possible extent and effectiveness of attack from the air was difficult to assess. Naturally the combination of a higher risk of claims and the disappearance of reinsurance capacity created an immediate demand for new capacity which did not involve enemy interests, and a rapid increase in reinsurance premiums.[11]

Fortunately, the proclamations prohibiting trading with the enemy made investment in British companies unattractive for German and Austrian investors, so there were overseas investors who wanted to dispose of interests in British companies – including British reinsurance companies. In these somewhat chaotic circumstances, Hatry and his associates acting through the Planet were able to acquire a German shareholder's controlling interest in City Equitable Fire Insurance Limited, a small British reinsurance company concentrating upon the reinsurance of fire and marine risks. Although almost ten years old, City Equitable's growth had been disappointing as premiums had amounted to only £80,000 in 1912 and 1913 and at 31 December 1912 its investments amounted to less than £51,000. Even so it provided Hatry's syndicate with a platform from which to take advantage of the heightened demand for reinsurance cover.[12]

Everyone assumed that the stock exchange's closure would be short-lived and that business would resume on a normal basis when the stock exchange reopened. Although new issues would not be possible while the exchange was closed, they would start again when it reopened. So, when City Equitable was acquired, Hatry and his associates assumed that the restriction on new issues would soon be released and that in due course they would be able to raise money by a new issue of shares. On this basis, of the total purchase price of £55,000, only £3,000 was paid immediately, leaving £52,000 to be paid when funds had been raised, with a deadline of 31 March 1915.[13] When the stock exchange reopened in January 1915, rumours began to circulate that the Planet would be offering shares for sale to finance a reinsurance venture. With this prospect in mind, the work of restructuring the company's share capital, board and management went forward. Apart from his longstanding associates, Lord Ribblesdale, Lord March and Arthur Bingham (later Lord Clanmorris), Hatry added four other directors: Sir David Burnett, Sir Douglas Dawson, Henry Grenside and Moir Milligan.

Sir David Burnett, a former Lord Mayor of London, became chairman. He was best known for having organised the public subscription that saved the Crystal Palace at Sydenham for the nation, and does not seem to have professed great commercial experience. A few months later, in April 1915, Sir Douglas Dawson was invited by his neighbour in Henley, Sir Frank Crisp, Hatry's solicitor, to become a director.[14] After a distinguished military career, and a period as military attaché in Vienna, Paris, Brussels and Bern, Sir Douglas had become a member of the Royal Household, as comptroller of the Lord Chamberlain's Department. In that role, he was involved in theatre censorship, and had been, for example, instrumental in the banning of Granville Barker's controversial play, *Waste*, which had explored contemporary attitudes towards abortion. More significantly from Hatry's point of view was Dawson's position as secretary of the Order of the Garter and the Order of Merit and as inspector of Vulnerable Points at the Horse Guards. Although Burnett and Dawson did not profess great commercial experience, they added to the impression of respectability that Hatry was trying to create. Moreover, Dawson was in an excellent position to intercede with the Treasury should any dispute arise over an issue of the Planet's shares.[15]

As far as management was concerned, the incumbent secretary of the company, Edward George Mansell, was appointed general manager. He had worked for City Equitable since it had been founded and was a genuine expert in reinsurance. He also proved to be an effective business-getter. The company's management would not depend upon Hatry. When Mansell was appointed general manager, the company's business had already improved with the result that premium income for the period ended 28 February 1915 was about double the income of the previous period. At the Annual General Meeting on 20 May 1915, Mansell exuded confidence in the future:

> To meet the further expansion of the business it was necessary that fresh capital should be raised, and … I am able to inform you that, since the subscribed capital of the company was increased from £50,000 to £250,000, further valuable contracts are already being entered into which will have the effect of very considerably increasing the income of the company, and I feel sure that at future annual meetings your directors will be able to report a constant and substantial increase in the company's annual income and corresponding profits.[16]

This increase in capital had been arranged privately and not by the public offer of a new issue of shares. Although brokers had been led to expect that new issues would be permitted, the chancellor of the exchequer had privately urged the Capital Issues Committee to veto all new issues and this is what happened.

However the capital had been provided, the new capital enabled the company to grow as Mansell had predicted. At the next Annual General Meeting, the board was able to report that premium income had more than doubled again, as had the profit. By the end of February 1916, the investment portfolio amounted to £106,000 and cash on deposit amounted to £30,000.[17] The initial judgement at the beginning of the war that there was money to be made in reinsurance had been thoroughly vindicated, although the realisation of this prospect must have been almost wholly due to Edward Mansell who was left in sole charge of the day-to-day management of the reinsurance business. The almost complete reliance on Mansell's knowledge of reinsurance was later to prove an embarrassment in the landmark litigation which followed the company's demise in early 1920.

The time had come for Hatry's next move.

Two opportunities presented themselves: a chance to sell City Equitable to Gerard Lee Bevan for a substantial profit and a chance to use that profit to buy a bank.

Of these two, the potential sale of City Equitable to Gerard Lee Bevan was the more remarkable for it initiated a close relationship between Hatry and Bevan, seemingly incompatible operators. A scion of one of the families which founded Barclays Bank, Bevan had been passed over for employment within the bank and his father had bought for him a partnership in Ellis & Company, a firm of stockbrokers. The firm had been founded by Thomas Ellis in 1778 and in the early years of the nineteenth century had been celebrated for raising a loan of £24 million for the government to finance Wellington's campaign against Napoleon. In short, it was one of the longest established stock exchange firms and was also one of its stuffiest. So stuffy was the firm that Osborne O'Hagan, one of the more successful promoters of new issues and one of Hatry's closest supporters, knew better than to try to do business with them:

> one of the leading firms of London stockbrokers, old-established and prosperous … so old fashioned was the firm's reputation that I never attempted to secure them for my underwriting list: new undertakings were the last thing I should have expected them to interest themselves in.[18]

At first sight, Bevan was suited to this type of firm. One of his biographers, Aylmer Vallance, painted him as a 'gilded old Etonian – civilized, politely arrogant, and certain the world owed much to him'.[19] So well suited was he to his firm that just before the war Bevan had become senior partner.

It was not surprising that stockbrokers would be interested in the broking business generated by the investment portfolio of a rapidly growing reinsurance company such as City Equitable, but it was surprising that a stuffy, blue-blooded City house should ally itself so closely with a young man in a hurry such as Hatry. That it happened at all was in part due to an improbable overlap between Bevan's and Hatry's circles of friends.

Gerard Bevan's principal aides in the acquisition of City Equitable were to be Theodore Barclay and Peter Haig-Thomas. Barclay was a member of another family associated with Barclays Bank who had become senior partner of a firm of stockbrokers, in his case Sheppards & Company. Haig-Thomas was a nephew of David Thomas, later ennobled as Lord Rhondda, who had extensive interests in coal mines in Wales which had been brought together as Consolidated Cambrian Limited, a company which had been floated on the stock exchange with the assistance of Ellis & Company in 1914.[20] These two different characters were united by a common experience: they had both won the Silver Goblets at Henley and had both rowed for Cambridge in the annual University Boat Race. Barclay had won the Silver Goblets in 1887, setting a record time of 8 minutes 15 seconds. Haig-Thomas had won the Silver Goblets in 1905. After his victory in 1905, Haig-Thomas had remained a notable figure at Henley and was to go on to become a distinguished coach of Cambridge crews and, in later years, Oxford crews in the Boat Race.

Hatry's partner, Bruce Logan, was also a notable figure at Henley. In 1912, he won the Silver Goblets and went on to win a silver medal in that year's Olympic Games. In the previous year, 1911, and in Barclay's presence, Logan had competed for the Silver Goblets, but had been eliminated at a preliminary stage, in a dead heat, setting a new record time of 8 minutes 11 seconds: 4 seconds inside Theodore Barclay's record time of 8 minutes 15 seconds which had stood for 25 years. Through this connection, Hatry was introduced to Bevan.

It may seem odd that Hatry and Bevan were able to form a successful business relationship. Bevan was a blue-blooded City insider convinced of his entitlement to success. Hatry was a young newcomer, who had already been bankrupted once and was ready to take risks to achieve the financial reward and social standing he so craved. That they succeeded together suggests that Bevan was not quite what he seemed. His biographer, Martin Vander Weyer, speculates that he displayed a blindness to risk which led to his being passed over for employment within Barclays Bank because he did not possess the visceral risk aversion and meticulous attention to formality expected of successful bankers. One of the partners at Ellis & Company commented in a written report to the Metropolitan Police that Bevan would trust anybody – not usually a qualification for successful trading.[21] Possibly because he felt a need to demonstrate that his family had erred in passing him over for employment within the bank, Bevan was attracted by the profits that could be achieved through the promotion of new issues, an activity that, as O'Hagan knew, would traditionally have been avoided by Ellis & Company. Both Bevan and Hatry had something to prove. Bevan wanted to live down his family's assessment of his abilities. Hatry wanted to achieve acceptance by the community of the City. They were both risk-takers.[22]

Bevan and Hatry found that they shared an ability to understand balance sheets. Bevan was to be remembered by Baron Emile d'Erlanger, an Anglo-French financier, as a man with an exceptional command of figures and a great ability to explain a business clearly and concisely. Many years later, George Greenfield, a literary agent who worked for Hatry after the 1939–1945 war, recalled that if doubts were raised about a proposition:

> in quarter of an hour he had plucked out figures, juggled with them and then proved conclusively that the problems did not exist. Of course, when the bubbles subsided, you realised that the problems had not gone away – but while you were the target of CCH's battery of wit and charm, everything seemed not only possible but likely as well.[23]

Greenfield's recollection is echoed by the memories of Laurance Lyon, who in 1920 was MP for Hastings:

> His slight, almost delicate appearance, his soft manner, and his gentle way of speaking, and a placidity which apparently nothing could ruffle, were all d'une pièce. But a curious and different look came into his eyes – actually – when he began to disclose and discuss the details of all his schemes; and especially when he went to the little blackboard, which was always a curious feature in his office, and with the aid of a piece of chalk, set out to demonstrate that his conclusions were correct; for he had a particular predilection for that system, which he asserted made for lucidity, and of which he claimed to be the inventor.[24]

However it happened, Bevan and Hatry formed a close understanding, the sale of City Equitable went ahead and Hatry achieved a capital profit of £200,000. Almost immediately, the profit was used in the next stage of creating Hatry's financial empire: the acquisition of Commercial Bank of London Limited.

Hatry aimed to become a company promoter and stock exchange operator in the fashion of Osborne O'Hagan. To enter into this trade, as O'Hagan would have explained, Hatry needed a company to serve as a platform for raising funds and managing faultlessly the documents and transactions that were involved in any public offer of shares.[25]

In 1916, this was not a straightforward matter. The wartime controls on new issues imposed at the government's request prevented Hatry from forming a new company to raise capital through a public offering. The solution presented to Hatry was the acquisition of an existing bank. At this time, O'Hagan's principal business interest was Associated Portland Cement Manufacturers Limited which he had created by taking over a large number of small cement works. In 1910, a controlling interest in that company had been acquired by John Phillips, Lord St Davids, who controlled the Old Broad Street Group of investment trusts which he had himself created. From that point, O'Hagan and Phillips had formed a partnership, collaborating to extend the cement group's domination of the cement manufacturing industry.

John Phillips was one of three remarkable brothers, all of whom were eventually ennobled. In February 1888, John Phillips had married Leonora Gerstenberg, one of two orphaned girls who inherited a fortune from their father, Isidore Gerstenberg, the founder of the Corporation of Foreign Bondholders which safeguarded the interests of British holders of foreign bonds. By the time of her marriage, Leonora's fortune had grown to about £100,000. With his wife's financial support, Phillips had acquired interests in investment trusts and in 1890 became a director of an early investment trust, Government Stocks and Other Securities Investment Company, which shortly thereafter was embarrassed by the Barings crisis. Phillips was appointed chairman and managed to rescue the company. Subsequently he became a director and then chairman of a series of other trusts, and was able to use their funds to support the shipping interests of his two brothers: Laurence, later Lord Milford, who founded Court Line, and Owen, later Lord Kylsant, who was to create the Royal Mail Steamship Group, one of the largest shipping groups in the country.[26]

In 1912, Phillips' investment trusts had acquired a controlling interest in Anglo-Japanese Bank Limited, a small bank which had been formed a few years earlier to finance trade between Japan and Great Britain but had failed to pierce the Japanese banks' monopoly of the trade because of language difficulties. On gaining control, Phillips had changed the name of the bank to Commercial Bank of London Limited with the intention of concentrating on domestic business. By the onset of war, the bank's business was still small and the directors decided that, for the duration of the war, it would not write new loans, concentrating on managing its existing commitments. So it was that at the beginning of 1916, Phillips controlled a small bank which was not making a return for its shareholders and was not expected to resume normal business before the end of the war. Two personal tragedies, the death of Leonora, his formidable wife, in March 1915 and the death of his elder son in France in May 1915, were sapping his enthusiasm for business so that, as O'Hagan knew, he was reducing his commitments by selling investments.

Hatry took his chance and bought Commercial Bank and then increased its size by taking advantage of another chance by acquiring Reuters Bank from Baron Julius de Reuter.[27] As was his normal practice, Hatry reformed the board of directors by introducing a number of his old associates and adding Peter Haig-Thomas to maintain the relationship with Bevan and City Equitable. This relationship was to prove especially valuable to Hatry as a company promoter needed a way of managing the market price for his newly floated shares to build the confidence of potential investors who would not buy the newly offered shares unless they expected there to be an active after-market. In the years which followed the 1914–1918 war, Bevan and

Ellis & Company were to collaborate with Hatry. Bevan arranged that City Equitable and Ellis & Company would take large positions in the shares floated by Hatry, either selling them slowly at a profit if there was demand in the after-market or buying more if there was selling pressure and the market price fell.[28]

Alexander Roger, the existing chairman of Commercial Bank of London, was keen to stand down. In 1915, he had become director general of Trench Warfare at the Ministry of Munitions and was absorbed by the process of setting up and managing the government-owned factories which would produce weapons specially designed for trench warfare for which no demand had been foreseen at the outset of war. Not only was Hatry good at forming relationships, however unlikely, he was also good at preserving them. Although Roger left the board of Commercial Bank of London, he was later to serve as a director of companies floated by Hatry and seems to have been the conduit by which some potential transactions were introduced to Hatry.[29]

In his place, Sir Charles Hobhouse had been appointed chairman. Until May 1915, Hobhouse had been postmaster general in Asquith's Cabinet, but had lost office when the first coalition was formed. In October 1915, he was told that he had an internal growth which was inoperable. He nonetheless underwent and survived an operation which found that his illness was not as serious as feared. By the time he was fully recovered, Asquith had resigned as prime minister and the Cabinet had been reformed. He was never to hold high political office again although he retained his seat in the House of Commons until the general election in 1918.[30]

Acquisition of Commercial Bank was another significant milestone for Hatry who thereafter directed all his energy to developing its business, moving his office to the City from 180 Piccadilly.[31] This led to the severance of his partnership with Deighton Patmore and Bruce Logan and the termination of his relationship with Patmore – a rare example of a relationship that Hatry was not able to preserve. This breach was later to be much regretted by Patmore's family, for without Hatry the insurance broking business withered and the wealth that Patmore had gathered was dissipated. In time this brought an end to Patmore's business career and to his marriage. Pursuing her fascination with poets, Brigit Patmore joined Ezra Pound's circle in Paris and Deighton Patmore became engaged in what would in later years be called alternative therapies.[32]

While the demise of Hatry's insurance broking partnership may have been a disappointment, by the end of December 1916 he had achieved much. Not only had he demonstrated that he could find solutions for business problems, his acquisition and then disposal of City Equitable followed by the acquisition of Commercial Bank had shown that he could implement his solutions in spite of adverse wartime circumstances. As a result, he had acquired a platform for raising funds to finance stock exchange operations and an organisation that he could use to execute transactions in shares. He had also begun to form the close team of professional advisers that any company promoter needed. J.D. Langton & Passmore, a firm of solicitors, and Ellis & Company, the stockbrokers, were to act in almost all of his share issues between 1916 and 1922.

This close team of publicly acknowledged advisers was surrounded by another group of committed supporters. This group included not only people who arranged loans with Hatry's assistance and went on to sit on the boards of his companies, but City names such as Sir Frank Crisp, the lawyer, and Osborne O'Hagan, the company promoter. Beyond them Hatry had formed connections with a wider circle which included prominent figures in the Liberal Party such as Viscount St Davids, the treasurer of the fund that financed Lloyd George's campaigns, and Arthur du Cros, a Conservative Party MP.

In December 1916 he celebrated his 28th birthday. Hatry's calculation that he would be able to make his fortune in the City was proving to be correct.

Notes

1 Kirkaldy, 1915; Lawson, 1915; Withers, 1915; Michie, 1999, pages 143 et seq; Kynaston, 1999, page 3 et seq; Roberts, 2013.
2 Michie, 1999, page 146.
3 *Financial Times*, 30 July 1914, page 8; 31 July 1914, page 3.
4 On the factors that made arbitrage trading in London attractive to Jewish immigrants from Germany, see Michie, 1999, pages 128–129.
5 Even if Eiser's firm had survived July 1914, its business would have been severely curtailed by the onset of war as arbitrage trading was to be forbidden during the war which caused much financial distress for specialist arbitrageurs (Michie, 1999, pages 156–157; Stock exchange General Purposes Committee minutes, 22 January 1915; LSX archive, Guildhall Library).
6 The stock exchange did not permit dealings in new issues of shares that had not been approved by a new committee established by HM Treasury. Contrary to expectations, the committee followed the private instructions of the chancellor of the exchequer and sought to exclude all new issues that did not serve the government's view of the national interest (letter dated 17 April 1915 from the chancellor of the exchequer cited in Beach and Victoria, 1932, page 329). For the loss of manpower and expertise, see Michie, 1999, pages 155–156.
7 The two principals were Oliver Clare and John Jarvis. In the 1930s, Jarvis was to play a prominent role in creating employment opportunities in Jarrow after the closure of the local shipyard.
8 On 26 August 1914, Bernard and Sigi Weinfeld left Liverpool for New York on board SS *New York* (TNA passenger list).
9 *Insurance Guardian*, February 1915, page 14; TNA file BT 31/18520/99222.
10 *Insurance Journal*, 15 October 1914, page 39; *The Times*, 28 September 1914, page 4.
11 *The Times*, 28 September 1814, page 14.
12 Vander Weyer, 2011, pages 93–94.
13 TNA file BT 31/18520/99222.
14 Vander Weyer, 2011, page 97 et seq.
15 Dawson, 1927, pages 349–350.
16 *The Times*, 26 May 1915, page 13.
17 *The Times*, 30 May 1916, page 12.
18 O'Hagan, 1929, volume II page 339.
19 Vallance, 1955, Manley, 1973.

20 Vander Weyer, 2011, pages 108–109.
21 The report was compiled at the beginning of Bevan's imprisonment. TNA, files PCOM 8/321; HO 144/2745.
22 Vander Weyer, 2011, pages 96–97.
23 Greenfield, 1995, cited in Vander Weyer, 2011, page 97.
24 Anonymous, 1927.
25 O'Hagan, 1929, volume II, page 454 et seq.
26 Davies, 1981.
27 Emden, 1951.
28 Vander Weyer, 2011, page 130.
29 For example, in 1920 Hatry managed the private offer of shares in United Brassfounders, a company which had been formed before the 1914–1918 war by the amalgamation of four foundries. During the war, the company's production had been given over wholly to the manufacture of trench munitions (the responsibility of Alexander Roger's section at the Ministry of Munitions) but after the war experienced great difficulty as it had sacrificed its accustomed markets.
30 David, 1977, page 258.
31 TNA file BT 31/22241/135481.
32 Patmore, 1968, pages 10–11.

References

Primary works: periodicals

Financial Times.
Insurance Guardian.
Insurance Journal.
The Times.

Primary works: contemporary books and papers

Anonymous. (1927), *By the Waters of Babylon.* (Hutchinson, London).
Dawson, Sir D. (1927), *A Soldier Diplomat.* (John Murray, London).
Hicks Beach, Lady Victoria (1932), *Life of Sir Michael Hicks Beach* (two volumes). (Macmillan, London).
Kirkaldy, A.W. (1915), *British Finance during and after the War 1914–1921.* (Sir Isaac Pitman & Sons, London).
Lawson, W.R. (1915), *British War Finance 1914–1915.* (Constable & Company, London).
O'Hagan, H.O. (1929), *Leaves From My Life* (two volumes). (John Lane, London).
Withers, H. (1915), *War and Lombard Street.* (E.P. Dutton & Company, New York).

Secondary works

David, E. (ed.) (1977), *Inside Asquith's Cabinet: From the Diaries of Charles Hobhouse.* (John Murray, London).
Davies, P.N. (1981), 'Business Success and the Role of Chance: The Extraordinary Phillips Brothers', *Business History*, volume 23 (2), pages 208–232.
Emden, P.H. (1951), 'Baron Paul Julius De Reuter', *Transactions, the Jewish Historical Society of England*, volume 17(1951–2), pages 215–223.

Greenfield, G. (1995), *A Smattering of Monsters: A Kind of Memoir.* (Little Brown, London).
Kynaston, D. (1999), *The City of London: Volume III: Illusions of Gold 1914–1945.* (Chatto & Windus, London).
Manley, P.S. (1973), 'Clarence Hatry', *Abacus*, volume 12(1), pages 49–60.
Michie, R.C. (1999), *The London Stock Exchange: A History.* (Oxford University Press, Oxford).
Panayi, P. (1990), 'The British Empire Union in the First World War', in Kushner, T. and Lunn, K. (eds.), *The Politics of Marginality? Race, the Radical Right and Minorities in Twentieth Century Britain.* (London).
Panayi, P. (1991), *The Enemy in Our Midst: Germans in Britain during the First World War.* (Berg Publishers, Providence, Rhode Island).
Patmore, D. (1968), 'Introduction', in Patmore, B. ed., *My Friends When Young.* (Heinemann, London).
Roberts, R. (2013), *Saving the City: The Great Financial Crisis of 1914.* (Oxford University Press, Oxford).
Vallance, A. (1955), *Very Private Enterprise: An Anatomy of Fraud and High Finance.* (Thames & Hudson, London).
Vander Weyer, M. (2011), *Fortune's Spear: The Story of the Blue-Blooded Rogue behind the Most Notorious City Scandal of the 1920s.* (Elliott & Thompson, London).

4 Hatry surfs a boom

December 1916 was not a good time for creating a new financial house.

The acquisition of Commercial Bank of London was concluded on 4 December 1916 when the shareholders approved an increase in its share capital, just as Herbert Asquith's time as prime minister was drawing to a close. Two days later, David Lloyd George became prime minister. Public unease about the performance of Asquith's government had been encouraged by campaigns such as the Strength in Britain movement which alleged that the government was disorganised, and that its procrastination had led to an appalling waste of manpower, shipping and men.[1] As *The Times* observed in an editorial: 'The country at large loathes party politics in the present emergency. Their one desire is to close ranks and get on with the war'.[2]

The war had already lasted longer than anyone had expected or wished, and there was growing apprehension that the challenges to be faced after the end of the war would be no less severe than any of the challenges created by the war. Planning for reconstruction had begun early in 1916 and had brought a realism over the difficulty of reintegrating into a peacetime economy men currently serving with the forces, reorganising industries whose current structures had been shown by the war to be inefficient, and recapturing overseas markets sacrificed to wage war. None of this would be made easier by the loss of the City's international prestige. As an American author wrote in a book reviewed by *The Economist* on 2 December 1916:

> It is at least a safe prediction that when the war is ended England cannot regain overnight, so to speak, the position which she lost as a consequence of the economic vicissitudes of 1914. It is an easy possibility that New York will retain many of its war-time functions and responsibilities as the central money market of the western hemisphere.[3]

In wartime, share trading on the London exchange was discouraged by government-inspired regulations that required that all transactions should be settled immediately in cash, not by credit, that there should be no trading in options or futures and almost no domestic share offers and no international offers. Stockbrokers' incomes had suffered partly because there was much less domestic business, but more importantly because much international business had gone elsewhere.[4] Why then did Hatry form his new organisation in such apparently unpromising circumstances?

Even though no one knew when the war would end, some were already anticipating the conditions in which normal business would be resumed after the war. A boom was expected, created by pressure from a backlog of transactions held up by the war. Since the declaration of war, many companies wanting to raise money for new ventures or the exploitation of new technology had been denied finance. Companies aiming to merge with others had deferred their schemes. Shareholders wanting to transfer ownership of a business by way of a flotation had been obliged to wait. By the end of 1916, many were frustrated by what they regarded as well-justified issues being thwarted by the negative attitudes of the Treasury's Capital Issues Committee. This frustration had been magnified by the number of issues that in the market's eyes had proved worthless after being approved by the committee in the mistaken belief that they would serve the nation's military interests. In short, a backlog of well-justified transactions was being built that would be released when normal trading was resumed. At that point, there would be many opportunities for company promoting houses that had established their capability.

In December 1916, although Hatry had some experience of stock exchange transactions and had begun to form a support team, Commercial Bank of London remained a new, untried organisation. On paper his team appeared to have many of the skills that a company promoter would require. For knowledge of company law, he had the support of Sir Frank Crisp of Ashurst Morris Crisp and Stanley Passmore of J.D. Langton & Passmore. For knowledge of the stock exchange's rules, he had the support of Ellis & Co. For understanding of stock exchange trading and promotions, he had the support of Osborne O'Hagan, the company promoter. Knowledge, however, was not sufficient; Hatry also needed an organisation which could manage a share issue.

Before the introduction of computers and the creation of the internet, share issues involved the transmission of many pieces of paper. To apply for shares, investors completed an application form. The promoter would allot shares to applicants, confirming the allotment by sending a notice – on paper. The applicant would pay for the shares – with a cheque. When payment had been received, the company would register the new owner as a shareholder and issue a share certificate – on paper.[5] To be successful, a promoter needed an organisation that could handle the prodigious number of documents – without error. Hatry had such an embryo organisation, organised by Ernest Treweek, a clerk, but at the beginning of 1917 it had not yet had chance to prove that it could cope. By setting up his new concern at the end of 1916, Hatry gave himself a chance of establishing its capability in good time to surf on the crest of the boom that was likely to follow the end of the war – whenever it came.

Although trading on the exchange itself was depressed and offered few opportunities for share offers, there were off-market opportunities that could be explored. Because the wartime restrictions were imposed by way of the London Stock Exchange's rule book rather than by public law, off-market transactions were not subject to the restrictive regulations and, although frowned upon, were not prohibited. When the exchange's restrictions had first been imposed in 1915, there had been a reluctance to find ways around them – it seemed unpatriotic. But as time had passed, the inflexibility of the Capital Issues Committee came to be regarded as perverse, so the mood had changed and investors were prepared to countenance propositions circulated outside the market. All the Treasury could do to respond to attempts to circumvent the stock exchange's restrictions was to issue plaintive notices which were reproduced in the financial press but cut no ice. Everyone knew that the Treasury had no power to punish offenders. This offered Hatry the chance to hone and then broadcast his new organisation's capability.

Almost immediately, good fortune favoured Commercial Bank of London. His solicitor, Stanley Passmore, introduced Hatry to a transaction involving two London department stores: Debenham & Freebody and Marshall & Snelgrove. Debenhams, which was controlled by the Debenham family, owned a substantial store in Wigmore Street in central London but owned no stores outside London, preferring instead to act as a wholesaler, supplying provincial department stores which remained independent.

In contrast, apart from its store in Oxford Street, London, Marshall & Snelgrove did not act as a wholesaler but owned a number of provincial stores which were located in Yorkshire. In 1916, Marshall & Snelgrove was not trading successfully and had become a significant debtor of Debenhams, its wholesale supplier. By entering into a joint working arrangement, it was planned that Debenhams' management would be able to improve Marshalls' buying and management so that Marshalls' performance would improve and the debt due to Debenhams could be reduced. Although the working arrangement fell short of a merger, it was recognised that a full merger might follow in due course.

Combining these two companies threatened to create a conflict between managing Marshalls' provincial stores and Debenhams' wholesaling business as the Marshalls' stores were in competition with independent department stores dependent upon supplies from Debenhams' wholesaling business. To avoid this, Marshall & Snelgrove agreed to transfer its provincial stores to Marshalls (Provinces) Limited, a new, independent company of which Stanley Passmore was to become chairman. Hatry was invited to manage the transaction and, in particular, to design the capital structure of the new company.[6]

Not only was this the first transaction for Commercial Bank of London under Hatry's ownership and its first fee (£25,000), ten years later the relationship with Marshalls (Provinces) Limited was to be the basis for Hatry's largest and arguably most successful amalgamation.

Commercial Bank's next transactions arose from an association with Sperling & Co – a company promoting partnership which had originally begun life in the early 1870s as a firm of stockbrokers. Like other firms such as Panmure Gordon and Foster & Braithwaite, Sperling & Co had developed its business by sponsoring new share offers. This work had been led principally by Edward Mackay Edgar, a Canadian who had been active in company promotion on the Montreal Stock Exchange before moving to England in 1906.[7] When the stock exchange's wartime restrictions threatened to eliminate new issues for the duration of the war, Sperling & Co had decided to forsake membership of the exchange to concentrate wholly on new off-market issues. Not surprisingly, this was regarded as treachery by other members who preferred to stay with the exchange.[8]

By the beginning of 1917, Sperling & Co had identified the shipbuilding industry as a possible hunting ground for profitable transactions.

Before 1914, the British shipbuilding industry had been the largest in the world. There had been 580 berths in Britain which could accommodate ships longer than 250 feet, whereas there had been only 341 on the mainland of Europe. About 60% of the gross tonnage of shipping launched in the world each year would be launched in Great Britain. In some years, the proportion launched in Britain had been even higher. During the war, the scarcity of shipping and high freight rates had encouraged a further expansion in capacity and the purchase of old ships at unprecedented prices. In 1917, it seemed certain that after the war this prosperity would continue as shipowners would have to make good the shortage of ships caused by wartime losses.

On its own, this would have been an enticing prospect for a potential investor, but for the company promoter another factor magnified the attractions of investment. While in aggregate the British shipbuilding industry was very large, it was composed of a large number of relatively small yards. Experience of wartime production demonstrated that small yards were inhibited by the size and, conversely, the value of large-scale production. This offered the prospect of amalgamating yards to create integrated ship and marine engine building combines, potentially enhancing profitability and increasing the capital value of the business. Searching for shipyards that could be grouped provided an opportunity for adventurous company promoters.

The first steps taken by Hatry and Sperlings to exploit these opportunities were taken during 1917 through the acquisition of interests in three yards: George Irvine's Shipbuilding and Dry-dock (West Hartlepool, Teesside), Joseph T. Eltringham & Co (Howdon, Tyneside) and H&C Grayson (Birkenhead, Merseyside). Acquisition of the interest in Eltringhams arose as a result of Hatry's association with Viscount Furness, whose offices were conveniently located in St James's a few steps away from the Cavendish Hotel. He had inherited his family's interest in the Furness Withy group and in 1916 decided that the group's shipping interests should be divided from its shipbuilding interests of which Eltringhams formed a part. The group's shipping subsidiaries bought out the Furness family's interest in return for the transfer to the family of the shipbuilding and other industrial investments. A further opportunity for the Sperling group was created in 1918 when Furness Withy decided to sell the Northumberland Shipbuilding Company.[9]

This company was also based at Howdon on the Tyne, and had been set up in 1898 by Rowland Hodge who bought and renamed an existing yard. He modernised and expanded the yard whose main business was in building large cargo steamers. Having exhausted his own sources of capital, in 1901 Hodge sold a controlling interest to the Furness Withy group but remained managing director and retained a substantial interest in the company's shares.

In July 1918, the purchaser of Northumberland Shipbuilding was Robert Workman, who was a London shipbroker and a member of the Belfast family which owned Workman Clark, a large concern which was renowned for building transatlantic liners. Workman valued the company's assets at about £850,000 but also knew that the company could expect an annual income of about £1.1 million in the first two or three years after the war from contracts to build ships for Italian and Norwegian shipowners. Understandably, Workman and Sperling & Co were attracted by the opportunity to buy the company for £830,000, or less than Workman's assessment of the value of its assets. But there was another attraction. Both Northumberland Shipbuilding's yard and Eltringhams' yard were based at Howdon upon Tyne so that the proposed acquisition would be a step towards an enlarged and integrated shipbuilding combine.

With the assistance of Kleinwort & Sons, a well-known merchant bank, Sperlings proposed that the acquisition would be financed partly by loans and partly by the purchase of shares in Northumberland Shipbuilding. Sperlings and Kleinworts would then recover their investment partly from the proceeds of the Italian and Norwegian contracts but also by selling the shares to the public. As the wartime controls on new issues remained in place, a flotation on the stock exchange could not be contemplated so it was necessary to place the shares privately off-market which was to be undertaken by Hatry as his role in the transaction.

With typical vigour, Hatry set about making the share offer known by circulating letters to prospective investors – the equivalent of cold calling a century later. This led *The Times* to report that a correspondent had complained of 'being the recipient of uninvited circulars'.[10] The paper's *City Notes* column warned that investors should be wary of a number of mysterious points in Hatry's circulars. For example, the paper noted that the circulars were voluminous and presented a glowing picture of the company's condition but omitted the detailed information which a formal prospectus would have provided. Although the authorised share capital was quoted, the issued share capital was not. Most mysteriously, the newspaper enquired why the company offering the shares for sale at 3 shillings, Canadian and General Trust Limited, was offering to buy them back at once at 4 shillings – a practice that *The Times* suggested was 'suggestive of catch penny finance rather than sound business'.[11]

Perversely, the complaints confirm that Hatry's organisation had succeeded in gaining the attention of prospective investors. Indeed, members of the stock exchange were extremely irritated by the example of selling shares by direct mail because of the benefit to Sperling & Co who were distrusted because they had forsaken membership. Business that otherwise would have been transacted through the exchange, earning commissions for members, was being diverted to former members. Pressure from the exchange's remaining members led the exchange to complain formally to the Treasury which was responsible for the Capital Issues Committee. Doubtless the complaints would have been muted if the offer had failed. Its success demonstrated that Commercial Bank of London could undertake such operations and laid the ground for Northumberland Shipbuilding to be used as the platform for Sperlings to build the group into the integrated shipbuilding combine they had planned.

Hatry had thus succeeded in his aim of establishing his organisation's credibility in time to exploit the expected boom in share trading on the cessation of hostilities. Ironically, Hatry's success in selling Northumberland Shipbuilding's shares contributed to a delay in the resumption of normal trading.

On receiving the exchange's complaint, the Treasury saw an opportunity to deal with its own concern that, with the end of the war, a return to unbridled share speculation would undermine the efficient allocation of resources to necessary reconstruction projects.[12] It therefore proposed to use public law to extend the wartime restrictions beyond the end of the war by introducing regulations under the Defence of the Realm Act that would have subjected all new issues to the oversight of the Capital Issues Committee by prohibiting trading in any issues (whether on-market or off-market) which had been made without the approval of the committee. This drew a horrified reaction from all quarters as it would retrospectively have outlawed trading in off-market issues made between January 1915 and January 1919, reduced the market value of those securities and undermined any bank loans which had been secured on them. Ridiculed by the press, the regulation was immediately withdrawn but the result was that it was not until March that the expected surge in new issues could begin. Moreover, it led to the Treasury's insistence that other constraints on trading, such as the ban on trading in options and futures, should be maintained for much longer than otherwise might have been the case. This meant in addition that cash settlement of trades remained in force for the time being.[13]

In spite of this delay and with the assistance of Sperlings, Hatry and Kleinworts, Northumberland Shipbuilding acquired controlling interests in William Doxford and Sons (Sunderland, Wearside), Fairfield Shipbuilding and Engineering (Govan, Clydeside), Blythswood Shipbuilding (Scotstoun, Clydeside), Edward Finch and the National Shipyards (Chepstow). In each case, the transaction was financed by a public offer of shares or debentures which to a greater or lesser extent involved Hatry and Commercial Bank of London.[14]

Sperlings' initiatives were not always successful. In 1920, Northumberland Shipbuilding tried but failed to acquire Swan Hunter and Wigham Richardson (Wallsend, Tyneside). A few months later, an attempt was made to control the cost of steel purchases by acquiring a steel manufacturer, as other groups had done. Its proposal to acquire Baldwins did not proceed. Northumberland Shipbuilding decided to withdraw following the government's decision to increase the rate of Excess Profit Duty which would have caused a material increase in Baldwins' outstanding liability in respect of wartime profits. As the government's decision was not announced until after a majority of Baldwins' shareholders had accepted the offer, Northumberland Shipbuilding was obliged to pay a substantial sum by way of damages (5 shillings per share to any shareholder who had accepted the offer). There was, however, some consolation in agreeing a contract for Baldwins to supply steel to the shipbuilding group.[15]

Nonetheless, Sperlings and Kleinworts had achieved their objective of establishing a shipbuilding combine, and with them Hatry had established his capabilities as a company promoter. When hostilities ended in November 1918, and the long-expected boom began to develop a few months later, Hatry was able to take full advantage.

During 1919, Hatry and Commercial Bank not only supported Sperlings' new issues, but they were also involved in a series of trading syndicates and managed the reconstruction or flotation of six businesses. Perhaps Hatry's most notorious association in 1919 involved James White, another promoter whose principal activity was property development. Like Hatry, he exuded a charm that brought the most unlikely people under his influence. Just before war was declared in 1914, he had persuaded Sir Joseph Beecham, the pill magnate, to underwrite the purchase of the Covent Garden market and estate in London, expecting that the purchase would be refinanced by a public offer of shares. Mirroring Hatry's experience with the Planet Insurance Company, White's plan to raise money by issuing shares came to nothing when new issues for non-essential purposes were prohibited for the duration of the war. This left Sir Joseph bearing the whole cost of the Covent Garden deal. Although White attempted to relieve him of this burden by proposing an interim arrangement in 1916, that scheme also came to nothing when Sir Joseph died unexpectedly before the documents could be signed. Sir Joseph's heir, Sir Thomas Beecham, the conductor, inherited the burden as the case descended into lengthy and complex litigation.[16]

By 1919, White was looking for other opportunities and formed a syndicate, of which Hatry became a member, to take advantage of speculation about the future of Mexican Eagle Petroleum which was owned by Sir Weetman Pearson (enobled as Viscount Cowdray in 1910), who had created it in 1909 to develop his interests in the Mexican oil fields. By 1919, Mexican Eagle represented about 75% of the value of the Pearson group and was larger than the Shell Transport and Trading group. It was known that for some time Cowdray had wanted to dispose of his interest in Mexican Eagle but had been prevented from doing this by the British government which in 1917 had eventually imposed restrictions preventing its disposal during the war. As the war ended, negotiations began with a view to the purchase of Cowdray's interest by Royal Dutch Shell, and as the uncertainty was reflected in the share price's volatility, White's syndicate aimed to take advantage by cornering the shares. By all accounts, this proved most profitable.

Later in 1919, Hatry was involved in another of White's schemes: to finance Dunlop's development in America. Before the 1914–1918 war, Dunlop Rubber had owned a subsidiary company in the USA which it was obliged to sell as a part of the government's programme of disposing of overseas assets to finance international purchases for military purposes. When the war ended, Dunlop, which was still led by Sir Arthur du Cros, decided to re-establish a subsidiary in America and sought advice on how this could be financed. White suggested that large numbers of small investors might be invited to buy Dunlop shares in small fractions which he proposed to call 'units'. The shares in question would be held by a trust on behalf of the investors and it was hoped that the London Stock Exchange would permit trading in the units backed by the trust. This scheme, which was similar to a number of dubious unit schemes organised in the USA, foundered in November 1919 as the exchange refused to approve trading in the units. It was to have a lasting effect, however, as the memory of the scheme led the exchange to resist future attempts to seek approval for trading in 'units'.[17]

Meanwhile, Hatry and Commercial Bank were vigorously pursuing various reconstructions and flotations, mostly for companies aiming to exploit new technologies or expanding markets for technologies developed during the war. British Window Glass was a new company which was raising money to exploit its exclusive rights to a process invented in Belgium for the manufacture of window glass. C.A. Vandervell was a leading manufacturer of electrical and lighting systems for motor vehicles which was raising money in anticipation of the increasing demand for vehicles. It was also innovative in using advertising to achieve recognition for its brand name ('CAV') boasting that it was one of the first to use pictures of brunettes in its brochures. Leyland Motors was a manufacturer of heavy lorries which had been used successfully to transport the Royal Flying Corps' aircraft from field to field in France and wanted to raise money partly to expand production of lorries and partly to begin manufacturing cars. Agricultural Industries was a company formed to finance the extension to all of the estates of the Dennis family in Lincolnshire of their modern farming practices which involved the installation of light railways and telephone systems.

Hatry would not have attracted work without successfully demonstrating his organisation's capability in handling new issues, but the volume of his work suggests that his services offered advantages not readily matched by his competitors. Two of his flotations exhibit what he offered.

In October 1919, Leyland Motors Limited (LML), a Lancashire vehicle manufacturer substantially owned by the Spurrier family offered for sale £750,000 7½% preference shares. In managing this issue, Commercial Bank of London was supported by Hatry's usual team: Ellis & Co as brokers[18] and J.D. Langton & Passmore as solicitors. Exceptionally for Hatry at this time, Leyland Motors was already a quoted company, having already made a public offer of preference shares in 1914, one of the last issues before the wartime restrictions were promulgated. That issue was managed from Preston and involved Clifford-Turner & Hopton of London as solicitors and John Prust & Co, also of London, as brokers. For the 1919 issue, they had both been supplanted by Hatry's team.

The 1919 prospectus stated that the new issue was required to permit the repayment of bank loans raised during the war to finance extension of the company's factory and to provide working capital to support the expected post-war expansion of business. This was probably true, but the structure of the transaction suggests that the Spurrier family had other objectives which were not acknowledged. The structure of the transaction was odd. As the shares of the existing company were already dealt on the exchange, it would have been possible for the company to vary its constitution by increasing its share capital and then issuing more shares. However, rather than do this, a new company was created to which the business of the old company was transferred, with the existing shareholders receiving shares in the new company in place of their shares in the old company.

There appear to have been two reasons for resorting to this device.[19] The first was to maintain the proportion of the company owned by the Spurrier family. On exchanging their shares in the old company for shares in the new company, existing ordinary shareholders received three new shares for each of their shares in the old company, whereas existing preference shareholders were only offered one preference share in the new company for each of their existing preference shares. The Spurrier family still did not own a majority of the new company's shares but owned a substantial and blocking minority. This had involved a considerable increase in the nominal value of the new company's issued share capital compared with that of the old company. As new money was not to be introduced by the existing shareholders in return for the additional share, this increase created a new problem. Potential shareholders would look to a prospectus to ensure that its share capital would be represented by net assets[20] and it was normal for companies to publish in prospectuses financial information demonstrating that after the new shares on offer had been issued, the company's net assets would be equal to or greater than the nominal value of the issued shares. In LML's case, this was done by including a statement of the net assets that the new company would have held as at 31 December 1918. As the issued share capital had been increased by issuing shares to existing shareholders without new money being subscribed, the gap was covered by a revaluation of the company's fixed assets. As the old company never published a balance sheet as at 31 December 1918,[21] and the prospectus gave little information about the revaluation,[22] the reader was left ignorant of the extent of the revaluation surplus included in the published statement of net assets.

Meanwhile, the statement suggested that the company's net assets exceeded the nominal value of issued share capital and thus satisfied potential investors' expectations.[23] However, the net assets of the new company would only exceed the nominal value of its issued share capital if all of the assets of the old company as shown in the statement were to be transferred to the new company. In LML's case this was not to be the case as the transfer agreement required that certain assets would not be transferred to the new company but would be held back by the old company. This was explained in the small print of the prospectus but not in the statement of net assets.[24]

Withholding some of the old company's assets from the new company provided another benefit for the Spurrier family. Leyland Motors had been extremely profitable during the war through securing the contract to supply all of the heavy lorries which the Royal Flying Corps required in France. In the 1919 prospectus, the company admitted that whereas the company's reported profit in 1914 had been £119,113, in 1916 alone it had been £312,377.[25] The assets withheld in the old company were eventually paid by the liquidators to the remaining shareholders (i.e. the Spurrier family) as a capital distribution which did not attract a liability to income tax. The effect therefore was that by holding back a balance that represented some part of the wartime profits earned by the company, the Spurrier family avoided a liability to taxation (including income tax and super tax) which would have arisen had the profits been paid out by way of dividend. None of this was evident from the prospectus.

This analysis strongly suggests why Hatry's services proved valuable to clients and why he was able so quickly to create a substantial business based on company flotations. He was not only good at showing how the weaknesses of company law and the stock exchange's rules could be exploited to achieve his clients' wishes, but he was willing to implement his ideas.

Agricultural Industries Limited (AIL), another share issue managed by Hatry in the autumn of 1919,[26] also demonstrates his willingness to exploit the vagaries of the law to meet vendors' objectives.

The company was created to farm extensive agricultural properties in Lincolnshire owned by the Dennis family. Over several decades, they had built an estate of about 2,000 acres on Deeping Fen around Deeping St Nicholas and in 1918 had the opportunity to acquire the nearby Nocton estate of about 8,000 acres. The family needed to raise money both to complete the purchase and to modernise the estate, as had already been done with the Deeping estate. In common with other farms in south-east Lincolnshire, the land was fertile and productive, but suffered from reliance upon man-made drainage, usually involving pumping. Unsurprisingly, in wet winters the land became muddy and, in the absence of suitable roads, hindered the marketing of the potato crop. Although potatoes could be transported by rail, farmers had to transport their crop to the station, which for remote farms could be problematic. Although the railway companies attempted to resolve this problem by offering discounts to cover the cost of carting potatoes to stations such as Boston or Spalding, a solution to this problem was not found until farmers began to lay light railways on their land. By avoiding the cost of major civil engineering works, light railways proved capable of transporting the heavy crops but also provided a way of moving employees, livestock and supplies to the remotest parts of the fens. The earliest light railway was installed in 1897 and ran east from Spalding; the Dennis family had installed light railways on their land at Deeping St Nicholas during the 1914–1918 war.[27]

In 1919, modernisation of the Nocton estate involved installing a light railway using the skills of the estate manager, Major Leonard 'Jock' Webber, who had seen service in France and proposed to use equipment from an army supply depot in Arras to create what was to be called the Nocton Estate Light Railway and eventually became the most extensive of the Lincolnshire potato railways.[28]

Hatry became aware that the Dennis family were looking for financial support to complete the purchase and modernisation of the Nocton Estate. Hatry approached the Dennises and proposed that they should raise money by way of a stock exchange flotation. This would not normally have been attractive to farmers as it involved sharing control of the land with other shareholders and risked a complete loss of control. Other forms of financing such as long-term mortgages did not pose the same threat and thus were more attractive.

To meet the Dennis family's wish to retain control of their land, Hatry devised a corporate structure in which all of the farming activities were to be carried on by subsidiary companies of a new holding company to be named AIL. Management agreements were devised by which the Dennis family was to control the appointment of directors of the subsidiaries and thus their activities for at least ten years. No member of the family was appointed a director of AIL itself. This was exceptional as investors often looked to such appointments as evidence that a previously successful management team would remain in control of the business after flotation. Failing to appoint Dennis family directors to the board was not a careless omission but a critical element of Hatry's scheme.

Under company law at the time, holding companies had no special power to require subsidiaries to provide information about their trading, so that Hatry's structure left the directors of AIL powerless to require information, let alone give directions to the subsidiaries.[29] Had members of the Dennis family who were also directors of a subsidiary become directors of AIL, however, they could have been obliged to disclose to their fellow directors information they held by virtue of being subsidiary company directors and the Dennis family's control of the land and the affairs of the subsidiary companies would have been at risk. It was therefore crucial to Hatry's scheme that members of the Dennis family should not become directors of the holding company.[30] This they never did.[31]

No other examples have been found of UK issues employing this corporate governance structure, although there were examples of issues in the United States where shareholders found that the company in which they had invested did not control the assets they may have expected.[32]

By offering the shares of AIL for sale through an independent company, Hatry exploited another loophole in company law and the stock exchange's rules as the law's requirements concerning prospectuses did not apply to offers for sale.[33] As a result, the offer document did not have to disclose the management agreements, so their existence and their significance were unknown to prospective investors.[34] When the offer documents were scrutinised by the stock exchange's committee, it was noted that because the disclosures were so limited, the reader could not work out how much profit Hatry was to earn from the transaction.[35] However, as the transaction complied with the existing rules, it was difficult to withhold approval and the transaction was cleared to go ahead. The stock exchange committee was sufficiently uncomfortable about the issue that within a fortnight the rules had been changed to eliminate the loophole that Hatry had exploited.[36]

AIL was the only Hatry promotion which eventually faced a formal legal challenge. In the 1940s, two speculators acquired shares in AIL and began to agitate for an enquiry to discover whether the group's affairs had been managed to disadvantage shareholders who were not members of the Dennis family. Eventually the Board of Trade agreed to the request for appointment of an inspector, but only after implementation of recommendations that inspectors should have powers to investigate all companies within a group of companies. The inspector's report for the first time disclosed the steps by which Hatry had safeguarded the Dennis family's interest in the land, and led shareholders to initiate proceedings against members of the family on the grounds that the flotation in 1919 had misled investors. While the judge was sympathetic to shareholders, he concluded that the governance scheme had been effective to safeguard the Dennis family. Although investors may have been misled, the fault was not the family's, so that the action was misconceived and the shareholders received no redress.

Analysis of the flotation of LML and AIL casts light upon the foundations of Hatry's ability to establish himself so quickly as a company promoter. Fundamental to his success was his reputation for achieving the objectives of vendors when others either could not or were unwilling to try. In the case of LML, Hatry achieved the Spurrier family's objectives of maintaining their influence over their company even though the family wanted to extract cash without incurring a liability to pay tax. In the case of AIL, Hatry achieved the Dennis family's objective of raising capital without ceding their control over the family's estates.

In these endeavours, Hatry was assisted by the state of company law's provisions in respect of prospectuses and of the stock exchange's own rules which generally were no more demanding than company law. In approving a prospectus, directors were expected to state everything with scrupulous accuracy and to ensure that no material fact was omitted. There was, however, some recognition that a prospectus was a marketing document which may colour the proposition put before potential investors:

> as Lord Chelmsford said in the Central Railway of Venezuela v Kisch: 'But although, in its introduction to the public, some high colouring,

> and even exaggeration, in the description of the advantages which are likely to be enjoyed by the subscribers may be expected, yet no misstatements or concealment of any material fact or circumstance ought to be permitted'.[37]

In addition, the Companies Act 1908 provided a list of detailed disclosures which had to be included in a prospectus, although the list was curiously limited as it did not include detailed financial disclosures.[38] The requirement for detailed disclosures was backed by provisions which could result in directors being liable to investors when incorrect information was provided in a prospectus.[39]

Since 1890, these limited requirements had been strengthened. In 1890, the court had found that a director could not be found guilty of misrepresentation in a prospectus if he could not be proved to have been fraudulent. Careless misrepresentation would not give rise to a liability to investors who had relied upon the prospectus. An 1890 Act had altered this aspect of the law, and its provisions were incorporated in the 1908 Act so that directors and promoters could find themselves liable for any untrue statement in a prospectus for which they were responsible.[40] By 1919, the phrase 'untrue statement' had been construed by the court on a number of occasions so that it was understood to encompass a 'misleading statement' and the omission of a material fact.[41]

Because the statutorily required disclosures did not include information which a potential investor would reasonably expect to be provided, such as information about financial performance and asset backing for the share capital, it was conventional for additional information to be provided, for example in the form of net asset statements and statements of past profits. However, as the law did not specify what financial information had to be provided, and there were no financial reporting standards, directors and their advisers were free to decide precisely how the conventions should be observed, if at all.

In the case of LML, for example, the prospectus included a statement signed by the company's auditors of the previous five years' annual profits which were described as: 'the profits … before allowing for Munitions Levy and Excess profits Duty … Income Tax, and Interest on borrowed money, but after charging Directors' remuneration and depreciation'.[42] In the case of AIL, previous years' annual profits were not disclosed. Instead, the annual average profits for successive three-year periods (1912–1914, 1913–1915, 1914–1916, 1915–1917, 1916–1918 and 1917–1919) were disclosed, presumably to obscure variations in annual profits. It was noted that the company's auditors had verified the annual profits, but the reported averages were not audited.[43]

None of this meant that directors were indifferent to the disclosures made in the prospectuses they approved. As the cases of LML and AIL show, the directors were aware of and interested in the objectives that the company promoter was attempting to achieve. They must, however, have been concerned that they should not risk liability as a result of misstatements.[44]

LML shows Hatry seeking for the Spurrier family a tax advantage which they evidently did not want to publicise. AIL shows Hatry seeking to provide safeguards for the Dennis family's control over their estates which might prove inimical to the interests of investors. Hatry's services were valuable not only because he was willing to associate with these objectives when others manifestly would not, but also because his approaches did not involve breaking the law; rather, he slavishly observed the details of all the law's current requirements. In spite of this slavish observance, however, the attention of potential investors was distracted. In this sense, Hatry's approach to promoting new issues is reminiscent of contemporary debates over the ethics of tax planning and the perceived conflict between legalistic and socially responsible interpretations of tax law.

As these flotations of LML and AIL were both underwritten by a range of City interests, they also demonstrate the City was willing to tolerate Hatry's exploitation of the weaknesses of the law and the rules, even though more established houses were not prepared to lend their names to the offerings.

By way of contrast, other company promoters operating in 1919 were able to find less questionable companies to promote. In November 1919, when Hatry was engaged in launching AIL, Frederick Szarvasy was floating Edison Swan Electric.[45] In December 1919, Oliver Clare and John Jarvis were floating Western Counties Shipping Limited.[46]

In December 1919, Clarence Hatry celebrated his 31st birthday and ten years of marriage. His position had been transformed. Whereas in 1909 he had been close to bankruptcy, in 1919, by prodigious efforts, he had created a substantial fortune.

Much of this had been achieved through his company, Commercial Bank of London, which he had established in Austin Friars, a quiet cul-de-sac which had also been the location of J.G. Eiser & Co, the stockbroking firm which his uncle had founded. Hatry had chosen to re-establish the family's commercial name at the scene of his uncle's ultimate embarrassment and continued in business there until 1930. By December 1919, Commercial Bank's flotations had proved highly profitable for the wide circle from which they attracted financial support and for his close associates such as Ellis & Co. Even those who were suspicious of the means by which Hatry's flotations obscured investors' risks were happy to share in the profits.

Hatry personally had achieved a measure of acceptance. By December 1919, he had become a director of London Assurance, one of the oldest and stuffiest insurance companies, whose board included general managers from all of the principal clearing banks and directors of the Bank of England – yet another sign that his approach to flotations was accepted. He was a member of the Executive Committee and the Council of the British Empire Union.[47] For a former bankrupt who was the son of German immigrants, this was a remarkable development for the British Empire Union had begun its life in April 1915 as the Anti-German Union, buoyed initially by a wave of anti-German propaganda after the sinking of the *Lusitania*. In its early years, the

Union had campaigned against German immigrants who were prominent in the City, arguing that it was too easy to become a British subject by naturalisation, as Hatry's father had done, and that they should not receive honours and privileges. Among its earliest targets were Sir Ernest Cassel and Sir Edgar Speyer, both of them merchant bankers, who the Union suggested should both be stripped of their membership of the Privy Council.[48] From time to time, members of the Union had campaigned for the naturalisation of German citizens to be rescinded retrospectively, which if it had occurred would have affected the status of Hatry, his siblings and their mother. Even if the mood within the Union had mellowed somewhat, that Hatry should be accepted in such circles suggests both that he had lived down his Germanic roots and that he had been eager to do so.[49]

The circumstances of his family had been transformed. In contrast to the uncertainty which followed his bankruptcy, he had also acquired the outward signs of success which were beloved of all successful company promoters. His wife and family were settled in Mayfair, at 56 Upper Brook Street, a capacious house which had been acquired from the family of Lord Duveen, the art dealer, together with all of its furniture.[50] They had acquired a country house. They had a string of race horses.[51] Admittedly, when they raced, the race horses were not usually the most fancied runners, but one, *Furious*, was to win a classic: the Lincoln Handicap in 1920, albeit against the odds. They had also acquired a racing yacht, *Westward*.

In 1919, *Westward* was renowned as the fastest racing yacht of its time. Commissioned by Alexander S. Cochrane, a New York carpet millionaire, she was built at the Herreshoff Manufacturing yard at Bristol Rhode Island, which was itself renowned as the yard that had built the yachts that had seen off all challengers for the America's Cup since 1893. *Westward* had been commissioned to sail across the Atlantic to compete in European regattas, and after her launch on 31 March 1910 she sailed across the Atlantic in 14 days. At the Kiel Regatta in June, she won the Emperor's Cup in a four-race series during which the Kaiser's Meteor IV suffered a broken bowsprit in a collision with *Westward* when her indomitable commander, Captain Charlie Barr, refused to give way. At the onset of war in 1914, *Westward* was at Cowes, having sailed there for the annual regatta and she was immediately seized by the British government. Always a wheeler dealer, Hatry had bought the yacht at a low price in 1919 as war surplus, and resurrected her original name, *Westward*. For the first time since the end of the war, the Cowes regatta included a race for the Royal London Yacht Club Cup – the class for the largest yachts. *Westward* crossed the line first, beating the King's yacht, *Britannia*, but the cup was awarded to *Britannia* when the rated handicaps were taken into account. *Britannia* displaced 221 tons and *Westward* 323 tons.[52]

Quite apart from its speed, its crew of 40 men, its monogrammed crockery[53] and its 20-seater dining table[54] ensured that *Westward* attracted a reputation for extravagance. It was almost too extravagant a symbol of success.[55]

Yet Hatry was not satisfied with these symbols of success and achievement – there were other signs of social acceptance that he craved.

In the early months of 1920, Hatry organised a syndicate to assist a Conservative MP, Laurance Lyon, to acquire *The Globe*, a London evening newspaper. Hatry had encountered Laurance Lyon, through an introduction from Sir Arthur du Cros who had been his predecessor as MP for Hastings and whom Hatry had encountered before the war in discussions over papers held by the Countess of Warwick. In the midst of negotiations over *The Globe*, Hatry enquired of Lyon how he might secure a baronetcy in the 1920 birthday honours list. Lyon agreed to speak to his party's chief whip, Sir George Younger, and arranged that Hatry should lunch with Younger at the Ritz. In his later description of the lunchtime conversation, Lyon recalled:

> I never saw such a change in anyone as in the would-be baronet. A quiet, almost restrained manner was usually one of his pleasantest characteristics. But a deep-rooted self-confidence was the mainspring of his actions; and, since an amazing power of persuasion was one of his chief assets, when in his office in the City he was never at a loss for word, or for an apposite argument. But at that luncheon he was tongue-tied, and obviously nervous and ill-at-ease. Apparently he could not come to the point, and Younger was not going to help him.[56]

Some days later, Sir George Younger told Lyon that appropriate investigations had been made and while nothing had been discovered which would disqualify Hatry, an immediate honour was problematic because he had 'never done anything for the public' and of course his health had prevented him from serving in the forces during the war. Hatry was therefore advised by Lyon to make one or two substantial donations to a hospital or some other charity and could then expect to be in the subsequent New Year's honours list.

Although Lyon thought that this response was positive, Hatry was disappointed for it was a check to his aim of establishing the family socially: 'We do things quicker than that in the City'.[57] He then went directly to Captain Frederick Guest, the Liberal chief whip, and enquired of him about a baronetcy.

At this time, the composition of each honours list was settled by a joint committee including the two chief whips of the parties represented in the coalition government: Sir George Younger and Captain Guest. Hatry may not have been aware of this committee or, if he was, he cannot have appreciated the effect he would cause. When Sir George spotted Hatry's name on Captain Guest's list of recommendations for baronetcies, he was taken aback and annoyed that Hatry seemed to have ignored his own suggestions and, as there were rumours of Lloyd George's susceptibility to financial inducements, wondered what Hatry had done to secure Guest's nomination. The inevitable result was that Younger vetoed Hatry's baronetcy.

Hatry's honour never materialised; nor did Lyon's attempted acquisition of *The Globe*. Although a purchase was agreed, the purchase price was not fully paid and the deal fell through. Within a year, Lyon was bankrupt and no longer an MP. *The Globe* merged with the *Pall Mall Gazette* and disappeared.[58]

Hatry never truly understood the behaviours of the City and politicians. An insider would not have committed the solecism of seeking the support of the Liberal Party's chief whip after misinterpreting as unhelpful the advice of the Conservative Party's chief whip. A wiser, more cautious reaction was precluded by his pressing desire for the grant of the baronetcy to which he believed he was entitled. Outward signs of social acceptance were important to Hatry as a demonstration of his family's redemption from the disasters which had befallen him, his mother and her sister's family, the Eisers. They were also important because at heart he remained an outsider. He must have suspected that in part he had succeeded because he was willing to contemplate transactions that established insiders would have avoided. For insiders he was convenient, because he could easily be sacrificed if undue risk led to disaster.

Few photographs of Hatry survive. Most of those few show him in sombre mood; only one shows him radiantly happy. It shows him in 1920 surrounded by friends, at the helm of the most extravagant sign of his financial success: *Westward*.

Notes

1 *The Times*, 7 December 1916, page 3.
2 *The Times*, 7 December 1916, page 9.
3 Review of AD Noyes, *Financial Chapters of the War*, in *The Economist*, 2 December 1916, page 1047.
4 Michie, 1999, page 149 et seq.
5 Lewcock, 1931, page 44.
6 Corina, 1978, page 77.
7 *The Times*, 9 October 1934; Kynaston, 1999, pages 70–71.
8 Diaper, 1990, page 75.
9 Diaper, 1990, page 78 et seq; Johnman and Murphy, 2002, page 26.
10 *The Times*, 7 October 1918, page 12.
11 *The Times*, 7 October 1918, page 12. In effect, the repurchase offer assumed that, after flotation, the market price of the shares would rise above the issue price.
12 Memorandum dated 1 November 1918 (TNA file T12200/37071).
13 Articles published in *Truth*: 5 March 1919, page 330; 19 March 1919, page 423. Swinson, 2017, page 97.
14 Diaper, 1990, pages 80–81.
15 Diaper, 1990, pages 80–81.
16 Beecham, 1944, page 142.
17 Application for listing files, LSX archive, Guildhall Library.
18 Some commentators have suggested that LML had decided that to develop its connections with City interests Gerard Lee Bevan should be invited to become a director with the implication that he introduced Hatry (Turner, 1971, page 14).

19 Some commentators have suggested as an alternative reason that Hatry suggested the creation of a new company to avoid the government's control of new issues (Turner, 1971, page 15). This explanation appears incorrect as the controls had been removed before the LML prospectus was published.
20 Rutterford, 2004, page 121.
21 The company was liquidated before publication of the required annual statement was due.
22 The prospectus reproduced a valuation report dated 22 September 1919 by Wheatley, Kirk, Price and Co, the valuers, which apart from stating that the assets had been valued 'at prices now ruling' gave no information about the basis of the valuation (*The Times*, 13 October 1919, page 20).
23 Net assets of the old company as at 31 December 1918 excluding the proceeds of the new share issue: £1,107,112. Nominal value of issued share capital: £1,100,000 (*The Times*, 13 October 1919, page 20).
24 The agreement provided for various sums to be withheld including the book debts as at 31 December 1918: £232,704 12s 2d (i.e. 21% of the stated net assets).
25 The level of the company's annual profits during the 1914–1918 war had not been reported in public before publication of the prospectus in 1919. To satisfy the Companies Act requirement that accounts should be filed each year, the company had taken advantage of a weakness in the Companies Act 1908 which did not specify that the accounts filed should be for the most recently completed accounting period – section 26(3), Companies Act 1908. Thus the company filed the 1915 accounts repeatedly (TNA file BT31/22241/135481). This incidentally demonstrates that the directors of LML were prepared to take a narrow view of their responsibility to comply with company law even before their association with Hatry began.
26 *The Times*, 3 November 1919.
27 Squires, 1987, pages 30–32.
28 Squires, 1987, pages 20–24.
29 Provisions concerning the relationship between holding companies and subsidiaries were first introduced in the Companies Act 1947.
30 This had the added advantage that members of the Dennis family were not directly responsible for any of the information published in connection with the offer for sale.
31 After the Companies Act 1948 came into force, the Board of Trade appointed an inspector to inquire into the affairs of AIL. The inspector's report described the governance arrangements put in place in 1919 and the family's subsequent observance of them (Inspector's report dated 17 January 1950, TNA).
32 The Piggly Wiggly Stores chain of convenience stores was formed by Clarence Saunders of Memphis, Tennessee, to exploit his concept of a modern self-service supermarket. In 1919, shares in Piggly Wiggly Stores Inc. were listed on the Chicago Stock Exchange and subsequently transferred to the New York Stock Exchange in 1922. Piggly Wiggly Stores Inc. did not own the Piggly Wiggly name or the patents on Saunders' innovations. They were owned by Piggly Wiggly Corporation, which was wholly owned by Saunders and a small number of investors. The principal asset of the company whose shares were floated in 1919 was the right to open new Piggly Wiggly stores (Davies, 2018, page 255 et seq.; Freeman, 2011).
33 Palmer, 1921, page 362.
34 Disclosure of such agreements would have been required if the transaction had taken the form of a share issue covered by a prospectus (Section 81(f), Companies Act 1908).

35 The relevant committee's papers do not suggest that the committee noticed the governance implications of the agreements (Application for listing file, LSX archive, Guildhall Library).
36 This is an exceptional example of the stock exchange's committee imposing a requirement which added to company law obligations (Stock exchange committee minutes, LSX Archive, Guildhall Library).
37 Spafford, 1921, page 13; Lobban, 1996.
38 Section 81(1), Companies Act 1908.
39 Section 84, Companies Act 1908; Palmer, 1921, pages 357–376.
40 Section 84, Companies Act 1908; Spafford, 1921, page 59 et seq.
41 Hemmant, 1910, page 84; Spafford, 1921, pages 80–82.
42 *The Times*, 13 October 1919, page 20.
43 *The Times*, 3 November 1919, page 19.
44 Palmer describes the effect of the company law provisions on prospectuses as 'onerous and exacting' (Palmer, 1921, page 362).
45 *The Times*, 6 November 1919, page 19; Kynaston, 1999, page 136.
46 *The Times*, 17 December 1919.
47 There is no evidence on Hatry's introduction to the British Empire Union. Horatio Bottomley, a notorious promoter, was a supporter of the Union and may have been the connection (*British Empire Union Monthly Record*).
48 Panayi, 1991, page 190. The Union initiated a legal action against Cassel and Speyer which eventually led to a trial in December 1915 before three judges, including Sir Horace Avory who 15 years later officiated at Hatry's trial. Cassel and Speyer were allowed to remain members of the Privy Council (*The Times*, 24 June 1915; 23 July 1915; 17, 18, 19 November 1915; 18 December 1915).
49 Panayi, 1991, pages 201–207.
50 *The Times*, 15 October 1919, page 15. The house, which had once been owned by David Ricardo, the nineteenth-century economist, had five reception rooms, 13 bedrooms, day and night nurseries, three bathrooms and three modern white-tiled domestic offices (Advertisement, *The Times*, 22 May 1926, page 23; British History Online: material taken from *Survey of London: Volume 40*, 1980, pages 210–221, downloaded 10 February 2007).
51 In owning racehorses, Hatry was copying his co-speculator, James White (Corley, 2004).
52 Beating the King's yacht was a solecism which may have explained the near-silence in the newspapers of *Westward's* involvement in the race.
53 Amery, 1946, pages 46–47; Maritime Museum, St Helier.
54 *Sunday Telegraph*, 1 August 1965, page 4.
55 In acquiring *Westward*, Hatry was again copying his fellow promoter and associate, James White, who earlier in 1919 had acquired HM *Steam Yacht Venetia* at the end of its wartime service. *Venetia* was a larger vessel but required a smaller crew of 30. White's maritime pretensions were to last no longer than Hatry's as *Venetia* was sold to Baron Henri de Rothschild in 1921, suggesting that White too suffered heavy losses in the stock exchange depression of 1920 (Beckwith, 2018, pages 314–315). In a previous generation, another company promoter, Whitaker Wright, had also owned a racing yacht which he named *Sybarita* and raced at Cowes (Hamilton, 2018, page 88).
56 Anonymous (1927).
57 Anonymous (1927).
58 *The Times*, 4 January 1921, page 16; 5 February 1921, page 4; 16 April 1921, page 5; 5 May 1921, page 10; 28 July 1921, page 16.

References

Primary works: unpublished documents

Guildhall Library: LSX archive.
TNA: Board of Trade papers.
TNA: Treasury papers.

Primary works: newspapers and periodicals

British Empire Union Monthly Record.
Sunday Telegraph.
The Economist.
The Times.
Truth.

Primary works: contemporary books and papers

Anonymous. (1927), *By the Waters of Babylon.* (Hutchinson, London).
Beecham, T. (1944), *A Mingled Chime.* (Hutchinson, London).
Hemmant, D.G. (1910), *The Companies (Consolidation) Act, 1908.* (Fourth Edition). (Jordan & Sons, London).
Lewcock, F.J. (1931), *The Securities Clerk in a Branch Bank.* (Sir Isaac Pitman and Sons, London).
Palmer, F.B. (1921), *Company Law: A Practical Handbook for Lawyers and Businessmen.* (Eleventh Edition). (Stevens & Sons, London).
Spafford, C.H. (1921), *The Law of Misrepresentation in Prospectus.* (Butterworth, London).

Secondary works

Amery, L.S. (1946), *In the Rain and the Sun.* (Hutchinson, London).
Beckwith, I. (2018), 'HM Steam Yacht Venetia: A Luxury Yacht in Royal Navy Service, 1914–1919', *The Mariner's Mirror,* volume 104(3), pages 302–317.
Corley, T.A.B. (2004) *'James White' in Oxford Dictionary of National Biography.* (Oxford University Press, Oxford).
Corina, M. (1978), *Fine Silks & Oak Counters: Debenhams 1778–1978.* (Hutchinson Benham, London).
Davies, P. N. (1981), 'Business Success and the Role of Chance: The Extraordinary Phillips Brothers', *Business History,* volume 1981, pages 208–232.
Davies, D. (2018), *Lying for Money: How Legendary Frauds Reveal the Workings of Our World.* (Profile Books, London).
Diaper, S. (1990), 'The Sperling Combine and the Shipbuilding Industry. Merchant Banking and Industrial Finance in the 1920s', in Van Helten, J.J. and Cassis, Y. (eds), *Capitalism in a Mature Economy: Financial Institutions, Capital Exports and British Industry, 1870–1939.* (Edward Elgar, Aldershot).
Freeman, M. (2011), *Clarence Saunders and the Founding of Piggly Wiggly: The Rise and Fall of a Memphis Maverick.* (History Press, Charleston).
Hamilton, D. (2018), *The Making of Whitaker Wright.* (Douglas Hamilton, London).
Johnman, L. and Murphy, H. (2002), *British Shipbuilding and the State since 1918: A Political Economy of Decline.* (University of Exeter Press, Exeter).

Kynaston, D. (1999), *The City of London: Volume III: Illusions of Gold 1914–1945.* (Chatto & Windus, London).

Lobban, M. (1996), 'Nineteenth Century Frauds in Company Formation; *Derry V Peek* in Context', *Law Quarterly Review*, volume 11(23), pages 287–334.

Michie, R.C. (1999), *The London Stock Exchange: A History.* (Oxford University Press, Oxford).

Panayi, P. (1991), *The Enemy in Our Midst: Germans in Britain during the First World War.* (Berg Publishers, Providence, Rhode Island).

Rutterford, J. (2004), 'From Dividend Yield to Discounted Cash Flow: A History of UK and US Equity Valuation Techniques', *Accounting and Financial History*, volume 14(2), pages 115–149.

Squires, S.E. (1987), *The Lincolnshire Potato Railways.* (Oakwood Press, Oxford).

Swinson, C. (2017), *Regulation of the London Stock Exchange: Share Trading, Fraud and Reform 1914–1945.* (Routledge, London).

Turner, G. (1971), *The Leyland Papers.* (Eyre & Spottiswoode, London).

5 Coming down to earth

While the boom lasted, Hatry made hay. At any moment in 1919, he was working on several deals in parallel, reaching a peak in October. In that month, when the relevant stock exchange committee considered applications to deal in shares, two were proposed by Hatry and he was a leading member of the syndicate that proposed a third. But the boom was too good to last – an end was inevitable.

It was precipitated by a series of policy changes. In November, the Bank of England increased bank rate from 5% to 6% to stem the price inflation that occurred as wartime price controls were relaxed and consumption demand pent up by the long years of war was released. The bank rate was to be raised again to the unprecedented level of 7% in April 1920.[1]

State spending was curtailed as the amount of government short-term debt in circulation was thought to be exacerbating inflation. As it became clear that the war had impoverished all the major belligerents apart from the USA, overseas demand for British goods fell, especially in Europe and the British Empire. By the end of 1920, prices were falling and by mid-1921 the British economy found itself in a deep recession with 2.2 million people unemployed and many more on short-time working. In spite of this, the government maintained its tough financial policies as it had become committed to returning as soon as possible to the gold standard at the pre-war parity against the US dollar ($4.86). This required an increase in the value of sterling and an extended period of fiscal and monetary restraint.[2]

Increasing the bank rate caused an immediate adjustment in the price of government fixed interest stocks, dismaying investors who had patriotically bought them during the war. Investors then realised the economic consequences of the government's severe fiscal and monetary policies would involve reductions in corporate profits and a general failure to realise the optimistic forecasts that had underpinned many of the company flotations in 1919. Share prices fell dramatically.

Sniffing trouble in the wind, Hatry chose January 1919 as the moment to sell shares in his own company, Commercial Bank of London. In the short term, the offer was a success. It was oversubscribed and, for a while, shares of Commercial Bank of London traded at prices above the offer price. If the offer had been attempted a month later, Hatry would not have been able to achieve the same price for the shares and in the longer term the offer was to prove an opportunistic embarrassment.

For company promoters like Hatry, the market's downturn was to bring trouble. He had a queue of share transactions in preparation which were instantly made problematic. Vendors were less likely to achieve the share price they had been led to expect. Underwriters could not be so confident that all the shares they had underwritten would be sold and thus would be nervous that they would have to buy the unsold shares only to find that in the falling market they could not resell them. Even the company promoter himself could expect losses. Of course, if a flotation still went ahead, the promoter would become entitled to a fee but most promoters did not regard their fees as their main source of income; they looked to the profits they could make after a flotation by trading in the shares that had just been offered for sale. If a flotation were successful, the issue would be followed by a period of active trading in which investors who had not been allotted shares when they were offered for sale attempted to acquire some so that they could participate in the company's future trading prospects. That was the promoter's opportunity to make the largest profits and most made they sure they kept shares for themselves to take full advantage.[3] In a falling market, the chances for such super-profits would quickly disappear and the promoter would be left with securities he could not sell and losses rather than profits.

Being left with shares which could not be sold was dangerous, especially if they had been financed by bank loans. For a start, the promoter would have to pay bank interest for as long as the shares were held without any prospect of immediate return. If the value of the shares fell below the balance of any loans, then the bank would insist either on additional assets being pledged as security for the loans or, failing that, on immediate disposal of the shares to repay the loan, so crystallising the fall in value as a realised loss.

In short, a prolonged fall in share prices was perilous for the company promoter.

At this point, in the spring of 1920, Hatry fell ill, requiring a serious operation which his later medical records suggest was an appendectomy.[4] To recover, he took a long cruise with his wife, intending to visit South America where a syndicate of which he and Bevan were members owned cattle ranches in São Paolo. He later recalled that as he left he instructed his lieutenants at Commercial Bank of London to sell all of its investment holdings.[5] It may be true that he later believed that this would have been the sensible course of action and it is what many merchant banks did. Immediate sales might well have cleared the bank loans and avoided what later became large losses. However, there is no evidence that his staff did anything of the sort, which may suggest that Hatry's memory was no more than wishful thinking.[6]

For the time being, the business continued with the transactions which had been in preparation. For example, in February 1920, the team managed the public offer of shares in a new company, Kent Portland Cement, which had been formed to build a new cement works in Kent.[7] But as the year wore on, and prices continued to fall, vendors understandably became more reluctant to contemplate a stock exchange quotation and Hatry's business suffered.

In the summer of 1920, however, Hatry had a piece of good fortune. He was approached by the owner of a Dundee jute mill and his auditor, who invited him to help them form a combine of jute mills which could be floated on the London Stock Exchange.[8]

At first sight, this was a surprise. Why would the jute families of Dundee choose to sell their businesses to public investors in the middle of a prolonged fall in share prices? They must have known that they would be selling control of their businesses for a price markedly lower than could have been achieved just a few months before. Such apparently perverse behaviour required an explanation which lay in the difficult position in which the jute industry found itself.

Before the 1914–1918 war, for many industries, coarse jute fabric had become the universal packing material. Coconuts for fairground coconut shies, coffee beans for roasters and grains of all descriptions would all be packed in various forms of jute fabric. More refined forms of jute fabric such as canvas would be used for tents, sails, munitions bags and sandbags.

Although the uses to which the product could be put were almost endless, the manufacture of jute cloth had proved commercially risky as it was prone to volatile swings in the supply and price of the raw jute fibre and in the demand for jute cloth.

Many of the uses for the fabric were dependent on weather conditions. A poor growing season would reduce the size of the crops, whether of coffee or grain, and would lead to unforeseeable reductions in the demand for sacks. In addition, the many military uses for jute fabric caused demand for jute cloth to be even more erratic. In years when there was a major conflict such as the Crimean War, the American Civil War or the Franco-Prussian War, demand might for a while appear almost infinite. When a war ended, the demand it had caused would disappear immediately. Jute mills responded by reducing their purchases of raw material which caused erratic movements in the market price for fibre. The jute farmers in Bengal, virtually the only source for jute, responded by reducing their annual planting until the price for fibre rose again.[9]

Attempts had been made by the mill owners to mitigate the effect of this volatility by finding other uses for jute cloth and some, such as the use of jute fabric as the backing for linoleum, had proved successful. Yet the demand was not large enough to render the jute business stable. Mill owners were constantly aware of the financial risks of this instability. Typically, raw fibre was bought in annual auctions, obliging the mills to forecast how much would be needed in the coming year. Underestimating demand might oblige a mill to supplement its annual fibre purchases at higher prices in mid-season, while overestimating demand might leave a mill with a costly excess of fibre in stock. The only measure which owners could employ to mitigate the effects of volatility was to cut or increase production, laying off workers as soon as production appeared to exceed demand. For the communities surrounding the mills, this caused considerable social distress and for the mill owners it brought a reputation for callous hard-heartedness.

In Britain, through historical accident, the jute industry was almost entirely based in Dundee. Confined to a narrow strip of land between the River Tay and the Sidlaw Hills, the industry consisted largely of small mills, although there were several larger mills developed in the mid-nineteenth century.[10] For the mills and the families who owned them, the 1914–1918 war had proved a most successful and profitable experience. From the beginning of the war, the government had commandeered all of the mills' production for tents, sandbags and munitions bags. Although this had sacrificed the markets that the mills had supplied in peacetime, it relieved the mill owners of any risk arising from unforeseen variations in demand. The owners were also relieved of the risk of fluctuations in raw fibre prices by the government's decision to purchase raw fibre centrally so that it could then be resold to the mills at prices related to the price which the government was prepared to pay for the finished canvas. Similarly, wage rates and the numbers of hours worked were set by government-appointed panels and, yet again, the prices paid for the finished fabric were adjusted accordingly. All the mill owners had to do was to maximise production and count the profit.[11]

This was good for as long as it lasted, which was for about 18 months after the end of hostilities in November 1918. Eventually, the government had to accept that it no longer needed canvas for so many bags of all descriptions. The central purchasing of fibre stopped early in 1920[12] so that the mill owners again had to cope with a fluctuating market and had little time for preparation as the main season for buying fibre was about to begin. Even worse, the government's purchases of jute fabric stopped, so the mill owners had to find again the overseas markets that had bought Dundee fabric before the war. Unfortunately, one government control was not abandoned: the wage councils remained in place so the cost of labour which had risen during the war was not easily reduced. This led to a dispute between the mill owners and the union over working hours which was settled unsatisfactorily as far as the owners were concerned with an agreement to experiment for four months with a working week of 48 hours over five and a half days (compared with the pre-war standard working week of 55 hours).[13] Worst of all, whereas prices for jute fabric had been controlled during the war, after the war the mill owners had again to face price competition. Ironically, the sharpest price competition came from new jute mills in Bengal, which had been established by Dundee engineers backed by money from the Dundee mill owners themselves and were of the most modern design, intended to minimise avoidable manhandling of fibre and cloth.[14]

In short, the jute mill owners feared that prospects for the Dundee industry after the end of the government's wartime management of the industry were not at all attractive and that the adjustment to peacetime conditions would be desperately uncomfortable. They knew that their older smaller mills were less efficient than the new mills in Bengal.[15] Whereas the newer mills were single-storey buildings, easing the movement of fibre and cloth, most of the Dundee mills were built on confined sites as multi-storey buildings where much manhandling of cloth and fibre was required between floors. Such mills could not readily improve their efficiency so reduction of labour cost depended upon a reduction of hourly rates from the levels to which they had risen during the war and a return to the pre-war standard working week – adjustments that were bound to prove contentious and difficult. Led by the chairman of Cox Brothers Limited, in 1919 the mill owners formed an employers' association whose rules obliged all mills to close if one mill faced a strike, as a way of maximising their chance of defeating the inevitable union resistance.

The creation of a combine did not reflect a confident view of the future or a need to raise funds to take advantage of attractive prospects. It was based on a realisation that there may never be a better time to realise the value of the jute barons' equity in the industry, which perhaps explains the involvement of the mill companies' auditor in the initial discussions with Hatry. Ominously, the calculation that disposal would be good for the mill owners suggested that it might be an unattractive acquisition for investors. Flotation of a new jute combine was unlikely to be straightforward.[16]

The Dundee jute barons were not ignorant of the ways of stock exchanges; they were seasoned investors who commanded substantial investment portfolios which were invested through stock exchanges outside Scotland.[17] They understood the weaknesses of the offer that they proposed to make to investors and that, if the offer were to be successful, they would need the assistance of a promoter with the skills to market a less than convincing proposition against the background of a falling market. Although some members of the mill-owning families were sceptical, for the majority, Hatry's developing reputation for exploiting the vagaries of stock exchange rules to achieve vendors' objectives seemed to qualify him as a candidate for the Jute Industries promotion. Jo Grimond recalled the reaction of one of his more sceptical relatives:

> When nineteenth century capitalists are criticised I think of the concern which my father showed for his work people and for the good name of the Grimond business. He disliked the idea of financial manipulation and neither he nor his Blairgowrie cousin, John, held any illusions about Hatry. Indeed the story goes that when the deed was done … Cousin John would have none of Hatry's cheques or bills or scrip but brought an attaché case and insisted upon taking his share in bank notes.[18]

The mill owners checked their view of Hatry with a former Dundonian, Robert Fleming, who had moved to London where he founded his own merchant bank and successfully created a number of investment trusts.[19] They then approached Hatry who, with alacrity, accepted the invitation to assist in the formation and flotation of a new combine.[20]

By October 1920, with less difficulty than had been expected, Hatry had secured the agreement of six families to the terms on which their mills should be merged into a single group.[21] There had been a fear that some members of the families might prove reluctant to sell at realistic prices but this problem had disappeared. With little time to prepare for the fibre buying season in July 1920, most of the Dundee mills had bought similar quantities to those used in 1919. By the end of September it was clear that demand for jute cloth was falling quickly which rapidly led to overproduction, the introduction of short-time working and reductions in the labour force.[22]

As demand fell, so did the market price for raw jute fibre which, as the directors must have known, threatened that the year-end profits would be hit by a reduction in stock values. In particular, Cox Brothers prepared its interim accounts on the basis of the historical cost of purchasing fibre so that account was not taken immediately of a reduction in the market price. At the end of each accounting period, remaining stocks of fibre would be valued at the market price ruling at that date so that there would be a charge to the profit and loss account if the market price had fallen materially. In the event, this is what was to happen.

The onset of short-time working emphasised the difficulty of the offer of the new combine's shares and the urgency of the launch which eventually took place on 11 November.

Under Hatry's guidance, the terms of the preference shares offered for sale were intended to be attractive.[23] The interest payable on the preference shares was set high by comparison with other share offers.[24] According to the offer document, the group's financial position was healthy. Its assets were valued optimistically on the basis of their replacement cost rather than their historical cost, so that the group's net assets were estimated to be £8,158,216, considerably in excess of the existing issued share capital of £2,000,000 before any account was taken of the new issue and the cash which would be subscribed. The effect was to distract attention from the possibility that the company was over-capitalised. Hatry intended that the total amount of the preference share capital should equal the cost of buying out the families' interests in their mills. As many of the family members were to be paid in cash, they must have regarded their payment as representing a fair estimation of the value of their interest and the ordinary share capital of £2,000,000 must have represented an additional burden. While this may have been justified if merger of the mills were expected to realise economies of scale, the pessimistic assessment of the jute trade which had led to the merger suggests that there was no additional value to be realised and that JIL was over-capitalised.[25]

Investors' attention was drawn to the exceptionally high profits that had been achieved during the war years rather than the difficulties of current trading, although the statement of past profits was accompanied by an acknowledgement that it was unlikely that such high profits could be fully maintained.

The formal, carefully worded prospectus was supplemented by anticipatory stories in newspapers before publication of the offer for sale[26] and by a series of advertisements placed in 93 newspapers and organised by the head of Hatry's new issues department, Charles Duguid, who had previously been City editor of the *Daily Mail*.[27] These advertisements emphasised the exceptional profits achieved during the war, but excluded the cautious words of warning that had been included in the offer for sale. Investors were being encouraged to suppose that the high profits reported during the war might continue. Duguid cannot have missed the irony of his involvement as, during his time at the *Daily Mail*, he had written a book warning potential investors on the interpretation of misleading articles on investment propositions.[28]

Finally, Hatry attempted to obscure the difference between the price paid to the jute families for their mills and the contribution expected from investors, which in large part represented his fee. Although the rules had been changed in December 1919 to close a loophole which exempted offers for sale from the full disclosure requirements applied to prospectuses, Hatry tried to avoid disclosure of a key agreement by careful timing. One of the agreements to acquire the six family-owned jute mills was not made public or appended to the application submitted to the stock exchange by Hatry for permission to deal in the shares on the floor of the exchange. As Hatry later explained, the agreement could not be shown to the committee because it had not been signed until after the application had been submitted (although it was contemplated). He cannot have expected that the omission would be overlooked as the missing agreement related to Cox Brothers Limited, the largest of the mill companies. When the omission was spotted, the exchange initially refused permission to deal in the shares. To ensure that the shares would be admitted to the floor of the exchange, Hatry was obliged to disclose the information he had withheld. However, Hatry's primary aim had been to deny information to potential investors and that he had achieved. The supplementary information which the exchange forced him to divulge was not published until after the deadline for investors to submit applications for shares. Although the stock exchange received complaints about this, the complainants do not appear to have received redress.[29]

For all of Hatry's efforts, the public offer of the shares of Jute Industries was not a complete success: only just over 70% of the shares were sold, leaving just under 30% to be taken up by the underwriters. The disappointing public response implied that trading in the after-market would be disappointing. So it proved. As underwriters attempted to dispose of the shares they had been obliged to purchase, the share price fell below the issue price. As a result, there was no prospect of Hatry realising profits on his own shares.

A few months later, when JIL's annual results were announced, the news for shareholders was even worse. Although there had been enough profit to pay the dividend due on the preference shares, there was to be no dividend for ordinary shareholders. Understandably, many shareholders were aggrieved by this and became suspicious that either the original offer had been misleading or the directors were not disclosing the full profit that had been made and retained by the subsidiaries. Relationships between the directors and shareholders became sour, and it was to be some years before shareholders were prepared to accept that the directors were telling the truth in saying that there was no profit. It was to take more years for the shareholders to accept that they had been sold shares at considerably more than their true value and that the company's capital should be written down.

The shareholders were justifiably aggrieved. Yet again Hatry had served the interests of the vendors; the jute barons had profited by seeking his help in selling their shares in 1920.

Others of Hatry's new issues in 1919 and 1920, such as Leyland Motors, suffered problems.

The first problem arose when the government sought purchasers for the large number of heavy Leyland lorries that had been bought during the war for the Royal Flying Corps. Threatened with the prospect of more than 1,100 second-hand lorries in varied states of repair shrinking the demand for new lorries and undermining the reputation of Leyland's products, LML decided to buy all of the lorries. This was a financial burden for which the company had made no allowance. It also became the subject of a political scandal when it became known that the government official responsible for selling the vehicles in France was a member of the Spurrier family and had previously been a director of the company. In debates in the House of Commons, the family connection was widely blamed for the low price that Leyland was able to negotiate.

This was not the limit of Leyland's problems. The company's post-war plans included the development of motorcars in parallel to its respected buses and lorries and came to fruition in the introduction of the Leyland Eight at the International Motor Show at Olympia in 1920. Nicknamed the 'Lion of Olympia', the car was claimed to be the finest car ever made. Whatever the truth of that claim may have been, it was certainly one of the most expensive. A chassis delivered to a coachbuilder cost over £2,500, whereas open tourer versions with two or five seats would be supplied from the factory for more than £2,700. At these prices, the car was more expensive than a Rolls Royce but proved unsatisfactory as it was not fitted with front brakes and suffered from heavy steering. After only 18 were produced, the car was withdrawn from sale and the remaining chassis were converted for racing at Brooklands by the designer J.G. Parry-Jones, who left the company. At the time it was rumoured that the cost of developing the car had exceeded all of the profit made by the company during the war.[30]

Although LML survived, it was to take the company a decade to live down the chastening experiences of 1920–1921. Its shareholders were as suspicious of the Spurrier family's motives as the shareholders of Jute Industries were of the jute barons' families. This suspicion was never successfully resolved as the preference shareholders refused to approve the directors' proposals to restructure the share capital and the company's development had to await the realisation of sufficient profit to make good the losses of the early 1920s.[31]

AIL also suffered problems. With the onset of a recession in the second half of 1920, land prices began to fall and with them the company's hopes of borrowing money to complete the modernisation of its estates. In seeking a way out, the holding company directors realised that Hatry's corporate structure, which was designed to preserve the Dennis family's control of the farming land and business, necessarily involved denying the holding company the power to intervene. In short, the holding company directors found that they were powerless to manage the group's affairs and thus to protect the interests of the holding company's shareholders. The result was a long-lasting stand-off between the Dennis family and the external shareholders which was not resolved until the early 1950s after a Board of Trade inspection of the company.

Another of Hatry's flotations, Kent Portland Cement Company, which had been formed to build a new cement factory, found that the construction cost was greater than expected and that, in the current state of the stock market, it could not raise additional money. The company, with its half-built factory, was eventually sold at a substantial loss to the Blue Circle Cement Group, which was managed by Hatry's friend, the former company promoter Osborne O'Hagan. Shareholders had again suffered.[32]

Hatry's companies were not alone in suffering the effects of the recession in 1920 – all businesses were affected in some way. But the newspapers noted that many investors had lost money by supporting his flotations and his reputation suffered. Often there was nothing he could do, but occasionally, as in the case of Amalgamated Industrials, he was able to defend himself. Amalgamated Industrials, a slightly bizarre grouping of shipbuilding, coal and iron companies, was floated in 1919. After a few months, a controlling interest had been sold by Hatry to a John Slater who proceeded to raise money by issuing more shares and to make a series of acquisitions of shipping and insurance companies. By the end of 1920, the company had become insolvent and was being wound up, to the accompaniment of newspaper articles proclaiming the demise of a Hatry company. Hatry responded with libel writs pointing out that at the time of the company's demise Hatry had not been involved – a point confirmed in the apologies which the newspapers were obliged to print.

Hatry's sensitivity to attacks on his reputation was understandable, but they did not pose an existential threat to his business. His reputation for promotions which stretched rules to their limits was tolerated by City houses which were happy to profit by supporting him covertly in transactions which they would not have sponsored publicly. Moreover, the trading problems of the businesses he had promoted were not exceptional. During the recession of the early 1920s, all businesses encountered difficulty.

While share prices were falling, financial embarrassment was growing for anyone who had built a portfolio of shares by borrowing money from banks. As a result of their deep involvement in Hatry's flotations, Ellis & Co, his stockbrokers, and City Equitable Fire Insurance, the insurance company that Hatry had sold to the senior partner of Ellis & Co, both held large numbers of shares in companies that he had floated. By mid-1921, Ellis & Co and City Equitable Fire Insurance had suffered losses on their holdings of Hatry-related shares and were under pressure from their bankers to repay their loans or provide additional security. Hatry desperately tried to persuade them not to sell their shares because that would tend to depress share prices further and increase the pressure on his own company, Commercial Bank of London. Although some relief was achieved by acquiring small insurance companies and merging their investment portfolios, by the end of 1921 the pressure had grown again and they were obliged to close, having become irremediably insolvent.

This caused an unexpected shock. Both businesses were chaired by Gerard Lee Bevan, who immediately absconded, to the professional delight of the many journalists who pursued him across Europe and to the horror of his former partners and co-directors who had little warning of the collapse.[33]

Within Ellis & Co, Bevan had been allowed to be an autocrat. Investment of the firm's funds had been directed by him without the involvement or knowledge of any of his partners. None of them knew of the extent to which he had supported Hatry's flotations or the risks he had taken.[34]

City Equitable's failure was attributed to an egregious failure of corporate governance. Reinsurance was a specialist business which was understood by the company's manager, Edward Mansell, but not by the company's directors. They had perforce to trust Mansell's development of the business which superficially had been justified by growth in premiums and profit, but he had abused the directors' lack of supervision by arranging personal benefits for himself. Equally, the directors had placed undue responsibility for the company's investments in the hands of Bevan. Although there was supposed to have been an investment committee, there were no records of it having met, let alone records of it having reached any conclusions. In practice, investment policy had been decided by Bevan alone without the other directors knowing what was done in their name. These discoveries, coupled with the excitement of Bevan's attempt to avoid arrest, turned City Equitable into a cause célèbre, which provided the plot for John Galsworthy's novel, *The Silver Spoon*. Landmark litigation followed as the liquidator tried to claim that the directors had been negligent and should be personally liable for the company's losses.[35]

Meanwhile the liquidators set about realising the remaining investments at what were to prove rock bottom prices, which meant that share prices for Hatry-related shares fell further and the stability of Hatry's own company, Commercial Bank of London, came into question. Eventually, early in 1922, it too went into liquidation, Hatry having failed to persuade his banks that this fate could be delayed. Desperate to preserve his reputation, Hatry was able to persuade all of the interested parties that there was enough value in the company's investments to meet all of its liabilities and the liquidation proceeded on the basis that it would prove to have been solvent. To achieve this required not simply Hatry's usual charm but also money, as he was obliged to buy off interested parties such as Sir Charles Hobhouse, the chairman, who might otherwise have objected to Hatry's proposals.[36]

As the liquidation proceeded, however, it proved difficult to realise investments at the prices that Hatry had hoped for and the liquidator lost patience with Hatry's entreaties, deciding to sell for whatever price could be achieved. For some, this was a welcome development. The Dennis family in Lincolnshire, for example, was able to buy a substantial holding of the shares of AIL for next to nothing and thus gained voting control of the company for much less than they had received when it had been floated in 1919.

For Hatry, the liquidator's actions were problematic. By selling investments for very low prices, the liquidator was failing to achieve the values that Hatry had told shareholders would be possible and were crucial because they underpinned Hatry's promise that the company would prove to have been solvent and that the shareholders would find that they had not lost money by investing in his company.

For a company promoter, such promises mattered. How good an operator could a promoter be if his promises of value could not be realised? If a promoter's supporters lost money by supporting his deals, would they repeat the experience? If Hatry were to stay in business as a promoter, he needed to honour his promises that Commercial Bank's shareholders would not lose their money. He found himself in a hole. To honour his promises and keep faith with his supporters, he needed to find a new way of making money.

Hatry had struggled mightily to avoid this outcome and, as he was later to claim repeatedly, in the effort he had lost most of the fortune he had amassed by the end of 1919.

This sounds far worse than it was. While it cannot have been enjoyable for Hatry, this substantial loss did not destroy everything he had created. After his bankruptcy before the 1914–1918 war, Hatry was determined not to expose his family to the ignominy that his mother had suffered and which his uncle and aunt suffered in 1914 when J.G. Eiser & Co was hammered. He may well have promised his wife that she would not have to cope with bankruptcy. Consequently, he had consistently transferred large amounts of money to his wife. By this means, the family's finances were protected. They remained at the house in Mayfair. His son was able to complete his time at Eton. The race horses were retained, although there were to be no more wins in classic races. When a rival promoter, Horatio Bottomley, was prosecuted in 1922, Hatry's wife was able to buy his stud at Alfriston in East Sussex.

One extravagance proved too much: Hatry did not race his yacht, *Westward*, after the 1920 season and it was eventually sold. Ironically *Westward* was sold to T.B. Davies, a South African who was a resident of Jersey. He was a friend of King George V who often sailed with Davies, perhaps recalling the time in 1920 when he had witnessed *Westward* with Clarence Hatry on board, outpacing his own yacht, *Britannia.* Under Davies' ownership, *Westward* was to be raced regularly but, as he wished, on his death was scuttled off the coast of Jersey. Never again was Hatry to own a yacht.

Although Hatry's circumstances were dire, his family survived. To rebuild his business needed the kiss of life.

Notes

1 Kynaston, 1999, page 61 et seq.
2 Price, 2007, page 145 et seq.
3 Such opportunities for profit remain significant for advisers involved in promoting new issues, as shown by the well-documented case of the privatisation of the Royal Mail in 2013. The vendor's independent corporate finance adviser, Lazard & Company Limited, earned a fee of £1.5 million for advice, while its associate, Lazard Asset Management, recorded a profit of £8.4 million on selling within 48 hours of the flotation shares which it had been allocated (House of Commons Business Innovation and Skills Committee report, July 2014; National Audit Office report, March 2014).
4 TNA file PCOM 9/383.
5 *Sunday Express*, 26 January 1930. This recollection was later to be challenged implicitly by the liquidator of Commercial Bank of London (which had been renamed Commercial Corporation of London), who suggested that Hatry had not foreseen the market's reversal (*The Economist*, 1 May 1924, page 723).
6 Kynaston, 1999, pages 54 and 96; Manley, 1976.
7 Cook with Cohen, 1958, page 65.
8 Pearson, 1961, page 112.
9 Lenman et al. 1969, page 37 and 40.
10 The largest mill, Cox Brothers Limited, was one of the largest employers in the UK: reputedly the 120th largest employer in 1907 (Wardley, 1999, page 105).
11 Walker, 1979, page 400 et seq.
12 *Dundee and District Jute and Flax Workers Guide*, July 1920.
13 Walker, 1979, page 420.
14 *Daily Herald*, 28 April 1919; *Dundee and District Jute and Flax Workers Guide*, May 1919.
15 Stewart, 2011, page 35.
16 Walker, 1979, page 439 et seq.; Tomlinson, 2014, page 104 et seq.
17 Investments were placed through brokers outside Dundee so that local brokers did not know what the jute barons were doing (Smith, 2000, page 14). Most of these investments were made through the mill companies and appear in the accounting records held by DUA (Lenman and Donaldson, 1971, page 2).
18 Grimond, 1979, page 24.
19 Fleming worked for Cox Brothers before establishing his first investment trust (Smith, 2000, page 12).
20 Gilbert, 1986, page 111; Greenfield, 1995, page 48.
21 Thomas Bell and Sons, Gilroy Sons and Company Limited, J.&A.D. Grimond Limited, John N. Kyd and Company, Cox Brothers Limited and Harry Walker and Son Limited. All of these companies, save for the last-named concern, were audited by one firm.
22 DUA holds an extensive collection of the accounting records of Cox Brothers Limited. These records include departmental trading accounts which for several years were prepared on a monthly basis. They also record the average cost per

unit of production on a monthly basis. These show that during September and October 1920, the average cost per unit of production was being monitored. They also show that action taken to introduce short-time working and to reduce the labour force avoided material increases in average cost. In other words, they demonstrate that management was aware that the trading position had worsened materially and was actively controlling costs. More limited records exist for Gilroy Sons and Company Limited. These two sets of records are consistent in showing a decline in trade and profit during the last months of 1920 (DUA).

23 *The Times*, 11 November 1920, page 20.

24 9% per annum, cumulative. Moreover, the initial payment due in May 1921 was to be paid at the full rate of 9% and not pro-rated to take account of late payment of cash by subscribers. The average yield on preference shares offered for sale was 8.1% in 1920 and 8.4% in 1921 (Thomas, 1978, page 44).

25 As proved to be the case in 1929, when JIL was obliged to reduce its capital. The capital structure designed by Hatry followed the practice adopted in the USA during the merger wave before the 1914–1918 war which had led to prolonged debates about over-capitalisation and stock watering. Mitchell, 2007, pages 67–68 and 71.

26 *Dundee Advertiser*, 24 September 1920, pages 1 and 8; 25 September 1920, page 9; *Dundee and District Jute and Flax Workers Guide*, October 1920.

27 *The Times*, 18 November 1920, page 17.

28 Duguid, 1904.

29 Application for listing file, LSE archive, Guildhall Library.

30 Turner, 1971, pages 15–18.

31 Turner, 1971, pages 18–19.

32 Cook with Cohen, 1958, page 65.

33 Vander Weyer, 2011, page 169 et seq.

34 Vander Weyer, 2011, page 249 et seq; Dawson, 1927, pages 351–352.

35 Vander Weyer, 2011, page 255 et seq; Dawson, 1927, page 349 et seq. Bevan's assumption of autocratic investment powers is described in Romer J's judgment in the litigation initiated by the liquidator of City Equitable Fire Insurance (in Re City Equitable Fire Insurance (1925) ChD 407).

36 Copy of letter dated 7 June 1922 from Hobhouse to Hatry (annotated to the effect that the original of the letter was subsequently 'torn up' in the presence of Hatry). Letter dated 7 June 1923 from Hatry to Hobhouse (records of J.D. Langton & Passmore, LMA).

References

Primary works: unpublished documents

Dundee University Archive: Jute Industries papers.
Guildhall Library: LSX archive.
London Metropolitan Archive: J.D. Langton & Passmore papers.
TNA: Board of Trade papers.
TNA: Prisons Commission papers.

Primary works: newspapers and periodicals

Daily Herald.
Dundee Advertiser.
Dundee and District Jute and Flax Workers Guide.

Sunday Express.
The Economist.
The Guardian.
The Times.

Primary works: contemporary books and papers

Dawson, S.D. (1927), *A Soldier Diplomat.* (John Murray, London).
Duguid, C. (1904), *How to Read the Money Article.* (Effingham Wilson, London).

Secondary works

Cook, P.L. with Cohen, R. (1958), *Effects of Mergers.* (George Allen & Unwin, London).
Gilbert, M. (1986), *Fraudsters: Six Against the Law.* (Constable, London).
Greenfield, G. (1995), *A Smattering of Monsters: A Kind of Memoir.* (Little Brown, London).
Grimond, J. (1979), *Memoirs.* (Heinemann, London).
Keyworth, J.M. (1985), 'Sir Arthur Wheeler', *Dictionary of Business Biography.* (Butterworths, London).
Kynaston, D. (1999), *The City of London: Volume III: Illusions of Gold 1914–1945.* (Chatto & Windus, London).
Lenman, B. and Donaldson, K. (1971), 'Partners' Incomes, Investment and Diversification in the Scottish Linen Area 1850–1921', *Business History*, volume 13, pages 1–18.
Lenman, B., Lythe, C. and Gauldie, E. (1969), *Dundee and Its Textile Industry.* (Abertay Historical Society, Dundee).
Manley, P.S. (1976), 'Clarence Hatry', *Abacus*, volume 12(1), pages 49–60.
Mitchell, L.E. (2007), *The Speculation Economy: How Finance Triumphed over Industry.* (Berrett-Koehler Publishers, San Francisco).
Pearson, M. (1961), *The Millionaire Mentality.* (Secker & Warburg, London).
Price, C. (2007), 'Depression and Recovery', in Carnevali, F. and Strange, J.-M. (eds), *20th Century Britain: Economic, Cultural and Social Change.* (Second Edition). (Pearson Education, Harlow).
Smith, B. (2000), *Robert Fleming, 1845–1933.* (Whittinghame House, Haddington, Scotland).
Stewart, G. (2011), 'Endgame for Jute: Dundee and Calcutta in the Twentieth Century', in Tomlinson, J. and Whatley, C.A. (eds), *Jute No More: Transforming Dundee.* (Dundee University Press, Dundee).
Thomas, W.A. (1978), *The Finance of British Industry 1918–1976.* (Methuen, London).
Tomlinson, J. (2014), *Dundee and the Empire: 'Juteopolis' 1850–1939.* (Edinburgh University Press, Edinburgh).
Turner, G. (1971), *The Leyland Papers.* (Eyre & Spottiswoode, London).
Vander Weyer, M. (2011), *Fortune's Spear: The Story of the Blue-Blooded Rogue behind the Most Notorious City Scandal of the 1920s.* (Elliott & Thompson, London).
Walker, W.M. (1979), *Juteopolis: Dundee and Its Textile Workers 1885–1923.* (Scottish Academic Press, Edinburgh).
Wardley, P. (1999), 'The Emergence of Big Business: The Largest Corporate Employers of Labour in the United Kingdom', *Business History*, volume 41(4), pages 88-116.

6 Arthur Collins to the rescue

For Hatry, salvation was to come in the unlikely form of Arthur Collins. In surviving photographs, he appears as a stout, confident, conventional man, in a three-piece suit, sporting a gold watch chain. His appearance is reminiscent of Alderman Joseph Helliwell, a character in J.B. Priestley's play, *When We Are Married*, about how pillars of the community in a northern town deal with the unwelcome disruption of their satisfying, respectable lives by the discovery that their marriages were not legally valid. For most of the early part of his career, Arthur Collins lived and worked in northern towns, although he was never an alderman. He was, however, a local authority treasurer, one of a class of men renowned for their prudence and their sobriety. If their stereotype were to be taken seriously, they were selected for advancement on the basis of their lack of imagination and entrepreneurial ambition. Collins was an exception. In his childhood, Collins obtained a scholarship from a National School which had enabled him to go to Bury Grammar School and thence to Owen's College, which was subsequently to become Manchester University. He then started work in the office of the borough treasurer of Blackpool, where he was trained by Mr Bateson, a past president of what was to become the Institute of Municipal Treasurers and Accountants (IMTA) and is now the Chartered Institute of Public Finance and Accountancy (CIPFA).[1]

In its early years, the institute did not offer a separate qualification; most students sat the examinations of the Society of Incorporated Accountants and Auditors. But as a part of its programme to establish itself as a professional body, the institute decided to become a qualifying body and Collins won first place in the first final examinations in 1905. To commemorate this achievement, he was later to endow the award of a gold medal to finalists who were placed first, to match similar awards in other accountancy bodies, a demonstration that the IMTA aimed to be as respectable as they. To this day, the Collins Medal is still awarded every year.

In the same year, Collins broke free from his mentor at Blackpool and moved to West Bromwich where he became deputy borough treasurer. Three years later, in 1908, he moved to the larger authority of Birmingham, where he became deputy city treasurer.

From the beginning, Collins was keen to establish a national position for himself, perhaps with the encouragement of Mr Bateson, his mentor. To do this, he followed the well-worn path of lecturing and writing widely on local authority finance, contributing to the IMTA's newsletters. On a number of occasions, he seems to have acted as an expert witness on local authority finance matters. As the institute's examinations were in their infancy, there was a dearth of support for those trying to qualify so he created Collins Correspondence Courses for students intending to sit the IMTA examinations, matching the Foulks Lynch correspondence courses that were taken by students preparing for the chartered and incorporated accountants' examinations. One result of this innovation was that a large proportion of the students sitting the institute's examinations and new members of IMTA recognised the name of Arthur Collins.

Towards the end of the 1914–1918 war, he became city treasurer of Birmingham on the retirement of his predecessor, and, at the end of the war, was elected to the council of the IMTA. In many professional bodies, there would then have been a long wait before a new council member was considered for advancement to office-holding, but in Collins' case, he was elected vice-president after only three years and became president a year later in June 1921. This is a powerful testimony to the position he had established within the profession but must also have been assisted by the fact that his mentor, Bateson, was still a member of the council and, as a past president, would still have been a part of the group that considered potential office holders.

Advancement to the presidency appears just to have been another stepping stone in Collins' career plan. His assumption of the presidency was noted in the July 1921 issue of the IMTA's newsletter, the *Financial Circular*. In the next issue, the *Circular* reported that a deputy treasurer had been appointed by the City of Birmingham to support him: J.R. Johnson, who also later became president of the IMTA. Six months later, in January 1922, the *Circular* reported that Collins had resigned his position as city treasurer with effect from 31 December 1921, with J.R. Johnson becoming acting treasurer. Collins continued in support as 'consultant' at a fee almost equal to Johnson's salary, a role he was to maintain until Johnson was appointed to the substantive role of city treasurer in 1923. By these changes, Collins had freed himself from his ties to Birmingham sufficiently to consider other activities.

This is precisely what he then did. On the first page of the first issue of the *Circular* to be published after the end of Collins' year as president, there appeared an advertisement for his new business: the Municipal Loans Bureau. The new bureau offered advice to local authorities on financial planning and assistance with the arrangement of new financing facilities, including assistance with sponsoring private bills to vary councils' powers to borrow.

The initiative was well timed. On returning from the war, servicemen had been promised by politicians that there would be new homes and communities in which their families could live happy and settled lives. To a large extent, honouring these promises fell upon local authorities. Social housing estates had to be built. Each estate had to be provided with the necessary infrastructure, such as water supply, sewage treatment and road connections. Schools had to be built. Corporation bus services had to be extended. Quite apart from all this activity, developments in technology were making other demands of authorities. Growing car ownership and use of lorries for distribution of goods were creating more traffic and a need to rebuild an inadequate road network. In the midst of all this activity, borough treasurers had to find the necessary finance. For most ratepayers, it was not acceptable to find the money by raising rates for they would bear the burden of creating infrastructure for the future that many of them would not be able to use. Borrowing long-term money at fixed rates was more acceptable because the cost would fall upon the future generations which would use the infrastructure that the money would provide. This brought borough treasurers into contact with a world of which most had little experience: the City.

The dangers inherent in this had been recognised, so authorities wishing to raise long-term money by means of issuing tradeable securities were required to seek the approval of the Ministry of Health, the government department which at that time exercised oversight of local authorities. But, in addition, local authority treasurers wanting to navigate their way through a financial world that was foreign to them looked for guidance from a knowledgeable source they could trust.

Collins' experience made him an excellent candidate to meet this need. He had served as treasurer of small and large authorities. He was acknowledged as an expert in local authority finance. Most newly qualified treasurers would have relied upon the support of his correspondence courses. Perhaps most significantly, as president of the IMTA he had enjoyed opportunities to meet the borough treasurers of all significant authorities.

Arthur Collins well understood the value to him of his network of contacts within the institute so that, after completing his year as president, he protected that network by arranging to become examinations secretary and subsequently, in 1928, secretary of the institute and editor of the *Financial Circular*. Indeed, the London office of the institute was to be located in his offices, its telephone number and telegraphic address (ARCOLSTER) being shared with Collins' bureau. Throughout the 1920s, he was to play a leading role in lobbying government on behalf of the institute, presenting its evidence to the Royal Commission on Local Government in 1925, and publishing annual reviews of local authority acts of parliament, many of which were sponsored by local authorities seeking revision of their powers to borrow money.[2] Arthur Collins was a man in a hurry who had planned to make the most of his opportunities.

This was the man who was introduced to Hatry in 1925[3] and was to provide the means by which Hatry redeemed his promise to the Commercial Bank's shareholders that they would recover the capital they had invested. The introduction came through Sir John Crisp, of the solicitors Ashurst Morris Crisp, who had taken over as Hatry's solicitor on the death of his father, Sir Frank Crisp. It is obvious that Collins and Hatry 'hit it off' immediately and why. They both had created new businesses from unprepossessing beginnings through exploiting new ideas, networking skills and unrelentingly hard work. Collins had done this in the world of local authority finance and Hatry in the City. The milieus were different but the strategies were similar.

By 1924, however, Collins' project had hit a stumbling block. His original advertisements for the Municipal Loans Bureau had suggested that he would assist local authorities to arrange new loans when they were needed, doubtless calculating that he would be able to negotiate more favourable terms for authorities and benefit from charging them fees. When he tried to do this he had been unable to break a virtual monopoly of the placing of municipal stock issues which was in the hands of three firms of stockbrokers: Mullens Marshall & Company, the government and Bank of England brokers Nivison & Company, in which Lord Glendyne was the principal partner, and J. and A. Scrimgeour & Company. The three brokers maintained their monopoly through their control of underwriting for new loan issues. City houses were eager to participate in underwriting as the new issues were generally well subscribed so that there was only a small risk that underwriters would be called upon to take up stock that had not been subscribed. By threatening to exclude houses from this lucrative trade, the brokers undermined opposition to their monopoly which extended to the arrangement of loans in London for the colonies. The monopoly was regarded favourably by the Bank of England as it facilitated the arrangement of prospective issuers of loan stock into an orderly queue.[4]

In his first attempt to break this monopoly, Collins had been supported by British Shareholders' Trust Limited (BST), a house which was chaired by the respected young Chartered Accountant Bernhard Binder. This organisation had been created in 1915 by provincial stockbrokers who were concerned that London brokers might freeze them out of sponsoring new issues on the London exchange. In 1923 and 1924, attempts had been made to break the monopoly both for local authority issues and for colonial issues. Both attempts had failed. In the case of local authority issues, the market, principally the specialist gilt-edged stock-jobbers, had declined to deal in stocks which had not been introduced by the usual route. In the case of colonial issues, although there was strong support from Conservative ministers, the introduction of BST was opposed by J. & A. Scrimgeour, who threatened that the firm would henceforth withdraw completely from the market.[5]

This threat was potent because it exposed the weakness of the BST proposition. BST did not have access to financial resources sufficient to guarantee that the whole of any loan issue would be sold, thus creating a risk that the authority might be left with unsold stock. The incumbent brokers, by contrast, were able to point to their track record of ensuring that stock was sold. If the incumbent brokers were to withdraw from sponsoring stock, authorities would be left to bear the risk that stock would not be sold.

This threat was sufficient for the Crown Agents to refuse to appoint BST and thus to uphold the existing monopoly. The downside of this outcome was that as the three existing brokers did not compete with each other on their charges to local authorities for sponsoring loan issues, the local authorities had no choice but to accept the terms they were offered.

Collins thus found himself seeking an operator who could sponsor new local authority loan issues and was not afraid to challenge an established monopoly. Hatry was prepared to take this on and took the chance.

His solution was that he would buy the whole of the loan that a local authority wished to raise and would take upon himself the risk of finding purchasers for the stock so that the local authority would not be left with unsold stock.[6] At the same time, he proposed to restructure the charges for arranging the issue, undercutting the three established brokers. He planned to do this by cutting out commissions payable to other parties who were used by the existing brokers to organise an issue.

Perhaps the most important change was to stop using a clearing bank as the receiving agent for the issue. The usual practice was that anyone who applied to buy a new loan stock would be asked to pay the money to a clearing bank which would issue a receipt and then hold the money subscribed until it was paid over to the local authority. In due course, the investors would tender the receipts to the local authority as proof that they had subscribed to the issue and would receive in return a formal certificate of ownership issued by the town clerk. In return for providing this service, the bank would receive a small commission.

Hatry proposed that one of his own companies should act as receiving agent. This had the advantage of avoiding the need to pay commission to a bank but would also allow Hatry's company to benefit from the chance to earn interest on the money which it held, even for a short period, on behalf of the local authority. Hatry's company would match the low rate of interest that a bank would have allowed the local authority but hope to earn more by using the money for itself. This income allowed Hatry to reduce the rate of commission his company would be charging the local authority for arranging the issue.

These details may seem arcane but they were important to the frugal borough treasurer. In return for issuing loan stock, a local authority would receive the money subscribed by investors less the costs incurred by whoever sponsored and managed the issue. The higher the costs, the lower the net amount received by the treasurer and thus the higher the effective rate of interest borne by the authority. If, in addition, a part of the stock issue was not sold, the effective rate of interest rose even higher. Hatry's proposal promised not only to free authorities from the risk of unsold stock but also to free them the existing brokers' control of costs.

As comfort, local authority treasurers knew that Hatry's approach was approved by Arthur Collins, a man they knew and trusted. They also knew that any proposed loan issue would be scrutinised by the Ministry of Health, although they probably did not realise that the ministry did not scrutinise the market wisdom of any proposed arrangements but merely their compliance with the ministry's formal regulations. Certainly the ministry did not consider the wisdom of Hatry's own company serving as receiving agent for a loan issue.

Hatry's experience made him ideal to offer his revised approach. From his association with Sperling & Co in 1918 when he was selling shares in Northumberland Shipbuilding, he had experience of selling shares off-market. From this experience he knew that, whatever the conventions of the formal market may have been, there were always people prepared to buy shares or stock if the financial proposition was sufficiently attractive. Even the most outwardly respectable houses would support unconventional issues privately if the deal was right. Not only did he know this, he knew how to find prospective supporters.

As it was important that any stock issued should be tradeable on the London Stock Exchange, Hatry still needed a broker who would sponsor the issues, and he was fortunate to be introduced by Sir John Crisp to Cecil Braithwaite, the senior partner of Foster & Braithwaite, a stockbroking firm which had specialised in sponsoring new issues.[7] Braithwaite was a cautious, well-respected broker whose principal interest was fly-fishing, which led him to write in his memoir of life as an angler:

> To me the soft sound of the rippling water, with the song of the birds, is a sweet lullaby, the best possible cure for the cares and worries of a business life. It is a lovely sensation, when you step into a train at one of the London termini bound for the North, on fishing bent; you feel friends with everyone you meet, from the fellow-passenger to the sleeping-car attendant.[8]

This gentle man was slightly distrustful of Hatry and, while prepared to cooperate with the local authority loan stock venture, never allowed his firm to become involved in any of Hatry's industrial issues. This caution stood him in good stead when in 1929, after Hatry's collapse, he was carpeted by the governor of the Bank of England for having supported Hatry's loan stock issue initiative.[9]

Having reached an understanding with Collins, Hatry's first step was to create a new company to lead the new business: Corporate & General Securities Limited (C&GS), which was to be a subsidiary of another new company, Aylesbury Trust Limited, and was to be chaired by the Marquess of Winchester, the premier marquess in England, who was introduced by Foster & Braithwaite.[10] Hatry then offered shares in Aylesbury Trust Limited to the shareholders in Commercial Bank, which by this stage was defunct. By this offer of shares in a new, potentially profitable business, Hatry redeemed his promise that investors in Commercial Bank would recover their capital and restored his reputation.

On 23 January 1925, newspapers carried reports of the first loan stock to be issued as a result of the collaboration between Arthur Collins and Hatry:

an issue of £500,000 4¾% redeemable stock (1943–1955) for Plymouth Corporation which had not been offered to the market but sold in full to C&GS.[11]

This was undoubtedly a shock for the specialist gilt-edged stock-jobbers on the stock exchange whose cooperation had not been enlisted in advance.[12] A stock had been issued which had been placed with investors without the assistance of the jobbers. As *The Economist* explained:

> The sale was made direct to the Corporation and General Securities Limited ... This company took the stock from the Corporation of Plymouth and placed it among investors, through the medium of well-known firm of Stock Exchange brokers whose connection with the House extends for a century. The firm, however, was not one of the three firms which, by convention, are called upon to handle the issues of British Government, Corporation and Colonial stocks. Permission to deal in the stock was duly obtained. When it came to a matter of dealing, however, the majority of jobbers hesitated as to what course they should pursue. The three firms already mentioned are in the habit of taking such steps as will ensure freedom of market in the issues with which they are connected. Until an issue becomes firmly settled into the hands of the more or less permanent investor, the issuing house takes up the position of what, in homely phrase, may be regarded as the nurse who looks after her baby until it is strong enough to stand on its own feet. Hesitation, however, was expressed on the point as to whether the Stock Exchange firm which had invaded the preserves of the three regular houses would feel called upon to maintain a free market in the same way as the latter do, and the jobbers in the Consol market, genuinely anxious for the interests of the public as well as of themselves, pointed out that unless some assurance was felt that investors could buy or sell with facility they, the jobbers, felt some disinclination to start dealing in a stock which might possibly prove the forerunner of various other Corporation loans offered in the same way.[13]

In other words, jobbers were afraid that the initial placing of the stock was to be handled outside the exchange so that they would not participate in the issue or profit from it. In meetings mediated by Foster & Braithwaite, jobbers were assured that there was no plan to exclude them from trading in stocks sponsored by Hatry. As their opposition disappeared, so the power of the three incumbent brokers to control the market for local authority loan stocks withered and the monopoly was broken.[14]

Hatry had realised that the existing brokers' monopoly depended upon the continued support of the jobbers and had called their bluff. By showing that he could place stock with investors outside the exchange, he showed that the loan stocks he promoted could succeed even though the incumbent brokers had not been involved. Moreover, if Hatry's approach proved successful, the jobbers would be denied any participation in and thus income from dealing in the issues. By opposing Hatry's issues in order to protect the existing monopolist brokers, the jobbers would therefore lose the income to which they would have become entitled by participation. They did not want to be excluded from what had been a profitable activity and to this end were ready to reach an accommodation with Hatry which brought an end to the existing monopoly.

This opened the way for Hatry, with Collins, to build this opportunity into a profitable business. They were to prove an effective team. Through his network of contacts with local authority treasurers and his reputation for understanding of local authority finance, Collins was able to advise local authorities and to introduce them to C&GS and Hatry. On encountering an authority, Hatry could begin to negotiate the terms of a possible issue. If any difficulty arose, the authority would refer to Collins as an independent consultant who could advise on the merits of Hatry's proposals and smooth out any difficulty by counselling Hatry on how he should improve his terms to win the business.[15] This was a successful partnership. Within a month of the stock issue on behalf of Plymouth, another stock had been issued for Rotherham and yet another for Chesterfield. In the next two months, they launched a further five issues for local authorities. In its first year of operation, C&GS was to act for 11 issues that amounted in total to £4,805,000 which represented 60% by value of all the issues authorised by the Ministry of Health in that period.[16]

This was merely the beginning. In the following three years, Hatry and Collins were to be involved in numerous issues. In 1928 they saw a possibility of extending their reach to empire issues, and in 1929, through introductions arranged by an Australian politician, Sir James Connolly, arranged an issue in London on behalf of City of Melbourne, the first overseas issue that they had arranged and yet another breach in the monopoly enjoyed by Messrs Mullens, Nivisons and Scrimgeours.[17]

The profit earned by C&GS was substantial and was used to finance a rebirth of Hatry's main business of sponsoring new industrial issues. It also created a substantial income for Arthur Collins. Quite apart from the fees earned by the Municipal Loans Bureau from advising the authorities that decided to raise new loans, C&GS paid Collins personally an annual consultancy fee of £5,000, together with an expenses allowance of £2,500.[18] The salary for his successor as treasurer of Birmingham had been only £1,250.

There was, however, a darker side to this commercial success. Hatry and Collins had annoyed three respected firms of stockbrokers who were not to forget that they had lost business as a result. Their monopoly was favoured by the Bank of England, whose governor, Montagu Norman, did not forget Hatry's role in destroying an arrangement which he had found helpful.

In 1929, he was to be instrumental in Hatry's undoing.

Notes

1 This and the succeeding paragraphs are based on an article that appeared in the members' newsletter of the IMTA on Collins becoming president (*Financial Circular*, July 1921).
2 *Financial Circular.*
3 *Sunday Express*, 26 January 1930, page 11. This article was described as Hatry's 'own story' and appears to have been based on evidence which Hatry prepared for the legal team representing him at trial (letter from Cecil Hatry to the chief general manager of Lloyds Bank, 3 February 1930, LBA, file HO/GM/Bea/25). The article suggested that Hatry's first conversation with Collins took place in January 1925.
4 Attard, 2004.
5 Kynaston, 1999, page 94; Crown Agents' papers (TNA file CAOG 9/108).
6 This approach was similar to that employed in the southern states of the USA by Rogers Caldwell (McFerrin, 1969, page 10 et seq).
7 Crisp assured Braithwaite that Hatry was 'entirely to be trusted' (Braithwaite's manuscript note of his meeting with the governor of the Bank of England, September 1929, envelope accompanying the Foster & Braithwaite archive, Guildhall Library; Michie, 1999, page 139; Reader, 1979).
8 Braithwaite, 1923.
9 Envelope accompanying the Foster & Braithwaite archive, Guildhall Library. Braithwaite's initial caution was to prove well justified as the relationship between Hatry and Braithwaite was frequently strained (letter from Braithwaite to Hatry dated 16 June 1926 complaining over Hatry's introduction of another broker, Cohen Laming & Hoare); disagreements over the presentation of C&GS's accounts in April 1928 (meeting notes and draft letter); disagreements over claims that Sir James Connolly would represent Foster & Braithwaite as well as Hatry on a visit to Australia in 1928 (letter from Frederick Braithwaite to Hatry dated 6 March 1929); disagreements over proposal to float further shares in C&GS in May 1929; management of a second Melbourne issue in September 1929 (letter dated 17 September 1929, Foster & Braithwaite archive, Guildhall Library).
10 *The Times*, 11 February 1931, page 5; C&GS Statement of Affairs, LBA, file B1403/a/5.
11 *The Times*, 23 January 1925, page 19.
12 *The Times*, 22 January 1925, page 19.
13 *The Economist*, 7 February 1925, page 251.
14 *The Economist*, 7 February 1925, page 251; letter from Hatry to Braithwaite dated 12 January 1935; letter from Braithwaite to Hatry dated 16 June 1926 (Foster & Braithwaite archive, Guildhall Library).
15 Negotiations with the Borough of Swindon provide an example of this process. Initial approach to Collins by Swindon: letter dated 11 April 1927 (TNA, file DPP 1/91). Discussion in December 1928: letter dated 19 December 1928 (TNA, file DPP 1/91). Introduction of the borough treasurer to Hatry on 7 January 1929: evidence of the borough treasurer, trial transcript, day two, page 2 (TNA, file DPP 1/91). Negotiations with the Borough of Wakefield demonstrate how Collins smoothed difficulties over pricing: file note dated 29 November 1928 (TNA, file DPP 1/91).
16 List of issues: Foster & Braithwaite archive, Guildhall Library; Connolly papers, NLA; Ministry of Health Annual Report 1924–1925, Cmd 2724, page 91.
17 Connolly visited Australia on behalf of Hatry and C&GS to see the Australian Loans Council, city councils and other local authorities with borrowing powers to solicit their business (*The Advertiser*, Adelaide, 25 September 1929, page 15).
18 C&GS Statement of Affairs (LBA, file B1403/a/5).

References

Primary works: unpublished documents

Guildhall Library: Foster & Braithwaite papers.
Lloyds Bank Archive: Lloyds Bank papers.
London Metropolitan Archive: JD Langton & Passmore papers.
National Library of Australia: Connolly papers.
TNA: Crown Agents papers.
TNA: DPP papers.

Primary works: newspapers and periodicals

Financial Circular.
Sunday Express.
The Advertiser, Adelaide, Australia.
The Economist.
The Times.

Primary works: government and parliamentary reports

Ministry of Health Annual Report 1924–1925. Cmd 2724. (HMSO, London).

Primary works: contemporary books and papers

Braithwaite, C. (1923), *Selected Extracts from Fishing Vignettes.* (Trout and Salmon Magazine, London).

Secondary works

Attard, B. (2004), 'Moral Suasion: Empire Borrowers and the New Issue Market during the 1920s', in Michie, R.C. and Williamson, P. (eds), *The British Government and the City of London in the Twentieth Century.* (Cambridge University Press, Cambridge).
Kynaston, D. (1999), *The City of London: Volume III: Illusions of Gold 1914–1945.* (Chatto & Windus, London).
McFerrin, J.B. (1969), *Caldwell and Company: A Southern Financial Empire.* (University of North Carolina Press, Nashville).
Michie, R.C. (1999), *The London Stock Exchange: A History.* (Oxford University Press, Oxford).
Reader, W.J. (1979), *A House in the City: A Study of the City and the Stock Exchange Based on the Records of Foster & Braithwaite, 1825–1975.* (Batsford, London).

7 Amalgamating department stores

In anticipation of the chance to revive his company flotation business, Hatry changed address, moving to Pinners Hall. This was a multi-occupancy building which had been completed just before the 1914–1918 war and stood at the far end of Austin Friars. It also fronted Old Broad Street and Great Winchester Street, boasting three addresses and as many exits.[1] In this, Pinners Hall recalled the office of Augustus Melmotte, the company promoter in Trollope's novel, *The Way We Live Now*, who found his office's several exits most convenient when avoiding aggrieved investors.[2]

At the same time, Hatry chose Austin Friars Trust as the name for the company he was to use in new flotations.

What he then needed was an idea, which on this occasion came from his friend and solicitor, Stanley Passmore. In 1917, Hatry had assisted Passmore in the formation of a new listed company to take over the provincial department stores that previously had been owned by Marshall and Snelgrove, of which he had then become chairman. In 1919, Marshalls Limited had recruited Ronald Gaze from Harrods to become managing director, and he had proposed to Stanley Passmore that they should create a national group of department stores. This was the idea that was put to Hatry in 1925.

Broadly, the retail trade in Britain consisted of three groups of businesses: small independent shops, multiple chains of shops and department stores.[3] Before the 1914–1918 war, there had been many thousands of small independent stores selling all manner of goods, mostly owned by the people who worked in them. There had also been a growing number of chains which owned a large number of branches under central management. Many of these chains were devoted to footwear and food, such as Lilley & Skinner, Freeman Hardy & Willis, Maypole Dairy, Home & Colonial Tea, Lipton Tea and International Tea. Other chains included multiple tailors such as Hepworths and Colliers, pharmacists such as Boots and Timothy White, and W.H. Smith. More than 16 chains owned more than 200 branches and the Co-operative Movement had more than 1400 local societies.

Finally, there were about 250 department stores stocking a wide range of goods, and depending on the store and its location, offering a more stately shopping experience. Most of the department stores were independent of each other and like the thousands of independent shops, relied upon obtaining supplies from wholesalers, whereas the multiple chains purchased goods centrally and directly from suppliers not from wholesalers.

A social upheaval as great as the 1914–1918 war was bound to affect this trade, although the statistics quoted by *The Economist* in its annual reviews suggested that the multiple chains and department stores had survived equally well. Few statistics were available but in 1920, the first year affected by the post-war recession, net profits for the largest multiple chains were about twice as high as they had been in 1913, the last year unaffected by the war. Net profits for a selection of the London department stores in 1920 were just over twice the level achieved in 1913. These comparisons are misleading, however, as they do not take account of the effect of wartime inflation. As 1920 pounds were worth about 2.22 of 1913 pounds, both multiple chain and London department stores had done no more than earn a net profit in 1920 that was similar to the purchasing power of that earned in 1913.[4]

What is worse, these figures obscure other differences between the multiple chains and the department stores because they do not reveal what had happened to sales and profit margins between 1913 and 1920. In many locations, there had been intense competition between the multiple chains and department stores. Sales had more than doubled but profit margins had been eroded by price competition which had exposed the department stores' key disadvantage. Because they relied upon wholesalers, department stores shared the total possible profit margin with the wholesalers and for equivalent goods sold at equivalent prices would earn a lower margin than the multiple chains. As the chains purchased directly from suppliers, they enjoyed the advantage of being substantial purchasers, and there is some evidence that they were able to negotiate higher discounts with suppliers than the wholesalers.[5] Of course, many department stores aimed to charge higher prices to achieve higher margins, which they justified by emphasising the benefits that customers enjoyed by choosing to shop in a department store, such as in-store cafés, lounges for customers and roof gardens. Other stores arranged special events to attract customers. Selfridge's in London arranged to exhibit the plane in which Louis Blériot had flown across the English Channel.[6] In 1879, Lewis's in Manchester had been the first to stage a Christmas grotto for children. In times of economic difficulty, 'benefits' and attractions such as these proved weak incentives for customers. Prices mattered more.

Department stores could also offer wider ranges of goods offering products of a quality that the multiple chains did not offer. There was of course no point in offering a wider range of goods if potential customers were not aware of what was being offered. Traditionally, department stores had attracted customers with extensive displays of merchandise in store windows. However, as attractions, window displays were increasingly supplemented by advertising which was used to develop the reputation of a store and not merely the goods which it offered for sale. The ability of local, independently owned shops to compete was limited by their ability to finance holding stocks of expensive items and the additional costs of advertising.[7] Of course, department stores could consider cutting out the wholesaler by purchasing directly from suppliers, but this would be expensive since stores would require their own buyers with knowledge of possible suppliers and could not guarantee that even if they attempted direct purchasing, the scale of a single store's order would be sufficient to command competitive prices. What is more, these challenges had to be faced in addition to the need to maintain the attractiveness of their premises after a period of under-investment during wartime.[8] When the post-war recession began in 1920, these disadvantages became severe and the department stores' profits fell.

Gaze's scheme proposed that department stores could be rescued from these disadvantages by amalgamation into a large group. The aim would be to form a group of sufficient size to order in quantities that would justify demanding lower prices from suppliers, just as the multiple chains had managed to do through centralising buying. Centralised stock-holding would enable individual stores to offer wider ranges of goods for sale. Better purchasing could be supported by advertising which would be beyond the means of an individual store. In short, Gaze was proposing that the department stores should bring in-house the margin that had hitherto been earned by wholesalers and to strengthen weaker stores by extending to them the policies and practices of the stronger stores.[9]

This idea was not completely new. There had been some amalgamations of department stores. Indeed, Marshalls, Gaze's company, owed its existence to an agreement in 1916 for a joint working arrangement between Marshall & Snelgrove and Debenham & Freebody, which had led after the war to a merger. There were other examples, mainly in London. Harrods in Knightsbridge had bought Dickins & Jones in Oxford Street. Barkers in Kensington had bought Derry & Toms and Pontings. Although these were local agreements and not of the scale that Gaze contemplated, the underlying aim of these mergers was to deal with the commercial weakness of one store by taking advantage of the better buying and management skills of another.

It is difficult to conceive an idea for which Hatry was better suited. He had experience of the negotiations necessary to form combines and of the financial manoeuvres necessary to finance them. That had been obtained in 1920 when he was the midwife at the birth of Jute Industries. He also had experience of the pitfalls that led negotiations to fail which he had obtained in 1921 when his attempts to form Esparto Paper Mills had foundered on the issue of the prices to be paid for acquiring the individual mills.[10] Moreover, Ronald Gaze offered himself as someone who had experience of managing a group of department stores, albeit in a clearly defined geographical region. Hatry himself would not be called upon to manage the new group.

So swift and positive was Hatry's response to this proposition that within a few months the first department stores that Gaze identified as candidates for amalgamation had accepted offers, with the result that on 17 December 1925 the prospectus of Drapery & General Investment Trust was published, inviting subscriptions for £1.2 million of debentures and preference shares. Apart from Marshalls in Yorkshire, the stores being acquired included Curl Brothers in Norwich, Dawson Brothers, H.C. Russell and Staddons all in London, Kennards in Croydon, Plummer Roddis in towns on the south coast and Pettigrew & Stephens based in Sauchiehall Street, Glasgow.[11]

Drapery Trust's prospectus proclaimed five principal aims of which the first was wider and keener buying by using combined purchasing power which it was hoped would enable Drapery Trust's stores to offer better value and the lowest selling prices. Drapery Trust also planned to pool technical knowledge for the benefit of stores and to employ experts whose services could not otherwise have been afforded by the individual businesses. Wider scope for advancement would attract ambitious staff 'of both sexes' to employment in the Trust's stores. Finally, it was intended that the group's deeper financial facilities would enable stores to take advantage of opportunities for expansion.[12]

Gaze's analysis of the department stores' condition had been proved correct. Store owners concerned about pressure on profit margins and the potential cost of refurbishing ageing stores enthusiastically accepted invitations to join the new combine. As further proof of the project's attractions, the offer of Drapery Trust's shares was successful and opened the way for more stores to be added to the group in what became a remarkable series of acquisitions. Within 15 months of the publication of the first prospectus in December 1925, Drapery Trust had acquired stores in Manchester, Birmingham, Gloucester, Ipswich, Southsea, Bristol, Reading, Southampton, Plymouth and Stratford on Avon, not to mention the Bobby & Co mini-group which owned stores from Margate to Exeter and Torquay, and from High Wycombe to Leamington Spa. To add to the complexity, an agreement had been reached with the Scottish Drapery Corporation with stores in Edinburgh, Dundee and Aberdeen. Each group of acquisitions had led to further fundraising by issues of preference shares in the major store companies which Drapery Trust had acquired.[13]

At breakneck speed, by the early months of 1927, Drapery Trust had become a major national group of drapers and department stores. Against the background of the unrest and fears for future security which were created by the General Strike and the coal strike, Hatry had been remarkably successful in selling to scores of highly individual store operators the idea of pooling their expertise. The group had grown to 11,000 employees in 65 stores recording 18 million sales transactions annually and had achieved the critical mass which allowed it to begin to reorganise to take advantage of the promised benefits of amalgamation. It was able to announce early in 1927 that: 'A department has been started for the purpose of developing a system of centralised cooperative buying from which it is anticipated that a considerable income will … be derived for the company and its subsidiaries'.[14] Even with all of these acquisitions, the group still lacked a flagship store in London – a lack that it was able to make good in 1927 with the acquisition of Swan & Edgar, in its new premises on Piccadilly Circus.

The rapid emergence of this new behemoth radically changed the retailing landscape. As was quickly realised, by stealing a march on other leading stores, Drapery Trust had been able to choose the most attractive department stores for its group. Others risked being left behind. The result was that Drapery Trust's example was followed by others. In 1926, James White persuaded Gordon Selfridge that his group should reorganise and expand along the lines chosen by Hatry. This led to the creation of Selfridge Provincial Stores in 1926 which took over a number of stores outside London which had previously been managed by Selfridge and the acquisition of the Bon Marché group of stores in South London. Its prospectus was launched on 8 November 1926, 11 months after Drapery Trust's.[15]

In the following year, another group, United Drapery Stores, was floated by Charterhouse Investment Trust, beginning with the acquisition of five department stores on the fringes of London. Its prospectus was launched on 30 May 1927.[16]

From the beginning, Gaze and Hatry must have understood that if their strategy proved successful it would become an existential threat to the wholesalers who supplied independent department stores, including one of the largest: the wholesaling business owned by Debenhams.

For very many years, Debenhams had consisted of three discrete activities: managing retail department stores, wholesaling and exporting. All of its three department stores were based in London: Debenham & Freebody in Wigmore Street, Marshall & Snelgrove in Oxford Street and Harvey Nicholls in Knightsbridge which had been acquired in 1919 when, like Marshall & Snelgrove, it had become a troublesome debtor for Debenhams' wholesale business.[17] It owned no department stores outside London but acted as a wholesale supplier to large numbers of what had until recently been independent department stores and, in many cases, manufactured the goods that it supplied as wholesaler. Its exporting business was an extension of the wholesaling activities in Britain and had offices in South Africa, Canada, Australia and China.

The advent of three large groups of department stores determined to purchase their supplies directly threatened the eventual destruction of Debenhams as a wholesaler. Moreover, the fact that Drapery Trust was acquiring a major store in London and that Gordon Selfridge's group had been formed around a major London store removed the distinction that Debenhams had previously enjoyed as a signpost for fashion. There was also a risk that the London stores of the new groups would have a pricing advantage over Debenhams if the new groups were able to purchase at better terms as they promised. Meanwhile, if the new groups succeeded, Debenhams' wholesale business would suffer so that Debenham & Freebody, Debenhams' flagship store in London, might not be able to meet the new groups' prices.

Whether or not Gaze and Hatry had foreseen the outcome, the time had come for Debenhams to rethink its approach. In 1926, the group's trading performance proved unsatisfactory, as the General Strike and the coal strike increased uncertainty and depressed sales. Profit was expected to be materially lower than the average of recent years and the growth of Drapery Trust's group suggested that in recovering the group would have to surmount aggressive competition.

For many years, the strategic direction of the group had been in the hands of two men: Ernest Debenham and Frederick Oliver who were closely identified with the policy of developing the wholesale business rather than creating a group of department stores outside London. They had first met at university, after which Debenham had entered the family business while Oliver was called to the bar. Debenham had later invited Oliver to join the company – an invitation that was readily accepted. Oliver's arrival was quickly followed by a decision to establish a bigger presence at the premium end of London's retail trade and the purchase in 1896 of Nicholays, the oldest fur business in London which held royal warrants from Queen Victoria and the royal families in Russia, Austria, Prussia, Belgium and Spain. On this foundation, Debenham and Oliver set about winning the patronage of people with social pretensions and at court by seeking and being awarded royal warrants from King Edward VII and Queen Alexandra, as well as the Prince of Wales (later King George V) and the Princess of Wales (later Queen Mary). Stunning presentation gowns, evening wear, garden party dresses, travelling costumes and tea gowns were produced by special designers from the group's own workrooms and fitted by French trained experts. Bespoke tailors looked after menswear.[18]

As Debenham and Oliver worked to improve the quality of the business, so it became more obvious that its existing premises were no longer fit for purpose; they no longer supported the image that the group was trying to create. This led in 1906 to George Trollope & Sons commencing work on a new building in Wigmore Street. Designed to offer all of the customer comforts that were expected of a modern store, the new shop was fitted with the latest Otis lifts, an elegant restaurant and gentlemen's smoking rooms. For female customers, a ladies' club room was provided, adjoining a suite of dressing and retiring rooms in which customers could read magazines and use telephones and postal services. To enter the new store was to enter a world in which luxury could be smelled, felt and seen. Often, customers' purchases sprang from individual indulgence and impulse. The salesman's job was to encourage the customer to see high fashion goods and expensive furnishings as necessities rather than luxuries. Price mattered to the shopkeeper as it determined the profit earned, but the salesman's function was to ensure that in the customer's eyes price was of secondary performance.[19]

The new store in Wigmore Street was the manifestation of the ruthless determination of Ernest Debenham and Frederick Oliver to place the customer in the right frame of mind to buy the expensive and luxurious goods that they aimed to sell. Customers entered through a spacious hall lined with cool grey-green and white marbles. On either side were large showrooms and, facing the entrance, manned by liveried footmen, was the marble staircase to upper floors. Oak woodwork and bronze metal work were everywhere. Air purification and vacuum steam systems provided a complete change of washed and warmed air three times an hour. As a demonstration of the class of business the store aimed to attract, the façade of the new building in Wigmore Street was capped with the royal coat of arms. The message was unmissable.[20]

These initiatives had been remarkably successful in their day. They served to justify Debenhams' reputation as a leading store where customers could find the latest fashions – a reputation that was important in supporting its credibility as a wholesaler which would enable its clients, the department stores, to offer a similar experience to their customers. However successful this strategy had been in 1906, it was challenged after the war by a growing cost-consciousness among the public which was to lead even Debenhams to organise discounted sales of unsold stock and later by the growth of the multiple chains and the advent of Drapery Trust. New ideas were needed.

This was the moment when Frederick Oliver announced his intention to retire. The first step was taken in 1926, when with the advice of Whitehall Trust, Debenham Securities was formed to buy out Frederick Oliver's interests. Ernest Debenham was left to become the chairman of the board of directors which was augmented by the inclusion of two men who were to become the future leaders of the group: Frederick Richmond and Maurice Wright, a Chartered Accountant.[21]

In 1927, as pressure grew from the development of Drapery Trust, Selfridge Provincial Stores and United Drapery Trust, Richmond and Wright saw that it was too late for Debenhams to build its own network of provincial department stores and that, to protect its wholesaling business, Debenhams should acquire one of the three new groups, so that its wholesaling organisation could become the foundation for a centralised purchasing department. Consequently, Richmond and Wright opened negotiations with Hatry for the purchase of Drapery Trust. On 18 November 1927, barely two years after publication of Drapery Trust's first prospectus, an agreement was signed between them which would lead to a combination of the two businesses.[22]

By this agreement, Debenhams Limited undertook to buy not less than 75% of Drapery Trust's shares at 30 shillings per share, paying a commission to Hatry himself of 1 shilling and fourpence per share. The total cost of this purchase was estimated at £2,350,000, which was in part to be financed by Hatry's company, Austin Friars Trust, buying a large block of Debenhams' shares, including the shareholdings of the existing directors, for £1,600,000 in cash. At this point, Hatry would control a large holding of Debenhams' shares. The intention was that this would be the prelude to increasing and reorganising the capital of Debenham Securities by means of Austin Friars Trust buying further blocks of shares and creating large numbers of new shares which would be offered for sale to the public.

The fusion agreement was initially announced in a brief press statement which provided almost no detail of the proposed transactions – a lapse that was not corrected until 3 December 1927, when the proposed transaction was explained in greater detail. As a consequence of this unfortunate delay, speculation grew in the newspapers about the reasons for the complexity of the transaction and the identity of the interests that would ultimately control the enlarged group.[23]

Among the many possible reasons for the transaction's complexity was the desire to secure the retirement of Ernest Debenham. Although the agreement with Hatry was signed on 18 November 1927, it took four days to persuade Ernest Debenham that the existing directors should sell their shareholdings to Hatry as a first step to implementing the agreement. Ernest Debenham understood immediately that he was not to be offered a seat on the board of the company which would be formed to take the group forward and that by agreeing to sell, he was accepting the end of his involvement with Debenhams. In discussing this proposal, he sought to impose conditions to ensure that control remained with former partners and that the group's policy with regard to staff and shareholders would remain unchanged, but on 22 November 1927, as speculation was growing, Ernest Debenham finally agreed to sell his 1,251,232 shares for £1,876,848. In effect, by this agreement, strategic direction of the group had finally passed to Frederick Richmond and George Maurice Wright.

Scars were left by what Ernest Debenham saw as an alliance between Richmond, Wright and Hatry to lever him out of his seat on Debenhams' board. When *The Times* reported that he had desired to sell his shares and that 'the purchase of his shares was the first transaction', he retorted immediately in a letter to the editor:

> A month ago I had no intention of retiring from the management of Debenham Securities. Indeed, I had every reason to hope that the connection of myself and my family with that business would be indefinitely prolonged. When the offer was made to purchase all or any of the Ordinary shares in Debenhams Securities, circumstances of no interest to the general investing public compelled me to accept the offer.[24]

Other personal considerations would have made this outcome difficult for Ernest Debenham to accept. His son, Piers, had also been a director of Debenhams and as he had been led to expect that he would succeed as chairman was shocked to find himself leaving the board with his father.[25]

In spite of these problems, Debenhams shareholders met on 18 January 1928 and approved the scheme which then went ahead. In February 1928, the last stage of Hatry's financial reorganisation was announced in the form of an offer for sale of 2 million cumulative preference shares, the offeror's role being taken by M. Samuel & Company Limited, the merchant bank. The management team of Richmond and Wright augmented by Ronald Gaze proved skilful in integrating the enlarged group, overcoming two particular challenges that might have led to disaster: the risk of losing financial control and the risk of obstruction by previously autonomous store managements.[26]

Maurice Wright, a Chartered Accountant, dealt with the first risk by reforming the group's accounting systems. He was notoriously parsimonious when it came to approving spending proposals but was able to ensure that trading debts and stock levels were constrained within the group's ability to finance them. Ownership by the new group did not lead to any relaxation of financial discipline.

Wright's work on financial controls was matched by work to coordinate the group's trading policies and practices: a task that fell to Fred Pope, a member of the Drapery Trust team who had been trained at Bon Marché in Gloucester. At the outset, the new group was no more than a federation of highly individual stores, each run by a managing director who may well have been drawn from the store's founding family and who could be expected to cherish inherited autonomy and resent outside interference. Ownership by the Debenhams group did not necessarily guarantee deference to central management. Pope won over the senior managers of the provincial stores one by one. Often the greatest problem was presented by the buyers in the largest stores who resisted Pope's policy that stock which proved slow to sell should be cleared as quickly as possible at bargain prices and that stores should build reserves to cover the risk of loss. Many buyers were unwilling to admit to mistakes in their ordering, preferring to hang on to goods at their original prices in the forlorn hope of eventual sales. With Wright's support, Pope was to overcome this resistance.

Thus the new management team overcame its challenges and ensured that the new group survived as the foundation for the store group that still exists.

On any assessment, this was Hatry's most successful series of promotions and demonstrates the circumstances in which his strengths could be used to full effect.

The initial business idea did not come from Hatry but came from Ronald Gaze of Marshalls. The initial judgement that the idea was commercially attractive was not Hatry's but Stanley Passmore's. Identification of the businesses that might become useful members of Drapery Trust was not Hatry's responsibility but Gaze's. Above all, it was critical to the eventual success of the project that Drapery Trust had in Ronald Gaze a person with the experience and skills necessary to make a success of the new organisation and later that Debenhams had a management team that was able to ensure that the enlarged group survived. Neither Drapery Trust nor the enlarged Debenhams group relied upon Hatry's contribution to management after the mergers had been accomplished.

Hatry's role was to design the corporate structure of the new group, arrange its financing and negotiate terms with the stores to be acquired. He was an enabler for a project that someone else had devised. In the formation of Drapery Trust, his role was to enable Gaze and Passmore to create the group they had conceived. In the formation of Debenham Securities, his role was to enable Richmond and Wright to realise the greater group they had envisioned but also to bring about the change in the strategic direction of

Debenhams that had become overdue. Hatry was not expected to play any part in the management of the group that he helped to create.

His effectiveness in these roles depended on three key capabilities: the ability to create and sustain a network of associations that enabled him to contact all of the parties whose support was necessary for the scheme to proceed; the ability and personal charm to persuade all parties to cooperate with the proposed scheme; and the ability to navigate around the relevant rules and laws. In the case of the Debenhams scheme, this last factor was especially important as the transaction was the first instance of a merger affecting a company whose shares were quoted and traded in both London and New York.

Hatry's success also owed much to Maurice Wright, who acted as a restraining influence. He ensured that the outcome Hatry proposed was a capital structure which could endure because it did not impose an unreasonable burden on the group's trading profit. If there was a risk that Hatry might be carried away by his own exuberance, Wright saved the transaction from it.

Nonetheless, Hatry looked back on the Debenhams transaction as a remarkable success for it had created what was to become one of the country's largest companies.[27] What was more, in the transaction, Hatry had collaborated with M. Samuel & Company, the merchant bank that formally offered Debenhams' preference shares for sale. This implied that to M. Samuel, and its chairman, Lord Bearsted, Hatry was regarded as an acceptable collaborator. As if to confirm this mark of commercial acceptance within the City, six months earlier Hatry had become a freeman of the City of London, as had Hatry's father Julius more than 25 years earlier.[28]

Hatry appeared to have achieved his ambition of restoring the commercial and social acceptance that had been his father's ambition in 1870 as an immigrant from Zweibrücken.

Notes

1 Announcement of proposed building: *The Times*, 3 March 1910, page 7. Opening of the building: *The Times*, 6 December 1913.
2 Trollope, 1875.
3 Jefferys, 1954, page 49 et seq.
4 *The Economist*, 11 June 1921, pages 1269–1270; 20 August 1921, pages 299–300.
5 Bellamy, 1946, page 329.
6 Scott and Walker, 2010, page 1108.
7 In 1925, Harrods' ratio of advertising to sales was 2.89%, believed to be the lowest of the large London stores (Scott and Walker, 2010, page 1112).
8 Porter, 1971, page 70.
9 Corina, 1978, page 98.
10 After the flotation of Jute Industries, Hatry was invited to manage negotiations to create a similar combine of paper mills close to Dundee. Although the negotiations continued for some time, it proved impossible to meet the existing owners' expectations of the value of their shares (Tullis Russell papers, St Andrews Special Collections).
11 Corina, 1978, page 94.
12 *The Times*, 17 December 1925, page 22.

13 Corina, 1978, page 97.
14 Corina, 1978, page 97.
15 *The Times*, 8 November 1926, page 22.
16 *The Times*, 30 May 1927, page 21.
17 Corina, 1978, page 84.
18 Corina, 1978, pages 60–62.
19 Corina, 1978, pages 64–66.
20 Corina, 1978, pages 67–74.
21 Corina, 1978, pages 94–95.
22 *The Times*, 19 December 1927; Corina, 1978, pages 190–191.
23 *The Times*, 3 December 1927.
24 *The Times*, 8 December 1927, page 25.
25 *The Times*, 15 September 1964, page 15.
26 *The Times*, 19 January 1928, page 19; 8 February 1928, page 20.
27 It was estimated to have been the 92nd largest employer in the UK in 1935 (1998, page 103).
28 Hatry became a member of the glass sellers livery company and a freeman on 17 June 1927.

References

Primary works: unpublished documents

St Andrews Special Collections: Tullis Russell papers.

Primary works: newspapers and periodicals

The Economist.
The Times.

Primary works: contemporary books and papers

Trollope, A. (1875), *The Way We Live Now.* (Chapman, London).

Secondary works

Bellamy, R. (1946), 'Size and Success in Retail Distribution', *Oxford Bulletin of Economics and Statistics*, volume 8, pages 324–339.

Corina, M. (1978), *Fine Silks & Oak Counters: Debenhams 1778–1978.* (Hutchinson Benham, London).

Jefferys, J.B. (1954), *Retail Trading in Britain 1850–1950: A Study of Trends in Retailing with Special Reference to the Development of Co-Operative, Multiple Shop and Department Stores Methods of Trading.* (Cambridge University Press, Cambridge).

Jeremy, D.J. (1998), *A Business History of Britain 1900–1990s.* (Oxford University Press, New York).

Porter, J.H. (1971), 'The Development of a Provincial Department Store 1870–1939', *Business History*, volume 13, pages 64–71.

Scott, P. and Walker, J. (2010), 'Advertising, Promotion and the Competitive Advantage of Interwar British Department Stores', *Economic History Review*, volume 64(4), pages 1105–1128.

8 Hatry turns 40

As Hatry was emerging from the excitement of the Debenhams transaction, the stock exchange was experiencing another boom which was characterised by shareholders' fascination with technology. Many companies were floated, offering a stake in new industries: gramophones, radios, performance cars and synthetic silks. Often these were 'shilling shares', designed with low prices to appeal to investors who wanted to take part in the boom but had little to invest. It would have been unrealistic to expect that Hatry would not participate in the frenzy that overwhelmed the market.

In February 1928, an Oxford Street store, Selfridge's, celebrated a 'double first': the first television department in the world and the first demonstration of the Photomaton in Europe.[1]

Television was the wonder of the year. John Logie Baird, the inventor, announced in January that the system had not only transmitted images between cities in England but it had also transmitted images between New York and London. It was a coup for Selfridge's that Baird was himself on hand in the store to demonstrate his system's achievements.

Meanwhile, a battery of Photomatons had been installed at the head of the escalators in the building's bargain basement so that they could be used by the public. This new invention had caused great public interest in New York when exhibited for the first time and had only been granted a patent in New York in January 1928. It provided a cheap means by which people could obtain a number of small photographs of themselves. As Selfridge's advertisements claimed:

> In a small space, roughly the size of a telephone booth, seated on a stool the height of which is regulated to suit the individual, the sitter looks into a frame of powerful light and a competent demonstrator gently asks him or her to turn to the right, to the left, to look up and down, to smile into the camera, and in the time it takes to read these words the performance is over. The sitter leaves the stool and a few minutes after, from a slot at the far end of the Photomaton, a strip of eight photographs is delivered, developed, printed and fixed automatically – all for the price of one shilling.

> Clear, extraordinarily natural and showing eight different expressions, these photographs are immeasurably above anything of their kind ever yet produced.[2]

Arranging to display these machines so soon after their launch in New York was yet another marketing coup for Gordon Selfridge.

The process behind these machines had been developed over many years by Anatol Josepho (originally Josephewitz), a Russian immigrant who had entered the United States from Shanghai in 1923. He had been born in Omsk, a town on the route followed by the trans-Siberian express, to a Jewish family which with many others had been somewhat summarily ordered to re-establish themselves in Omsk. As a boy he had become fascinated with the Brownie box cameras which were becoming widely available and told his father that he wanted to learn all he could about photography. This led his father to arrange for him to his enrol with a local technical institute. At the age of 15, in 1909, he decided that he wanted to travel and persuaded his father to give him the money he needed to travel to Berlin – a journey that was then being made by many other Russians who were aiming for Bremen to catch ships to begin new lives in North and South America. Once in Berlin, Josepho had found a photographic studio and persuaded the owner to employ him to learn the trade. As he learned how to use a portrait camera and glass negatives, as well as the arts of developing and printing, he evolved the idea of creating a faster, more efficient and less costly way of creating images that would make photographs available to the average working man. Josepho was captivated by the hopes and ambitions of the hundreds of America-bound customers who came to the studio for portrait photographs and in 1912 resolved to join them, boarding a ship bound for New York. On this occasion, his good fortune deserted him and he could not find a job so returned to Europe, setting up his own studio in Budapest.

Using the technical background from his Russian school, Josepho began to experiment, developing a primitive prototype for a self-contained machine that could be operated by a coin and would produce cheap photographs. During the 1914–1918 war, with other Russians in Austria-Hungary, Josepho was put under strict military surveillance, which constrained his freedom to develop his business. There were, in any event, few customers. Finding time on his hands, he concentrated on developing a new photographic paper that would produce a well-toned positive image without the requirement for a negative, and redesigned his machine to use the paper.

After the end of the war, Josepho returned home to his father in Omsk, but found that, following its invasion by the Red Army in 1919, the town had been pillaged and no longer provided a base for his business. He carried on travelling, taking the train eastward to Mongolia and then to Shanghai, which was known at the time as the 'Paris of the East' where he again set up a studio. There he used 5x7 inch negatives, generating penny photographs in horizontal strips. Although his studio was a financial success, he was still absorbed by his vision of an automatic photographic machine. During his time in Shanghai, he completed detailed design drawings for a machine and resolved to travel again to America to seek backers. He landed at Seattle, stayed for a short while in Hollywood to get motion picture experience and then travelled to New York on the east coast. He managed to raise $11,000 which was a substantial sum for the time, as a reasonably sized house could be bought for as little as $2,000.

With this money, Josepho was able to build prototypes in his Harlem loft and used three machines to open a Photomaton studio in September 1925 on Broadway between 51st and 52nd streets, not far from the current location of the Museum of Modern Art. The studio was an immediate success. Crowds, as many as 7,500 people a day, would line up to have their photographs taken, paying 25 cents for a strip of eight. The store was open until 4 a.m. every day, with most of the business taking place at night. His studio was described as 'Broadway's greatest quarter-snatcher'. The booth appealed not only to the 'average working man' who wanted cheap photographs but also to the more prosperous: the governor of New York and a senator were happy to have their photographs taken in the studio. In April 1927, *Time* magazine reported that in just over six months 280,000 customers had posed for automatic self-portraits in Photomaton booths. As experience of the process grew, so people realised that its small images could be used in many ways that its inventor had not foreseen. They became popular as support for job applications, they could be used to prove identification on driving licences, travel cards and passports, and the imaginative used them to personalise birthday or greeting cards. As each photograph cost no more than 3 to 4 cents, the Photomaton quickly established a reputation for excellent value as it became possible to use photographs for purposes which previously had been impracticable because of cost.[3]

For investors, Photomaton was an exciting prospect. It offered a solution for a problem that many had seen as a business opportunity, the production of inexpensive images, which had attracted and defeated many other inventors. By the beginning of 1927 the new technology had proved popular with the public and, like other successful technologies, as people gained experience they were soon thinking of applications far beyond Josepho's initial dreams. Although patents had not yet been granted, applications had been submitted, and it looked as if patent protection could be achieved – a key consideration for investors. Josepho himself did not have the means to develop or exploit the machine so entered into an agreement by which others would carry on the work; he sold the rights to exploit the machine in America and Russia to a syndicate led by Henry Morgenthau.[4]

Morgenthau was a well-known businessman who had made his fortune before the 1914–1918 war by dealing in New York real estate. In the presidential election of 1912, he had been a significant supporter of Woodrow Wilson and after Wilson's success had hoped to be appointed to his Cabinet but was rewarded by the offer of appointment as ambassador to the Ottoman

Empire. His first reaction was to turn down the offer but was persuaded to accept by his Zionist friends who pointed out that the Ottoman Empire's territories included the Holy Land and that as ambassador he would be able to influence the future of the Holy Land which the Zionist movement intended should be the location of a new independent state for Jews.

As matters turned out, his lasting reputation was built on an entirely different issue. Abandoning the discretion usually expected of ambassadors, he publicly expressed outrage at the Ottoman Empire's genocide of the Armenian people, ensuring that evidence of the genocide was broadcast widely and campaigning vigorously for an end to the atrocities but also for support and succour to be given to the surviving refugees.

After relinquishing his diplomatic role, Morgenthau built on his experiences in Asia Minor by becoming one of the founders of the American Red Cross, while also gaining a reputation as a shrewd businessman. He returned to the family's real estate activities and acquired an interest in the Underwood Typewriter Company which, under his direction, became the world's largest manufacturer of typewriters. Among the community of émigrés from Asia Minor and Russia, he was lionised and was a natural source of financial support for exploitation of Josepho's invention, the Photomaton. In March 1927, a syndicate led by Morgenthau paid $1,000,000 for the American rights to the machine to be followed later by royalties paid for use of the paper that Josepho had invented. On 28 March 1927, the *New York Times* reported the story, quoting Morgenthau's claim:

> I believe that through Mr Josepho's invention, we can make personal photographs easily and cheaply available to the masses in this country. We propose to do in the photographic field what Woolworth's has accomplished in novelties and merchandise, Ford in automobiles … [5]

The new owners were as good as their word. Plans were announced for 70 studios to be set up nationally, the first being opened quickly in Atlantic City and Coney Island, the location for amusement parks serving the New York area which were then at their most popular. A factory to manufacture the machines was opened in Long Island City, Queen's. As experience grew, the syndicate elaborated the product. The reverse side of the photographs was sold as advertising space. The stools on which customers sat while being photographed were fitted with weighing machines so that the customer's weight could be printed on the photograph. Photographs could be printed on mirrors. The studios sold envelopes and mounts so that images could be sent anywhere by mail directly from the studio.[6]

Meanwhile, Josepho turned to selling the rights to the machine outside America. It might have been thought that Gordon Selfridge was an obvious candidate to buy the rights. After all, he was the first to exhibit the machine in London so must have understood the machine's commercial potential. However, he no longer had the funds to contemplate such a purchase. On

All Fool's Day 1927, he had bought a controlling interest in Whiteley's, a large department store in Bayswater which had been rebuilt just before the 1914–1918 war but had since then been declining in what had proved to be a declining area. The cost of the acquisition, rumoured to have been £10,000,000, was probably exorbitant but was made much worse by Gordon Selfridge's response to an elderly lady shareholder who asked at a meeting whether Whiteley's dividends would remain at 25%. Selfridge answered that they would and that he would personally guarantee their payment for 15 years. He was to regret his undertaking which left him penniless.[7]

The way was open for someone else to acquire the rights to the Photomaton – a chance that Hatry seized. On 24 March 1928, Hatry signed an agreement by which he acquired the patent rights in the Photomaton machine for the world (excluding the USA, its dependencies and Russia) and one-third of the common stock of Morgenthau's company, Photomaton Inc. The purchase price was $1,500,000, which was partly paid in cash but supplemented by a promise of ordinary shares in a new company, Photomaton Parent Corporation (PPC), whose shares were to be listed on the London Stock Exchange and were offered for sale a few days later. Importantly, three of the seven directors of the new company were also directors of Debenhams, signifying that it was intended that a large number of the machines should be placed in Debenhams' stores.[8]

Although the agreement was to prove lucrative for Hatry, it involved a large initial capital outlay which he wanted to recoup as quickly as possible. He did this immediately by selling the assets bought from Morgenthau's company to the new British company, PPC. Payment was taken in the form of 5,600,000 five shilling shares in the new public company which he would be free to sell to the market when the shares were offered for sale. Within a month of the offer, the market price of the shares had risen to 17 shillings, compared with the price of 10 shillings which had been assumed at the time of Hatry's deal. If all of these shares were sold at the top of the market, Hatry had made a further considerable profit. In addition, Hatry's agreement entitled him to purchase more shares at a price of 10 shillings. If these shares were also sold at the top of the market, a further profit of £140,000 would have arisen. As these would all have been capital profits, no income tax would have been payable.

Although as a result of these transactions PPC found itself owning the international rights (outside the USA and Russia) to the Photomaton machine, they did not provide it with any of the money that it would need to exploit those rights. However, trading in the company's shares had shown that there was a great deal of interest in the company and that further sales of shares would be well received. Interest was maintained by a sustained advertising campaign which stressed the technological advantages of the Photomaton, the commercial opportunities that it presented and the disadvantages of the many other machines that competitors were launching, such as the Granville-Bradshaw Patent Semi-Automatic Photographic Studio launched by Coin

Operated Machines Limited of Finsbury Circus, London.[9] Eventually, just over two months after trading began in PPC's shares, another share offer was announced. A new company, Photomaton Far East Limited, had been formed to acquire from PPC the right to sell or operate Photomaton machines in the Far East, including territories such as China, India, Japan, Egypt, Ceylon and Malaya, which the offer sale claimed together had a population of 871 million. The offer suggested that if the company sold a minimum of 1,000 machines, it would earn a capital profit of £450,000, and thereafter would receive an annual income of £150,000 in royalties on the sale of sensitised paper strips for use in those 1,000 machines. It was also suggested that if the company operated 250 machines itself, the additional annual profit would be £250,000. The offer was intended to raise £390,000 from the sale of shares and debentures. The offer was heavily oversubscribed which suggested that the market's appetite for Photomaton had not been exhausted.[10]

The opportunity to repeat the sale was not missed. Two weeks later, another offer was announced following very closely the example of Photomaton Far East Limited. On this occasion, the new company was called Photomaton (Lancashire and Midland) Limited and had been formed to acquire from PPC the rights to exploit the machine in 17 counties in England and Wales, together with the Isle of Man and Northern Ireland. The offer suggested that the territory in which the company would operate was equal to the best in the United Kingdom:

> embracing as it does such industrial centres as Manchester, Liverpool, Belfast, Birmingham and the Potteries, and such holiday resorts as Blackpool, Southport, Douglas (IOM), Llandudno, the North Wales Coast and the Lake District.
>
> Official approximate estimates and records of the number of annual visitors to some of the most important seaside resorts in the Company's territory have been obtained and justify the following figures. Viz: Blackpool – 5,000,000, Southport – 1,500,000 and Douglas (IOM) – 500,000; whilst it is known that the number of annual visitors to other important pleasure resorts in the Company's territory is large.[11]

The issue aimed to raise £250,000. It was heavily oversubscribed.

A week later, a further offer was announced. On this occasion, the new company was to be called Société Continentale Photomaton, and it was to offer debentures and shares to raise £662,500.[12]

So it went on. A further English regional company, Photomaton (Eastern and Central) was also announced at the end of June 1928, and deals were negotiated to sell rights to companies in Italy, South Africa, Australia, New Zealand, Canada, Central America, Scandinavia, Spain and Portugal.

Meanwhile, efforts were being made to place machines and to establish a sustainable business which would realise the profits which had been forecast and these efforts were to some extent successful – so much so in France, for example, that the word 'Photomaton' is still used by many to refer to a photo booth. In England, by the end of 1928, PPC had reached agreement with Boots Pure Drug Company to install Photomaton machines in the chain's branches and was experimenting with mobile booths that could be used where 'crowds congregate' and in towns too small to justify permanent installations.[13] But, as a member of PPC's team later suggested in a court case, the impression grew that PPC was in business to sell shares rather than machines.[14]

PPC suffered from Hatry's weaknesses. In the cases of Drapery Trust and Debenhams which benefited from his strengths, the companies had been firmly under the control of people other than Hatry and it was they who made the key commercial decisions about how much should be raised from share offers, which ventures should be pursued and which controls should be imposed. In the case of PPC, most of the responsibility devolved upon Hatry. In practice, he was not interested in detailed day-to-day management which was left in the hands of others. This was dangerous partly because he made mistakes by judging people quickly on the basis of weak evidence but also because he was not a good supervisor.[15] Hatry was easily bored by the need for careful monitoring of results. He was interested in financial transactions involving his company's shares, although his judgements on the share issues that should be attempted were settled more by reference to what the market would bear and by the prospect of personal profit than by what his companies needed and could afford. The result was that PPC was over-capitalised, having issued more capital than it could afford, and poorly organised with a dysfunctional management structure. The division into regional companies may have been useful in terms of company promotions but was unhelpful in exploiting the patent rights as each of the regional companies would have to assent to agreements with department store groups or multiple chains. Eventually the division into regional companies had to be unravelled. In August 1929, British Photomaton Trading Company was formed to acquire Photomaton (Lancashire and Midland) Limited and Photomaton (Eastern and Central) Limited which had only been formed one year earlier. Its purpose was not to raise new money but to ensure that the rights under the Photomaton patents in the United Kingdom, Northern Ireland and the Irish Free State could be managed by a single company with a single management team.[16]

Implicitly, the reorganisation proposed in August 1929 acknowledged that the flotations in 1928 had endangered the business's ability to extract full value from the Photomaton patents. Hatry's eagerness for immediate cash receipts had been gratified at the expense of longer-term benefit for both himself and investors. Yet again his judgement either of business prospects or of the people who might advise him had proved disappointing.

Quite apart from the instant gratification of profit, the Photomaton transactions brought Hatry two other benefits: a new relationship and a further business opportunity.

The new relationship sprang from Hatry's association with Henry Morgenthau and the real estate dealing families of New York – he met Grigori Benenson.

Benenson's family traced its history to a series of rabbis based in Minsk, like Omsk, a town on the trans-Siberian railway. His father, Ossip, who had been fluent in both Russian and Yiddish, had become a successful timber merchant. As Grigori would later tell his grandchildren, he and his father would sledge across snow and ice into forests to negotiate deals with the bailiffs of the great landowners. They would buy hundreds of trees, paint their own sign on them and return after a week or two with their peasant labourers wielding axes and saws. Once felled, the trees were dragged to the riverside where they would lie untouched until the rivers became passable again with the spring thaw and the tree trunks could be floated by way of the Dnieper River to the Black Sea. All of the business was conducted by word of mouth as the gentile landowners trusted that Benenson, a Jew, would pay up at the end of the season. A transaction was never dishonoured. Grigori Benenson inherited his father's way of business, and in the late 1920s still kept all particulars of his deals in the inside pockets of his capacious overcoat.

In the late 1880s, at about the time of Hatry's birth, Grigori Benenson gambled and moved his family to Baku, a port on the Caspian Sea largely populated by Armenians in Azerbaijan. In the largely anti-Semitic Russian Empire, Jews were expected to live and not travel outside a territory known as the Pale of Settlement. For them, the Caucasus appeared to be an oasis, for there the Jews were merely a minority among other minorities. Throughout the nineteenth century, many Jews from the Pale left for the Caucasus, but the move became more attractive at the end of the 1870s. By the Treaty of Berlin in 1878, which followed the end of a war between Russia and the Ottoman Empire, three Armenian provinces, Kars, Ardahan and Batoum, were ceded to Russia. This territory was valuable because of its potential for producing oil and offered many young people such as Benenson the chance to make a fortune from prospecting for oil. By the time that Benenson and his family moved to Baku, Russia and its Persian dependencies were producing half of the world's oil supply and Batoum on the Black Sea had become the world's busiest oil port. Within a few years, Benenson had established himself as a leading oil prospector.

In 1904–1905, disorder was spreading throughout Russia following anti-Jewish riots in Kishinev, now known as Chisinau, the capital of Moldova. In Baku, disorder started with the workers striking over conditions in the oilfields. As the military garrison in Baku had been depleted by the transfer of troops to fight in the Russo-Japanese War, the disorder was not immediately suppressed and led to sabotage and firing of oil wells. As the risk of anti-Jewish riots grew, Benenson joined others in fleeing. Some went to Palestine as the pogroms had encouraged the growth of Zionism. Benenson went to St Petersburg where, at a distance, he tried to manage his family's continuing interests in timber and oil prospecting.

There Benenson became involved in the exploitation of new goldmines on the banks of the Lena in Siberia. By coincidence, in St Petersberg he met an Englishman, Frederick Cripps, who was the son of a Liberal politician who became Lord Parmoor and brother of Stafford Cripps, who was to become chancellor of the exchequer. Frederick Cripps was sent to Russia to open an office for Boulton & Company, a merchant bank based in London. For many years, Russia had been unknown territory for the British, with a reputation for being despotic and backward-looking. It was also thought unfriendly and unpredictable after the Dogger Bank incident in 1904, a bizarre sideshow of the Russo-Japanese War, when a Russian fleet had fired on British trawlers, unaccountably mistaking them for a Japanese fleet. In part to serve as a corrective to the impression of antagonism, the tsar had sailed to Cowes in 1909 for a state visit which had revived interest in investing in Russia. Cripps' mission to St Petersburg on behalf of his partners was intended to capitalise on this opportunity.[17]

Cripps' office was close to the Benenson family house, and when by chance he met Cripps, Grigori found a kindred spirit. Cripps was willing to take risks, as might be expected of a cavalry officer who was later to gain distinction at the Battle of El Mughair in November 1917 as the last British cavalry officer to lead a cavalry charge in battle.[18] Together they became involved in the exploitation of the new goldmines on the banks of the Lena, and then, through Imperial & Foreign Corporation, the company they founded together, in the arms trade between England and Russia which grew as the tsar re-equipped the Russian army in the years of growing tension before the 1914–1918 war.

Although Benenson's business was profitable, life again became threatening for him and his family. Unrest in the Lena goldfields led to riots and to a massacre when the police fired on rioters and their families. Liberal members of the Duma, Russia's parliament, saw an opportunity to destabilise the tsar's government and commissioned a lawyer, Alexander Kerensky, to undertake an investigation. Kerensky's report described the extreme conditions in which the goldfield workers had lived and outraged many who called for action against those, like Benenson, who had profited from the goldfields. For Benenson, life had again become too hot so in 1913, with Cripps' encouragement, he took his family to London.

Just before leaving, Benenson was attacked by a former mistress who threw vitriol in his face and damaged his eyesight for which he required medical attention, which he was advised could best be found in Hamburg.[19] While there, Benenson made the acquaintance of Max Warburg, whose bank maintained offices in both London and New York and was able to arrange continued access for Benenson to his assets in St Petersburg. When his sight had been restored, Benenson returned to St Petersburg with his wife and was still in St Petersburg in 1917 when the tsar was deposed by the communists.

In the period of unrest that followed, his house was requisitioned and, with his family, Benenson was placed under house arrest. Good fortune did not desert him, however, as he and his wife were lucky enough to be given a chance to travel to Sweden. While under house arrest, they were visited by a commissar, Comrade Goukovsky of the Department of Foreign Trade, who had met Benenson before the war at Monte Carlo. On that occasion, Goukovsky had lost all of his money at the gambling tables and in despair had approached Benenson for help. Refusing to give money which he feared might just be gambled away, Grigori had taken Goukovsky to the Hôtel de Paris opposite the casino, where he had instructed the porter to buy a ticket and see Goukovsky on to a train. In 1917, Goukovsky told Benenson that he was now in a position to repay the debt and offered to take the family with him when he left the next day to attend trade talks with the Swedish government. The family was thus enabled to return to London with such assets in the form of jewellery and gold that they could carry.

When the war ended, it was evident that Benenson would have to rebuild his fortune as the pre-war trade with Russia had more or less been brought to an end. Partly influenced by his association with Max Warburg, Benenson decided to move to New York, although he retained interests in London through his company Imperial and Foreign Corporation which continued in business, notably involved in importing radium from Czechoslovakia. Seeking friends in New York, Benenson's experience in Armenia and his Zionism commended him to Henry Morgenthau, who introduced him to real estate trading. Within five weeks of arrival, Benenson had bought 165 Broadway for $10 million, half of which he was able to pay in cash. The building which had previously been known as City Investing Building became the centre for his business and was forthwith to be known as Benenson House. It was to be demolished in 1968 to make way for One Liberty Plaza, on the fringe of Ground Zero.

This was the man whom Hatry met during his visit to New York. They found they were soulmates. In business, where others might have prevaricated, they were prepared to take risks to make profits. But more than this, they shared family experiences. Just as Clarence Hatry's father, Julius, had moved to London to save the family business after Lorraine had been ceded to Germany at the end of a war, Benenson had moved to Armenia after Armenian territory was ceded to Russia at the end of a war. Both families knew what it was like to seek financial success as outsiders in an alien environment. Both men knew from personal experience what it took for an outsider to recover from adversity and to succeed.

In 1929, Benenson was to be one of Hatry's most substantial supporters when he most needed them.

Hatry's second benefit from the Photomaton episode was the realisation that the coin-operated machine trade offered him business opportunities.

One of the curious aspects of Photomaton's development in England was that in the early stages, few were placed in railway stations; most were placed in department stores. While this was convenient because of Hatry's close association with Debenhams, it ignored the experience of Josepho's original studio in Broadway in New York, which found that many customers were happy to visit the studio at night when department stores would be closed. Railway stations might have been expected to be popular locations for Photomaton machines – they were frequented by large numbers of people and were open for long hours. In practice placing large numbers of machines in railway stations was difficult. Although the railways had been grouped in a small number of regional companies during the 1920s, they had originally been built and run by a large number of small local companies. As a result, the rights to place machines on stations were controlled by a series of legacy contracts agreed with the original management companies and it was not always easy to reach central agreements to place machines on all stations in the railway network.

This was another ideal business opportunity for Hatry, who had good reason to understand the ways of bringing together companies in a fragmented industry. On 13 November 1928, a company was incorporated to serve as a holding company for interests in the automatic machine industry, and two months later Associated Automatic Machine Corporation (AAMC) announced that it had acquired controlling interests in a number of automatic machine companies, and that it had made a conditional offer to acquire shares in the oldest and largest automatic machine company, British Automatic Company.[20] In subsequent months, AAMC acquired interests in other companies, including the Peerless Weighing Machine Company which operated more than 3,000 machines of an American design which produced a printed and dated statement of a customer's weight. Within a short time, AAMC could boast that while on the last day of 1928 it managed 1,061 machines, by the end of January that total had grown to 2,450 machines and it expected that by the end of 1929, after including machines operated by British Automatic Company and Peerless Weighing Machine, that total would have grown to 8,000. The directors also expected that it would be possible to achieve an annual profit of £27.12s.9d per machine but acknowledged that this depended upon being able to maintain the quality of the sites operated as their number grew.[21]

In business terms, for Hatry, 1928 had ended on a high with his latest creation, AAMC, becoming a success. His business success was to be matched by a grand party for a personal landmark: his 40th birthday in December.

The party was held at his family's new home in 5 Great Stanhope Street, which proved to be as extravagant a sign of success as *Westward* had been in 1920. Although Hatry had only spent £20,000 in buying the property, he spent twice that amount in preparing the building for his family's occupation. The building had been completely remodelled with every modern facility but the most memorable feature was the new building's 30-feet, 25,000-gallon swimming pool[22] which had been lined with white marble. Hatry had conceived the notion that on waking in the morning he should be able to walk as few steps as possible to take a swim. This required that the swimming pool should be built at the top of the house. His first architect said that it was impossible to build such a swimming pool, as did a second architect. Hatry was determined so sought further advice. A third architect proposed a solution: the insertion into the building of a system of girders from which the pool could be suspended. It was this proposal which was accepted at phenomenal expense. Close to the swimming pool was a small gymnasium fitted out as the interior of a boat. The lounge hall was panelled in Tudor style with an oak-beamed ceiling. The dining room was in Georgian style with raised plasterwork, fluted columns and a hearth formed of coloured marbles in mosaic. The centre panel of the marble chimneypiece was a carving of Aphrodite supported by dolphins. The winter garden, 35 feet by 12 feet 6 inches, was lighted through alabaster bowls on Ionic columns and heated by electric panel radiators. Ingenious artistic arrangements gave the impression that the garden was of much greater length than it really was. Marble and decorated plaster with burnished steel and delicate high reliefs adorned the ballroom which was 52 feet long by 22 feet and had a balustraded gallery for musicians. The study in Queen Anne style led downstairs to a cocktail bar planned as a Tudor inn – 'The Great Stanhope Arms'.[23]

Just as *Westward* had been, the new house was an outward sign that Hatry had built a fortune and could overcome all manner of difficulties.

On his 40th birthday, he had arrived … again.

Notes

1 *The Times*, 21 February 1928, page 13.
2 'Advertorial' under the heading 'Ben Trovato by Callisthenes' (*The Times*, 20 February 1929, page 10).
3 Bloch, 2012.
4 Bloch, 2012.
5 *New York Times*, 28 March 1927, pages 1 and 10.
6 Goranin, 2008; Bloch, 2012.
7 Selfridge was encouraged to acquire Whiteley's by James White, the company promoter who had helped Selfridge to create his chain of provincial department stores and with whom Hatry had collaborated in 1919 (Woodhead, 2012, page 216).
8 *The Times*, 29 March 1928, page 9.
9 *The Times*, 8 September 1928, page 16.
10 *The Times*, 8 June 1928, page 22; 12 June 1928, page 22; 16 June 1928, page 21.
11 *The Times*, 19 June 1928, page 22.
12 *The Times*, 26 June 1928, page 22.
13 Statement issued by the directors (*The Times*, 3 December 1928, page 26).
14 *Financial Times*, April 1930, page 5; 5 April 1930, page 5.
15 'Hatry was apt to take a fancy, first to one person and then to another … ' opening statement by D.N. Pritt KC on behalf of the former managing director of PPC (*The Times*, 3 April 1950, page 5).
16 *The Times*, 8 August 1929, page 16. This approach was subsequently commended by Price Waterhouse & Company and Spicer & Pegler & Company, accountants who were commissioned to investigate PPC after the Hatry collapse in September 1929 (*Financial Times*, 10 January 1930, pages 4 and 7).
17 Cripps, 1957, page 80.
18 Cripps, 1957, pages 116–117.
19 Cripps, 1957, page 94.
20 *The Times*, 21 January 1929, page 21.

21 *The Times*, 7 February 1929, page 23.
22 *Sunday Times*, 13 June 1965, page 25.
23 *Illustrated London News*, 26 January 1930, page 118.

References

Primary works: unpublished documents

St Andrews Special Collections: Tullis Russell papers.

Primary works: newspapers and periodicals

Financial Times.
Illustrated London News.
New York Times, New York, USA.
Sunday Times.
The Times.
Time, New York, USA.

Secondary works

Bloch, M. (2012), *Behind the Curtain: A History of the Photobooth.* (www.panmodern.com/photobooth.htm downloaded 1 January 2018).
Cripps, C.F. (1957), *Life's a Gamble.* (Odhams Press, London).
Goranin, N. (2008), *American Photobooth.* (W.W. Norton, New York).
Woodhead, L. (2012), *Shopping, Seduction and Mr Selfridge.* (Revised edition). (Profile Books, London).

9 Keeping up appearances in 1929

In January 1929, as so often, the prevailing mood was captured by a New Year cartoon in *Punch*.[1] An old sailor is pictured cavorting on an exiguous raft waving a pipe, the usual signifier in cartoons for Stanley Baldwin, the prime minister. The raft is encircled by sharks with large sharp teeth. In the cartoon, the sharks are not identified but readers would have been able easily to think of imminent risks for the government. Internationally, there were to be negotiations over the payment by Germany of the reparations due under the Treaty of Versailles. Domestically, local government reforms were to be implemented involving a major reform of the poor law. The need for rationalisation of many industries was generally accepted but was proving intractable. A general election was to be held; the first after the right to vote had been granted to all women by a 1928 Act. No one could be certain what the outcome would be. As the King was very ill and his recovery was not assured[2] it was possible that before the end of 1929 there might be both a new inexperienced government and a new inexperienced monarch. The cartoon leads the reader to ask not whether the raft will sink but why the sailor looks so jolly.

For Hatry, there was but one shark: his businesses were short of cash.

This was not a new experience. It had happened to him before, when the post-war boom broke in 1921. In the boom, trading in the shares he floated had boosted the profits made by charges for the flotations themselves. Substantial profits could be made by trading in a rising market. When the market peaked and began to fall, the flow of profit ceased and left traders with holdings of shares that could only be sold at a loss. Traders who were tempted to avoid crystallising the loss by holding onto their shares risked concentrating their wealth in assets whose value would decline for so long as the market fell, which was why in retrospect Hatry wished that in 1921 he had told his colleagues to sell everything immediately. Otherwise, there would be no flexibility to consider new projects. This effect would be worsened if the holdings were financed by loans, as Hatry's were. Paying interest to finance holdings of shares whose value was declining and which offered little prospect of profit was not an attractive business strategy.

For Hatry, this was not unfamiliar – he had fought his way out of such difficulties before. For his team, however, it was a new and unfamiliar challenge.

None of them had any experience of corporate finance businesses before they had joined Hatry at Austin Friars Trust. This left them ill-prepared when the first nine months of 1929 were dominated by a conflict between his business's cash shortage and the opportunity to pull off the rationalisation of yet another industry against all conventional City expectations. While Hatry's team saw the reconciliation of this conflict as a challenge to their financial skills, it was more seriously to prove a test of their character. For most of that time, the conflict was hidden from public view so that its final disastrous conclusion on 20 September came as a shock for which there had been little warning in public.

As the new year began, there were persistent doubts on the stock exchange about the stability of some of the smaller companies that had been floated in the 1928 boom.[3] At the end of January, these doubts crystallised in the announcement of worrying news of two promotions: Ner-Sag Limited and Blue Bird Holdings Limited.

Ner-Sag Limited owned the right to a bed design which it was claimed would never sag. After months during which the directors had failed to issue any reports on the companies' trading, accounts had been presented in which the directors admitted that they had been unable to determine the company's financial position from the accounting records. The shareholders had rejected the accounts to express their displeasure at both the information vacuum and the directors' failure to monitor the managing director, Mr Brandreth, whose whereabouts were unknown. For their part, the directors had presented a bankruptcy petition against Mr Brandreth.[4]

On the same day, 29 January, it was reported that Blue Bird Holdings Limited had failed to make cash payments for shares of other Blue Bird companies that had been promoted in the previous two years and which it had promised to acquire. The promoter, Mr Claud Lorang, had attempted to explain why the cash raised by the flotation of Blue Bird Holdings had not been available, but as *The Economist* observed, 'These explanations do not altogether lighten the shareholder's darkness'.[5] Blue Bird Holdings[6] was an example of what *The Economist* called 'parent finance' – a technique for milking the maximum cash from highly speculative promotions. Companies would be formed, allegedly to exploit a new invention or process, and then floated. After flotation, the company would sell some of its entitlement to exploit rights within a particular territory to another company whose shares would in turn be offered to the public. Apart from Blue Bird, there were many examples of this practice, including some, such as Photomaton, floated by Clarence Hatry.[7]

Nervousness about speculative promotions was heightened in February[8] by an increase in bank rate from 4½% to 5½% and by some rash speculation about what would happen if the Labour Party were able to form a government. Inevitably, this combination of fears led to a fall in share prices which disproportionately affected shares floated in 1927 and 1928. Hatry's flotations were also affected by the price reductions, not least the Photomaton shares which bore comparison with the discredited shares in Blue Bird Holdings.

These price falls continued after Easter, encouraged by the fact that some of the weakest companies floated in 1928 and early 1929, such as Poso-graph Great Britain Distributing Limited, a photographic portrait company, were already being wound up.[9]

Meanwhile, Hatry and his principal company, Austin Friars Trust Limited, continued to announce new corporate transactions as if the market falls had not disrupted the business at all. In January, the acquisition of British Automatic Company and Peerless Weighing Machine by Associated Automatic Machine Corporation (AAMC) had been announced, reinforcing the appearance that AAMC was continuing to build its network of automatic machines. In February, there had been the announcement of a new holding company to carry through a fusion of companies involved in the light castings industry[10] and in April the announcement of a new stock to be issued by the Melbourne Board of Works, a significant departure as it was Hatry's first issue on behalf of an overseas public authority and was the first transaction in Australia to flow from a mission sponsored by Corporation & General Securities (C&GS) and Hatry during 1928.[11]

At about the same time, the formation of the light castings combine presaged in February took shape in the form of Allied Ironfounders, which had been formed to take interests in companies which largely produced cast iron goods for use in the building trade. The goods produced comprised not only castings for external and internal drainage purposes but all kinds of highly finished porcelain enamelled baths, artistic fireplaces, stoves and ranges for cooking by coal, gas and electricity. It was claimed that the companies to be combined were market leaders in the supply of cooking apparatus for hotels, restaurants and institutions. This industry had suffered a considerable fall in profits during the previous 18 months brought about by severe internal competition. It was hoped that the new combine would eliminate this fratricidal competition and secure more economical production and distribution.

The new combine was in some ways similar to the jute combine which Hatry had helped to create some years before, comprising a number of family companies which came together for largely defensive reasons. Just as Jute Industries was based in Dundee, at the heart of Allied Ironfounders were three Scottish companies: Light Castings Limited of Stirlingshire, which was managed by the Steven family; Falkirk Iron Company Limited, managed by the Kennard family; and Forth and Clyde and Sunnyside Iron Companies of Stirling, managed by the Brown family. Future management of the new group was to be in the hands of these families, just as the Dundee jute barons' families managed Jute Industries. As happened in the case of Jute Industries, Hatry spent some months attracting other companies to join the combine, which was able to announce a public offer of debenture stock in May 1929. Only 75% of the stock offered was taken up, a result that *The Times* regarded as 'satisfactory' in view of 'the present condition of the market', observing that 'much less than 75% would have been subscribed by the public if the issue had not been on behalf of a merger company which seeks to rationalise an important section of the iron industry'.[12] With its similarity to previous transactions, the Allied Ironfounders transaction showed the Hatry group continuing to trade as normal. Even more importantly, it introduced Hatry to another industry that needed further rationalisation: the steel industry.

The 1914–1918 war had demonstrated the high economic cost of the fragmentation of the British steel industry between many small, poorly capitalised family-owned companies. After the end of the war, there had been a sharp decline in the demand for steel from shipbuilding and its other traditional customers, followed by an increase in demand from newer industries such as automotive and aircraft manufacturers. Small, locally focused steel mills dominated by their family owners had found difficulty in responding to these changes in demand and in rationalising their businesses unless external interests, such as bank creditors, had the leverage to oblige families to accept change.

Someone suggested to Hatry that this industry needed his attention[13] and that if he could succeed in rationalising the industry it would be an achievement of national importance. Hatry's initial research confirmed this view and appealed to his vanity as an opportunity to succeed where so many rationalisation schemes had failed. He began his work by forming a syndicate to provide the capital he would need to acquire companies before they could be restructured and then began to search for companies prepared to be founding members of the combine. His search quickly encountered the resistance of the existing owners who had experience of protecting their interests by jockeying for position in any new combines. Hatry's overtures eventually found one company, United Steel Companies Limited, which was prepared to talk about a new combine, albeit on its own terms.

United Steel had been formed in March 1918 around a close association between Steel Peech and Tozer Limited and Samuel Fox and Company which both produced rails and other products for the railway industry, although Samuel Fox was also famed for its umbrella frames. Those two companies had found that it was cheaper to expand their capacity by associating with other mills and suppliers. Accordingly they had invited the Frodingham Iron & Steel Company, the Workington Iron & Steel Company and the Rother Vale Collieries to join and had formed an association with United Strip and Bar Mills which was a major customer for United Steel's metal.[14]

By 1928, United Steel had survived a difficult period and had completed the programme of capital development which had been planned in 1918. But in the most recent three years, the company's profits had fallen from £153,959 in 1925 to a loss of £42,564 in 1927. In none of those years did the profit cover the cost of interest due on the debenture stock and on stock issued by United Strip and Bar Mills which the holding company had guaranteed (about £258,000 annually), let alone meet the sums which should have been set aside for debenture redemption and sinking funds (about £48,000). In these three years, the total commitment which could not be covered from the annual profits was about £800,000. Meeting that surplus commitment had left the company drained of cash.[15]

The clear implication of these results was that the company needed not only to reorganise to return to profit but also to restructure its finances to reduce the burden of the fixed interest debt which had been contracted in 1918 to pay for the modernisation of its plant. This implication had been accepted by the company well before Hatry arrived on the scene and had already led to managerial changes. After its formation in 1918, United Steel had retained individual management of its branches, any necessary coordination being achieved through representative committees culminating in a central management committee. In 1927, when contemplating how a return to profitability should be achieved, it had been agreed that the necessary economies might best be achieved by placing the final supervision of all the branches in the hands of a single managing director responsible for the whole group. It was also agreed that the new managing director should be recruited from outside the company so that any cost-cutting would be managed by someone unprejudiced by a connection with an individual branch who would be able to be impartial and, where necessary, drastic. The person appointed, Robert S. Hilton, had for nine years been managing director and deputy chairman of Metropolitan Vickers Company Limited. In parallel with Robert Hilton's appointment, the person who had led the company in accomplishing the internal reforms and had been a director since the company's formation in 1918, Walter Benton Jones, became chairman.[16] Together, Hilton and Benton Jones formed a partnership which was to lead the reformed business until the beginning of the 1939–1945 war.[17]

Having accomplished that internal reorganisation, the board had turned to the financial changes that were needed and, with the support of its banks, had negotiated a Scheme of Arrangement which was announced in February 1928. This Scheme provided temporary relief from the company's interest burden. All payments to sinking funds were to be suspended for three years, and the company would only pay interest to the extent that its profits, after agreed provision for depreciation, would permit such payments. As part of the arrangements, the company's bank had agreed to stabilise the existing loans and had provided a substantial special credit.

That United Steel had been able to negotiate such an arrangement demonstrates that its new management had convinced its banks not only that the business was fundamentally profitable but also that its muscular management was capable of restoring the company to a satisfactory profit-earning position within the three years, during which the moratorium would be in place. The relief was, however, only temporary – a permanent financial rearrangement had still to be accomplished.

This was the position which Hatry found when he approached United Steel early in 1929 to propose that his syndicate should purchase the business. Unsurprisingly in view of the work that the directors had done to secure the company's future, Hatry's proposal was roundly rejected, but the directors suggested that they might be interested in a sale of the company if that led to a reconstruction of the capital so that the company was left just with one class of capital, having repaid its fixed interest loans. The directors suggested that any sale should be conditional upon an agreement to meet the requirements of a financial reconstruction and that a substantial deposit would be required which would be forfeit in the event of non-completion.

The directors had seen in Hatry's intervention a chance of avoiding the drawbacks of the conventional approach to a capital reconstruction. Company law permitted the court to approve schemes to reduce companies' capital but required that any proposal should be approved by a majority of the holders of each class of a company's shares, not just the ordinary shareholders. The consequence was that holders of each class of shares had to be persuaded that any proposed arrangement was advantageous to them. This was never an easy negotiation and, in the late 1920s, Leyland Motors was only one of many companies whose schemes failed to secure approval because one class of shareholders believed they were to bear an unreasonable share of any reduction in the capital. In practice, schemes which were approved tended to write down the worth of ordinary shares by more than preference shares because preference shareholders were able to hold the ordinary shareholders to ransom by refusing to approve a proposed scheme.

In United Steel's case, Hatry found a solution for this conundrum. A new holding company would be created with the simple capital structure desired by United Steel's directors. He proposed to make a cash offer for all of the existing company's shares at a price that offered a premium to the current market price. Alternatively, the offer would include an option for shareholders to accept shares in the new holding company, rather than cash in return for selling their shares. In principle, the percentage premium would be the same for holders of all classes of share. When the existing shares had been acquired, the business of United Steel would be transferred to the new holding company. For the syndicate Hatry was organising to finance the scheme, the total cash cost of acquiring the old companies would depend upon the number of shareholders who opted to receive shares in the new company. If for any reason that option became less attractive than cash, shareholders would opt to receive cash immediately and the cash that the syndicate had to find would increase.

Hatry believed that the ordinary shares of the new company would be more attractive to existing ordinary shareholders because the interest burden of the existing fixed interest shares was to be removed, so that the new company would be able to pay dividends on ordinary shares. He also believed that the offer would be attractive to existing preference shareholders because it offered a way of realising some value from their existing holdings at a time when the market price had been depressed by the moratorium on interest payments.[18]

The directors accepted Hatry's new proposal which was announced publicly in April 1929.[19] Austin Friars Trust offered to buy all of the debentures, obligations and shares of United Steel and the preference shares of United Strip and Bar Mills for cash at varying rates of discount to their nominal values but at a premium to their current market price. Austin Friars Trust also undertook to provide further capital to pay off United Steel's bank loans, which totalled £2.9 million, and to provide additional working capital. The offer was conditional upon acceptance by 90% of the holders of each and every class of security.

Although the proposed financial reconstruction was welcomed by the newspapers as a necessary prelude to rationalisation, the novel character of the scheme led to lengthy exchanges of correspondence as holders of the various classes of security shared their doubts and debated the relative merits of the options available to them.[20]

In the event, although the offer was accepted by most shareholders, the required percentage of acceptances had not been reached by the deadline date. As the shortfall in acceptances was small, the deadline was extended. On 20 May, when sufficient acceptances had been received, the offer became absolute.[21] The next step was to send the transfer forms to shareholders so that the formalities of the purchase by Hatry could be completed. It was promised that the forms would be in shareholders' hands by 31 May. Only when the forms were returned would the proportion of shareholders opting to receive cash rather than shares and thus the total cash cost of the scheme become known.

This was of course one day after the date chosen for the general election and meant that shareholders would be completing their forms after the result of the election was known. If the election result increased the uncertainty surrounding the future trading of United Steel, shareholders might be more inclined to accept cash for their shares rather than shares in the new holding company. Although the shareholders' choice might not affect the stability of the new company, it would affect the amount of cash that would be required to complete the transaction. If more shareholders opted not to accept shares in the new holding company, Hatry would need more cash immediately to pay them.

In the event, distribution of the formal transfer documents was delayed until after an announcement by Austin Friars Trust on 14 June that its offer was to be varied. Shareholders who preferred to accept shares in the new holding company were not obliged to accept ordinary shares but were to be offered the additional option of receiving preference shares carrying the right to a fixed dividend each year. Although this was a departure from the conditions laid down by the directors of United Steel, it was a small encouragement to existing shareholders to accept the non-cash option. This slight delay in sending out the promised documents did not attract negative comment in the newspapers, and the transaction went ahead. Shareholders were given until 12 September to complete their formalities after which Austin Friars Trust would withdraw its offer. Although the delay in circulating the formal acceptance documents was a hiccough and could have been interpreted as a sign of underlying problems, to a casual observer the steel transaction seemed to be proceeding satisfactorily.[22]

After this, Hatry and his group attracted little attention until August, when a series of coincidences returned attention to the Photomaton companies.

On 3 August, *The Economist* reported on the condition of the Red Triangle group of cement companies. This combine had been formed in November 1926 by Henry Horne, a company promoter, on the rebound from the failure of his attempt to acquire the Blue Circle group, a combine of cement manufacturers led by Hatry's friend Osborne O'Hagan and Lord St Davids. Horne's objective was to raise profits by modernising the equipment of its constituent cement manufacturers and centralising distribution. In 1928, Red Triangle had attempted to undercut the prices of the Blue Circle group, a strategy that cost the Red Triangle group dear and could not be sustained in view of the cost. The Red Triangle group had given up this struggle in November 1928. Although a dividend had been paid in respect of trading in 1928, the group's profit did not cover the dividend nor provide for the modernisation that was required. To make good this deficiency, there had already been two calls for shareholders to provide additional capital and in July the directors had persuaded shareholders that costs should be reduced by integrating the group's four manufacturing companies.[23]

For Photomaton, the Red Triangle group's experience was significant because of the similarities between the two groups. Both had been formed by syndicates led by company promoters: Clarence Hatry in the case of Photomaton and Henry Horne in the case of the Red Triangle group. Horne believed that by acquiring interests in selected concerns, financial trusts could bring pressure to bear to maximise efficiency and improve profits. But success required an ability to identify companies whose profits could be improved, an ability which experience showed that Mr Horne and his organisation did not possess. As a result the Horne group failed to achieve the promised improvement performance. Red Triangle's annual accounts were opaque so shareholders were ill-informed about the group's true trading position. Photomaton had delayed publishing its first annual accounts which encouraged shareholders' suspicions that the group's results had been disappointing. Finally, both the Red Triangle group and Photomaton had suffered significant falls in the market price for their shares. By August, the shares in British Cement Products which had reached a high of 90 shillings in 1928 and had stood at 67 shillings and sixpence in January 1929 had fallen to 31 shillings and threepence.

Concerns about Photomaton were increased by the announcement in mid-August that the regional Photomaton trading companies were to be merged into the newly created company: British Photomaton Trading Limited. This looked like a direct parallel of the merger of the Red Triangle group's manufacturing companies and suggested that the Photomaton companies were not trading unsuccessfully. *The Economist*'s comment was incisive. By analysing the agreement by which British Photomaton Trading was to acquire the previously separate trading companies, the report suggested that the new agreement protected the balance sheet of Photomaton Parent Corporation by justifying the valuation of its holdings of shares in the regional trading companies rather than benefiting external shareholders. *The Economist*'s report observed drily that Photomaton Parent Corporation had still not published its first accounts.[24]

This coverage raised questions not only about the stability of the Photomaton companies but also the efficacy of Hatry's financialised approach to rationalisation – not at all helpful in the context of the steel scheme. The market price of Photomaton shares continued to slide, suggesting that there were persistent sellers of the stock.

Hatry's group of companies did not attract further attention until the early part of September when the prices of Hatry-related shares again began to fall. At first there was no explanation for the falls, although there was a suggestion that the renewed selling of Photomaton shares had started on the mainland of Europe. As late as Friday 20 September, the newspapers were still describing the falls as a reaction to the end of the 1928 boom and calling for the companies to explain matters in a statement.[25]

There was no warning of the next day's news. On Saturday 21 September, the newspapers were dominated by news of the collapse of the Hatry group. It had ceased to trade. Investigating accountants were at work. Dealing in Hatry-related shares had been suspended by the stock exchange. Clarence Hatry and his key associates had visited the director of public prosecutions for a voluntary interview, although the City of London Police were not prepared to make a public statement on the outcome of the interview. That had to wait for the newspapers published on Sunday and Monday which reported that on Saturday morning Hatry and his colleagues had appeared at the City of London Magistrates Court, accused of fraud.

For the general public, there had been no warning.

Notes

1 *Punch*, 2 January 1929, page 27.
2 He was convalescing in the house of Hatry's associate Sir Arthur du Cros: Craigwell House, Aldwick, near Bognor Regis.
3 Kynaston, 1999, pages 138–140.
4 *The Economist*, 26 January 1929, page 172. He was subsequently apprehended and prosecuted (*The Times*, 18 February, page 7).
5 *The Economist*, 26 January 1929, page 169.
6 Blue Bird Holdings owed its origin to a garage and car sales company founded by Malcolm Campbell, the racing driver who famously competed for land speed records in cars, all of which he named 'Blue Bird'.
7 *The Economist*, 19 January 1929, page 111. Hatry had first adopted this practice before the 1914–1918 war when Union Emigrants Association (Italy) Limited had been incorporated.
8 7 February 1929.
9 *The Economist*, 29 June 1929, page 1461.
10 *The Times*, 16 February 1928.
11 *The Times*, 29 April 1929, page 22.
12 *The Times*, 8 May 1929, page 23; 13 May 1929, page 24; 17 May 1929, page 20.

13 The suggestion may have been made by J. Ivan Spens and/or Peat Marwick Mitchell & Company, Chartered Accountants, both of whom worked with Hatry on both the Allied Ironfounders flotation and the steel scheme.
14 Andrews and Brunner, 1951, pages 102–118.
15 Andrews and Brunner, 1951, pages 156–157.
16 Peddie, 1969, pages 18–21.
17 Andrews and Brunner, 1951, pages 162–166.
18 Andrews and Brunner, 1951, pages 159–161.
19 *The Times*, 13 April 1929, page 17.
20 *The Times*, 26 April 1929, page 29; 27 April 1929, page 19.
21 *The Economist*, 11 May 1929, page 1057.
22 *The Times*, 15 June 1929, page 19; *The Economist*, 22 June 1929, page 1406.
23 *The Economist*, 3 August 1929, pages 230–231.
24 *The Times*, 8 August 1929, page 16; *The Economist*, 17 August 1929, page 320.
25 *The Times*, 20 September 1929; *The Economist*, 21 September 1929, page 531.

References

Primary works: newspapers and periodicals

Punch.
The Economist.
The Times.

Secondary works

Andrews, P.W.S. and Brunner, E. (1951), *Capital Development in Steel: A Study of the United Steel Companies Limited.* (Basil Blackwell, Oxford).

Kynaston, D. (1999), *The City of London: Volume III: Illusions of Gold 1914–1945.* (Chatto & Windus, London).

Peddie, R. (1969), *The United Steel Companies Limited, 1918–1968: A History.* (C. Nicholls, Manchester).

10 Keeping the plates spinning

In the early 1950s, an American psychologist, Donald Cressey, undertook a series of interviews with convicted embezzlers to identify the common features of fraudulent behaviour and the conditions that predisposed them towards criminal abuse of trust. His research found a small number of factors that were present in most if not all of the crimes his interviewees had committed. All of them had faced a financial problem which had threatened them with personal disaster, either financially or reputationally. All of them had believed that the problem could not be shared with others, leading them to become isolated from dispassionate advice. All of them had been presented with a way out of their problem that was unorthodox and potentially criminal. All of them had persuaded themselves that the way out could not be regarded as criminal – often because money was only being borrowed for a short time rather than stolen.[1] Although not included in the research, Hatry's experience followed precisely the stages that Cressey identified.

While in public Hatry's organisation appeared to be trading normally, activity was becoming frenzied in private. The team came to resemble music hall comedians condemned to keeping plates spinning on top of improbably long poles. As the frenzy continued, and the team's plight became more desperate, so the conditions identified by Cressey fell into place and Hatry's nemesis grew nearer.

Maintaining the public appearance of normality was important both for Hatry and his creditors. Problems in securing the cash needed by the group multiplied and led his team to resort to increasingly outlandish devices to surmount them. The options available would have been more limited if information about their difficulties had leaked. Keeping them private suited Hatry's financial creditors, whose options would also have been limited by any leak of information. It was in the mutual interest of Hatry and his key creditors to keep matters discreet – and they did.

To the outsider, Hatry's shortage of money would have seemed unlikely. Throughout 1928, after the successful merger of Drapery Trust with Debenhams, Hatry had been constantly busy. Quite apart from the Photomaton deals, he had launched the London Public Omnibus Company, sponsored share issues by Alvis Cars and Retail Trade Securities and a private placement of shares by International Bitumen Emulsions, a company aiming to exploit a new road surface product. At the same time, he had been involved in more local authority loan issues. How could he be short of money when there had been so much activity?

What was not evident to the outsider was that Hatry's business was vulnerable. Some of the companies had suffered falls in the market price for their shares in response to disappointing trading results. In one instance, Glasgow Bonding Company, Hatry had bought back a substantial majority of the shares to avoid further losses for shareholders,[2] while in another instance, London Public Omnibus Company, a controlling interest had been sold to London General Omnibus Company.[3] In both cases, Hatry's company, Austin Friars Trust, had not recovered the cash which Hatry had originally invested in the flotation.

Moreover, Austin Friars Trust relied on the profits earned from speculative trading in the shares he floated. Business vendors were less inclined to use the services of individual company promoters such as Hatry, preferring the services of the new, more cautious houses such as Charterhouse Investment Trust. To win new business, Hatry was obliged to compete by reducing his regular charges. Even the local authority loans business was not as profitable as it had once been, which had led to accusations by disbelieving directors of Corporation & General Securities (C&GS) that its accounts had been manipulated to exaggerate reported profits.[4] As for the industrial share issues, to achieve the profit that both he and his shareholders expected, Hatry had become more reliant on whatever additional profit he could earn after an issue by trading in the shares which had been floated. If for some reason there was no chance to trade successfully, he risked becoming financially embarrassed. Although the initial offers of Photomaton shares had been successful, the market had become more suspicious of the prospects for the many new technology shares which had been floated. Although the directors of Photomaton issued a series of what were intended to be reassuring statements about the company's progress in creating a worldwide network of companies to exploit the technology, they had not been able to maintain investors' confidence in the company's prospects. As a result, Photomaton's share price had slipped back and Hatry could not sell the Photomaton shares that he had kept back for trading. Indeed, he had been buying the shares in an attempt to support the share price. As a further sign of the difficulty, although the last Photomaton company to be created, Photomaton (Central and Eastern) Limited, had been incorporated in June 1928, its shares were never offered for sale to the public – the prevailing market sentiment was too negative. Hatry was left with less cash than he had expected.

His position was eased by a stroke of luck: he received a call from Abraham Cory Allibone, the town clerk of the Borough of Wakefield. In 1925, almost four years earlier, Wakefield had been one of the first authorities to raise money by issuing bonds with Hatry's assistance. The first issue, of £250,000, had proved so successful that in 1926 it was followed by a second issue of £750,000.

In the autumn of 1928, Mr Allibone and his colleagues had prepared a forecast of the council's cash requirements during 1929, chief among which was the obligation to repay the outstanding amount (£515,000) of an old loan stock which had financed the town's waterworks and was due to be redeemed on 1 September 1929. To meet this obligation and to raise additional funds for the waterworks, another loan was called for and as Hatry's services had proved satisfactory in 1925 and 1926, Mr Allibone contacted C&GS, Hatry's company, to seek advice on the appropriate time to make an issue and the terms which C&GS might offer.[5]

This must have seemed like a gift to Hatry. Knowing that his companies were short of cash, to be invited to advise an authority on raising money was too good an opportunity to miss. At an initial meeting on 29 November 1928, Hatry advised that although Wakefield Council might not need the money until September 1929 or later, there was nothing to be gained by delaying a bond issue. The cost of borrowing was unlikely to fall and might be affected by the uncertainty caused by the impending general election. If the council had no immediate need for the money raised by an issue, C&GS would be able to invest the funds on the authority's behalf at an attractive rate of interest. Hatry did not say how the funds would be invested, but there can be little doubt that he intended that his own companies would use the money to meet their own obligations. This would be especially valuable to him if he could avoid giving Wakefield any security for what in substance would be a loan to him by the authority. In effect he would be borrowing additional money without pledging any of his assets. Mr Allibone and his colleagues did not question the wisdom of lending such a significant amount to Hatry without security, displaying a naivety which was later to be criticised in the House of Lords.[6]

Hatry's use of Wakefield's funds mirrored a practice that had been perfected some years earlier by Rogers Caldwell in Tennessee. In 1917, he opened Caldwell & Company to buy and sell 'securities, stocks and bonds'. From the beginning he bought public utility bonds under depository agreements which provided that the proceeds of the bonds should be left on deposit with banks acceptable to Caldwell until the funds were needed to pay for construction on the projects being financed. So that it became easier for the funds to be used as working capital for Caldwell's own business, in 1919 he created the Bank of Tennessee which was to do nothing but hold the proceeds of bond issues. Just as local authority issues increased materially in the UK during the 1920s, so there was an increase in utility bond issues in the southern states of the USA – an increase which allowed Caldwell's business to thrive. Funds from municipal deposits had increased from $1.5 million in December 1918 to over $5 million in December 1924 and exceeded $12.5 million in December 1925. Between 1926 and 1930, Caldwell's company handled more than 1,000 trust agreements of this type.[7]

Although prepared to accept Hatry's advice that it would be prudent to issue new bonds quickly, Mr Allibone and his colleagues were initially disappointed by the terms proposed by Hatry and C&GS. However, after an intercession by Arthur Collins, revised terms were accepted by the council. It was agreed that a new 20–30 year stock of £750,000 would be offered for sale to the public at an issue price of £95.10.0 per £100 of stock. C&GS guaranteed that, after all charges, Wakefield would receive £94.15.0 per £100 of stock. In other words, Hatry limited his charges to 15 shillings per £100 of stock. Perhaps his experience of the two previous successful issues coloured Mr Allibone's judgement, but he did not insist that the deal with C&GS should be formalised in the form of a written contract as had been done on previous occasions. The issue simply went ahead during January 1929 and dealings opened on 21 January. At this point, Wakefield Council and C&GS agreed how to deal with the money that had been raised. Subject to two payments of £50,000 to be made to Wakefield in February and May 1929, the remaining cash was to be held by C&GS until the end of August 1929 when most of the money would then be required to redeem the retiring loan stock. It was agreed that C&GS and Mr Allibone would meet in August to agree precisely how to deal with the cash then remaining.

This deal relieved the immediate cash pressure on Hatry by placing between £650,000 and £700,000 of Wakefield's money in his hands for eight months, while leaving his assets free of pledges to Wakefield and available to back any loans which he could arrange with his bankers.

It did not relieve him of all pressure, however. He still had stock on his hands that could not easily be sold at a profit in the market. In the early months of 1929, this problem became larger.

In 1928, Photomaton had merely been one of many new issues linked to new technologies, several of which tried to capitalise on the public fascination with speed in the air, on water and on land. By January 1929, several of these issues such as Ner-Sag Limited and Blue Bird Holdings were in difficulty, which was causing a slide in share prices. Between January and June 1929, some shares lost most of their value.

Hatry's promotions were not immune to these developments. Although shares in Photomaton Parent Corporation lost only 8.3% of their value between January and June 1929, shares in Far Eastern Photomaton lost 71.4%. Nonetheless, in January 1929 the initial public offering of Associated Automatic Machines Corporation Limited (AAMC) was successful, to the extent that, later that month, Hatry was able to use shares in the company as part of the consideration for the purchase of British Automatic Company Limited (BAC), one of the largest of the automatic machine operators. While this was welcome, Hatry still needed to realise cash for his holdings of Photomaton shares.

In January, an opportunity was provided by the AAMC's acquisition of BAC. As soon as the acquisition had been completed, the existing directors were replaced with directors nominated by Hatry. The new board agreed that financial decisions should be made by a small group of directors (including Hatry) which gave him control of BAC's assets in a style reminiscent of Gerard Lee Bevan's control of City Equitable Fire Insurance some years previously. This power was used immediately to strip out all of BAC's cash and marketable investments so that Hatry's companies could use them to solve the cash problem. The same power was used to install Hatry himself and a co-director as trustees of the British Automatic Staff Pension Fund. Within a day, the pension fund's holdings of gilt-edged securities had all been replaced by shares in companies floated by Hatry. This was another small relief from the burden of holding unsaleable shares, brought about by transferring the risk to the staff expecting to benefit from the BAC pension fund.[8]

In the same month, Hatry formed Iron Industries Limited with an authorised share capital of £650,000. On 4 February, Austin Friars Trust applied for 500,000 of the 650,000 shares, paying for them with a cheque. Once paid, the cash was immediately loaned back by Iron Industries. Subsequently the authorised share capital of Iron Industries was increased to £700,000 and the remaining shares were all then issued to Austin Friars Trust which then used them as security for bank loans amounting to £600,000. In effect, loans had been raised against little more than Austin Friars Trust's promise to repay the loan.[9]

In succeeding months, the cash pressure on Hatry's companies did not abate and led his team to more extreme measures to secure relief. When the new issues by Allied Ironfounders were planned, Hatry took his fee in the form of shares in the new company as normal rather than in cash, although they could not be sold until after the company had been floated and dealings on the exchange had begun. To realise their value, Hatry sought a loan from National Bank offering the shares as security. This proposal was rejected by the bank on the reasonable grounds that the shares were worthless as security until they could be traded on the exchange, as the bank would be unable to realise the shares. This rejection was circumvented by Hatry who persuaded the bank to accept undertakings from stockbrokers that they would buy the shares on a default even if exchange dealings had not begun. The bank was not told that the brokers only agreed to do this on receiving Hatry's guarantee that he would buy the shares back from the brokers. Unbeknown to the bankers, Hatry had made the transaction circular.

In May, in another reckless move, Hatry sought the agreement of the directors of C&GS to raise money by a further public offer of £400,000 of its shares. On this occasion, Hatry's proposition was opposed by Frederick Braithwaite, the senior partner of Foster & Braithwaite, the stockbrokers who had supported Hatry faithfully in 1925 when he had begun to sponsor the issue of local authority loan stocks. The remaining directors all supported Braithwaite who argued that it would be impossible to achieve a reasonable price for the shares in a declining market. No offer was made, but, embarrassingly, Hatry had jumped the gun. Assuming that the directors of C&GS could not possibly refuse to agree another public offer, he had already gone ahead. The underwriting for the proposed issue had been arranged. What was worse, the formal agreements with the selected underwriters had been used as security for a loan of £400,000 from Westminster Bank. Not only had he misled the bank, he had antagonised his fellow directors, people who might otherwise have acted as his friends.[10]

From mid-April, calculations about the group's cash flow requirements were overshadowed by the steel scheme which envisaged as a first step that an offer would be made to acquire the holdings of existing investors in United Steel Companies Limited and United Strip and Bar Mills Limited. It was also envisaged that the offer would be made by a syndicate formed for the purpose, which would also pay off the two companies' bank debt and introduce funds to increase the group's working capital. The cost was to be recovered by making a public offering of shares in a new holding company, but until the public offer had been completed, the syndicate would have to bear the cost. In retrospect, it was foolhardy for Hatry to have attempted this project. Before taking it on, he was already short of cash and was trying to raise money by unconventional and desperate means, losing friends in the process. To cope with the additional burden of the steel scheme and survive, his estimates of the likely cost had to prove reliable and he had to form the syndicate which would cover the immediate cash requirement.

Hatry hoped that a substantial amount of the cash that needed to finance the offer would come from M. Samuel & Company, a merchant bank which had been founded by the Samuel family which had created Shell Oil and whose chairman was Marcus Samuel, Lord Bearsted. The proposed scheme had first been put to M. Samuel in February 1929 by Daniels[11] and raised several times in subsequent meetings. Eventually, on 8 April:

> Hatry wished to know whether he had our approval to make an offer on the lines discussed, it being understood that when he sees what acceptances he has received he will come to us with a clear proposition and with a knowledge of the amount of money actually required. In view of the fact that the offer stipulates for 95% acceptances, there appears no risk, and we agreed to the course proposed.[12]

The transaction stumbled at the beginning. Benton Jones, the existing chairman, spoke carelessly to journalists about the negotiations surrounding the scheme and, to avoid inaccurate speculation in the newspapers, the offer was announced early.[13] This was an embarrassment. Although Hatry had received offers of the financial support he needed to undertake the steel scheme, those offers had not been confirmed in a formal syndicate agreement, partly because it had not yet been possible to assess all the costs of the scheme. *The Economist* estimated that the cost would be of the order of £7 million but that included an underestimate of the steel companies' bank loans. By contrast, it took no account of the alternative offered to shareholders: the option of taking ordinary shares in the new holding company rather than cash in payment for their existing holdings of shares.[14]

At inception, no one knew how attractive this option would prove to be and how far it would reduce the cash requirement that the syndicate would have to meet. Whether the cash option proved more attractive to shareholders was to depend upon their view of the new group's prospects. If they believed that the company would be successful and able to pay dividends, then it might be more beneficial for shareholders to opt to take shares rather than cash. Any event which made future trading less certain would increase the risk that the company would not earn sufficient profits to declare dividends on the ordinary shares and might encourage investors to accept the immediate cash option.

Understandably, Hatry's team monitored public reactions to the offer and quickly became concerned that shareholders might not reject the cash option in sufficient numbers to keep the cost of implementing the scheme within their original estimate. The offer of an immediate cash payment was proving too attractive to shareholders for whom United Steel's existing moratorium on dividends denied any prospect of immediate income from the shares, especially when Hatry's offer gave no information about the income-earning potential of the new holding company. In certain quarters of the City, support for the steel scheme was further undermined by the opposition of Montagu Norman, governor of the Bank of England.

It is not hard to explain Norman's distrust of Hatry and his schemes. When in 1925, Hatry had succeeded in breaking into local authority loan issuing which previously had been controlled by three broking firms, he had destroyed a system that Montagu Norman had encouraged and found useful. In the absence of the direct control that had been applied during the war, the three firms had cooperated with each other and the Bank of England in a private queuing system that ensured that local authorities' issues did not compete with other issues by the United Kingdom and Empire governments. Norman's antipathy towards Hatry was reactivated at the end of April by the announcement of a new issue by the Melbourne Board of Works, the authority responsible for the water and sewerage services for the city and suburbs of Melbourne in Australia. This was the first issue arranged by Hatry for a public authority outside the United Kingdom and a further breach in the governor's preferred arrangements.[15]

Independently of his concern for ordering issues of stocks by public authorities, the Bank of England's private banking operations had led Montagu Norman to become involved in attempts to reorganise steel companies which could not service their bank loans.[16] From these experiences, Norman had good reason to understand the importance of rationalisation and the difficulties which stood in its way. Against the background of the local authority issuing initiative, the governor was sceptical that any scheme promoted by Hatry could offer a solution to the industry's problems and suspicious that Hatry's steel scheme involved paying existing shareholders too high a price for their shares. Accordingly, he made it his business to lobby City houses against supporting the steel scheme.

The scheme's prospects were complicated by another factor: the outcome of the general election to be held on 30 May. It was generally assumed that if the Conservative Party won there would be no change in policy towards industrial reorganisation and the steel scheme could go ahead unhindered. There was, however, no confident expectation of the view that would be taken if the Labour Party were to win.

By the week of the general election, Hatry was nervous of the prospects for his scheme's success, so nervous that he decided to challenge Montagu Norman to his face, arranging to meet on the day before the general election, Wednesday 29 May.[17] Presumably Hatry had hoped that he could persuade the governor to desist from lobbying against the steel scheme but he may also have hoped that the governor would agree to help to arrange support for the syndicate; at least the governor thought that he was being asked to do this. In the event, Hatry gained nothing. The governor refused to stop lobbying, refused to help with financing the scheme, and instead concluded that Hatry was looking for a way out of his obligations under the scheme. In relating the meeting to several merchant bankers two days later, the governor wrote disparagingly of Hatry as 'dangerous and perhaps ailing'.[18]

On election day, Hatry spent the evening with his wife at an election party arranged by Gordon Selfridge at his Oxford Street store. As he was fixing his black tie in his dressing room at 5 Great Stanhope Street, he heard the first results as they were broadcast by the BBC; they were disappointing. The Labour Party was winning seats. Hatry reassured himself and his wife by reflecting that the early results were usually misleading and would in the course of the evening be overtaken by Conservative victories in the shire constituencies.[19]

Anticipating a Conservative victory, Gordon Selfridge had not stinted in planning the party. He had invited all the most influential men of business with whom he was acquainted:[20]

> There must have been 2000 people at that show. There was plenty of room for them, plenty of loudspeakers, two bands and as much Cordon Rouge as the entire 2000 could drink, besides solid sit-down suppers for all who wanted it. The whole affair was magnificently organised.[21]

Gradually, those present realised that the Labour Party's earlier victories were not going to be redressed by Conservative victories in the shires. The effervescent atmosphere did not survive as Conservatives lost their seats or suffered reduced majorities. At one stage, the Labour and Conservative parties were equally matched with the Liberals a poor third, but gradually the Labour Party drew ahead. It became clear that the Labour Party was winning. As the party fell flat, so the guests made their excuses and left. There was little to celebrate.

As they strolled back to their home, Dolly asked Hatry if he was worried by the Labour victory. He answered that it was 'a very bad omen'.[22]

This view was widely shared in the financial community, as no one knew how far a Labour government would go in implementing its more radical plans. Everything seemed a little less certain than a day earlier.

The stock market reacted to the general uncertainty by marking down prices – a reaction that endangered the steel scheme by increasing the attractions for shareholders of Hatry's cash offer for their shares. Needing to check the reactions of his financial supporters, Hatry's first step was to go to the biggest contributor to the syndicate, Lord Bearsted, the chairman of M. Samuel & Company, the merchant bank that had offered £4 million. Bearsted's answer to Hatry's question was a shock, although he acknowledged that there had been discussions about a contribution from the merchant bank. M. Samuel & Company would not be contributing to the syndicate. Bearsted maintained his denial against all Hatry's charm and pleading.[23]

Without warning, Hatry was left without half of the cash he needed to implement the steel scheme which had already been announced. This was bad enough, but for Hatry the underlying significance was worse. He had been proud of his collaboration with M. Samuel at the beginning of 1928 over the reorganisation of the capital of Debenhams. It was a mark of respect and implied that Bearsted, a man of acknowledged distinction in the City, accepted Hatry as an equal or at least as a person with whom it was entirely appropriate to do business. Accordingly, Hatry had trusted that Bearsted's word would be good enough as many understood was the normal practice between men of the City:

> When I was banking in New York about thirty years ago … one always had to have a lawyer at one's side, and everything countersigned in legal from, before making the slightest commitment. In London, I have on occasion signed an underwriting agreement without any more than verbal agreements noted on a piece of paper, for most of the issue. In this small circle we all know and trust each other and every man's word is his bond. Whilst this standard remains, the City will always hold its own.[24]

For Hatry, rejection implied that Bearsted did not regard him as a member of the 'small circle' in which all members would 'trust each other'. Hatry was right to interpret the conversation in this way. Some days later, unknown to Hatry, Bearsted visited the governor at the bank and told him that he 'entirely' mistrusted Hatry.[25] In short, Bearsted's rejection of Hatry's scheme was a brutal demonstration that, for all his efforts, Hatry had not achieved the social and commercial acceptance which it had been his father's ambition to achieve and which he had inherited.

It carried another implication. If Bearsted's rejection placed Hatry outside the small circle of people who trusted each other, then, as an outsider, Hatry could not trust the circle's members. From this point, Hatry and his team knew they were on their own. They alone must find a solution to their problem which could no longer be shared.

Two of Cressey's conditions had been met. The team faced a problem that was potentially disastrous both financially and reputationally. Moreover, rejection by Bearsted meant that they were isolated; the problem could not be shared.

They were left to choose between two equally unpromising courses. If action were taken quickly, the unforeseen election result could be used as a pretext for abandoning the steel scheme. This outcome might have been regretted by the City but it would have been understood. Unfortunately, the terms of the offer had not included a *force majeure* clause contemplating withdrawal in material unforeseen events so that if Hatry withdrew, offerees would have been able to sue in a manner reminiscent of the Baldwins transaction in 1920. Even if they did not sue, his reputation would be seriously damaged. Withdrawal might have been understood but would have been damaging and personally embarrassing for Hatry.

Alternatively, the team could continue with the scheme, hoping that new contributors could be found to replace M. Samuel. As the final formal offer had yet to be circulated to shareholders, there was a still a possibility of adjusting the terms of the offer to increase the attractions of the new shares in contrast to cash. If these efforts failed, then the scheme would still fail and in the time devoted to the vain hope of raising more money, the cost of failure would have risen.

On returning to his office at Pinners Hall, Hatry discussed the position with his key associates, Edmund Daniels, John Gialdini, Albert Tabor and John Dixon.[26]

Edmund Daniels was the managing director of Austin Friars Trust, Hatry's principal trading company. When war had broken out in 1914, Daniels had attempted on 15 occasions to enter the forces but had been rejected as medically unfit and had instead served in the Red Cross. After the end of the war he found employment as a bank clerk, and in 1919 he was appointed as a clerk in the securities department of Commercial Bank of London, becoming principal of the department in 1920. On the death of the department's manager in 1920, he was appointed manager and was later retained in that role by the liquidator, although at a reduced salary.[27] Daniels had first been brought to Hatry's attention by his handwriting on an office memorandum. Hatry pursued an amateur interest in graphology and was proud of his ability to interpret handwriting. He was so appalled by Daniels' writing that he said Daniels should be dismissed immediately – a reaction he was persuaded to reverse as it was so capricious.[28] Hatry then learned that in spite of his handwriting, Daniels was conscientious and a steadfast family man, serving as scoutmaster of a local troop near his home in Surrey. He had been appointed managing director on the creation of Austin Friars Trust in 1925 and had worked closely with Hatry since then.

Daniels proved to be an accomplished sycophant. Each day he would be the first to arrive at Pinners Hall and the last to leave.[29] He had a reputation for copying Hatry, patronising Hatry's tailor and copying his mannerisms. Although he looked like a perfect City gentleman, he had no experience of corporate financial transactions other than those he had handled with and for Hatry.

John Gialdini had been brought into the company by Daniels and shared similar habits, even managing to look a little like Hatry.

In 1929, Albert Tabor was 36. He had served with the forces in France throughout the war and on demobilisation had joined a small company trading with the Levant with which he remained until 1925. He then went into business on his own account as an import and export dealer, through which he made the acquaintance of Daniels and through the intercession of a friend was given the chance of joining Austin Friars Trust and becoming manager of C&GS. Whatever his titles may have been, he seems to have been regarded by Hatry's other staff and by people outside the company as no more than a clerk.[30]

John Dixon was a company secretary. He also had been rejected for military service during the war, as he had a weak heart and defective eyesight, so had seen out the war years as the company secretary of the Chesterfield Tube Company, the company which Hatry's competitor, Szarvasy, had floated in 1906. When Hatry acquired an interest in that company at the end of 1919, he had been recommended to Hatry who was looking for an assistant secretary of his Secretarial and Registration Department. Subsequently, he was appointed secretary and then managing director of Secretarial Services Limited, which provided secretarial services to all the companies Hatry floated. While this was an unglamorous role, it was critical to the success of Austin Friars Trust and not insubstantial, involving the management of a staff of 80. By all accounts, Dixon was a competent and conscientious company secretary but had little experience of corporate finance.[31]

Small wonder is it that Daniels, Gialdini, Tabor and Dixon, bound together by their admiration for Hatry to whom they owed their livelihoods, were eager to persuade him that there was a chance, however slim, to prove to Bearsted that he was wrong. They pointed out that shareholders would not respond immediately to the formal offer when it was sent to them. Some would wait until the offer's deadline which could be set some weeks ahead. In the meantime, the team would have time to gather the balance of the money that would be needed to honour the offer; in particular to buy shares from holders opting for the cash alternative. Grasping at this straw, the team decided to soldier on.

Believing themselves to be outsiders, Hatry's team were deprived of dispassionate advice and listened to their private preferences. Hubert Meredith, a journalist who discussed the scheme with Hatry at about this time, recalled:

> As he sat opposite to me, smoking away at his pipe, the financier disappeared and in his place there seemed to me to be a very vain man undertaking a colossal task, not with the idea of making money out of it, but with the object of showing the world what a great man Clarence Hatry really was.[32]

Hatry was suffering the consequences of his own choices. A vain, insecure man, his judgement of people was not always sound. Strikingly none of the four other members of his core management team had any senior experience of corporate finance other than as members of his team. These were men who would tend to reinforce Hatry's vanity rather than challenging and testing.

However irrational the decision may seem, the team almost won through. By Friday 21 June, almost a month later, they had managed to replace most of the cash that Bearsted and M. Samuel had originally promised to provide. In part this had been done by persuading them to lend £1 million, rather than the £4 million which had originally been promised, but this was subject to four conditions. Neville Chamberlain was to be appointed chairman of the new holding company, as Hatry had proposed. M. Samuel should approve the names of the proposed underwriters. M. Samuel should approve the formal terms of the new loan. Finally, M. Samuel & Company had insisted that the loan should be guaranteed by Parent Trust and Finance, led by Sir Arthur du Cros.[33]

Hatry had not yet been able to satisfy all of these conditions, however, and there remained a gap of £900,000 that was proving difficult to fill.

On Sunday 23 June, the team met yet again to contemplate failure, on this occasion at Hatry's home. Reviewing all the avenues that might be open, they confirmed that there were none left that had not been tried or that offered any chance of success.

Recollections of what happened next were later to be hotly contested, perhaps inevitably in view of the atmosphere becoming emotionally charged. Hatry recalled that a way out was suggested by John Gialdini, who had been recruited by Edmund Daniels.[34]

When an investor applied to subscribe to a loan issue, each application had to be sent to a receiving agent and would be accompanied by a payment, typically in the form of a cheque. In return, the receiving agent would issue a receipt to the investor for the payment accepted for the amount of stock allocated to the investor. Formal stock certificates would be issued by the town clerk of the local authority in return for the receipts which had to be submitted to the authority within a period specified in the terms of the issue. During the specified period, banks and others would accept the receipts as formal evidence of the investor's title and, for example, would be prepared to lend money against them.

In the case of all loan stock issues managed by Hatry, C&GS was nominated as the receiving agent and held supplies of the receipts so that they could be issued to investors.[35] The way out suggested either by Daniels or Gialdini involved using the spare receipts held by C&GS, completing them as if they had been issued in return for cash subscribed by investors and then using the fraudulently completed forms as collateral for additional bank loans. If they needed more receipts than had already been printed, it would be a simple matter to order some more to be printed. Provided the fraudulent receipts were all recovered before the end of the period during which receipts could be exchanged for certificates, no one might ever notice that the receipts had been used in this way.

In this, the Pinners Hall team were in part relying on the inattentiveness of the clearing bank's staff. Early conversion of loan stock receipts into certificates was shunned by securities clerks, as, once converted into certificates, any change in ownership had to be registered – a time-consuming process. As a result, they tended to hold the receipts until the last possible moment.[36] There was one further motive for this practice. Share transfers were subject to stamp duty which became payable on completion of a transfer. Holding back transfers thus avoided the expense and inconvenience of stamping the transfer.[37] Hatry later suggested that at first he was unpersuaded. The scheme was plainly fraudulent, adding to the risk of failure the threat of prosecution and disgrace, if ever it were discovered. It may also be true that Gialdini lost his composure. Certainly the others all recalled that he burst out that they were within an ace of success after colossal efforts. However dangerous it may be, Gialdini saw the temporary use of loan receipts as the only way of avoiding a complete failure which would bring about a big crash in which the public would lose enormous sums. He had a pistol in his flat and rather than face such a crash he had made up his mind to blow out his brains.

Some have suggested that the team had adopted the approach before.[38] This seems unlikely. If it had been a usual part of the team's approach, it would also have been normal for the team to have printed enough blank receipt forms to allow for some to be used illegitimately as security for loans. On this occasion, at least, that had not been done, so one of the first steps in implementing the scheme on 24 June involved Tabor ordering the printing of additional receipts.

Whoever was responsible for suggesting the way out matters little. Hatry was the undoubted leader whose decision would have been followed whatever it might have been.

However, if the suggestions were theirs, Daniels and Gialdini had brought two sources of hope to the embattled, isolated team. The use of fake receipts offered a way out of the predicament which would avoid the unthinkable prospect of failure. Avoidance of a market collapse offered a rationale for discounting the taint of criminality. A belief that they were saving small investors from the losses that would flow from a market crash offered a superficially respectable motive. Moreover, trusting that the fake receipts could be recovered before anyone noticed them made the approach look like borrowing rather than stealing. How could borrowing be a crime?

Cressey's two final conditions had been met. A way out had been found, however desperate. Moreover, the team had found a rationale that allowed them to believe that what they proposed could not conceivably be regarded as a crime.

By the end of the meeting, they had all assented. They left the meeting having resolved to put this latest plan into operation.[39]

From the beginning the scheme was foolhardy. It involved descending into criminality – an irreparable and disastrous mistake. To avoid the humiliation that would follow discovery, everything had to work like clockwork. Most importantly, the issue of shares in the new steel holding company had to be completed so that the cash could be used to recover the fraudulent receipts. If this were not done, the fake receipts would be discovered by the local authorities when they were asked to convert the receipts into formal certificates. The deadline for this was 30 September.

Deep in their minds, they must have known that this was vulnerable to the slightest variation from the timetable. It was not only criminal but also unrealistic and impracticable.

Notes

1 Cressey, 1952, page 139 et seq.
2 Glasgow Bonding Company was floated in 1925 to establish a large bonded warehouse in Glasgow to take advantage of the demand for bonded accommodation in which to store maturing whisky. Demand had been augmented by the Immature Spirits Act 1915 which required immature whisky to be held in bonded warehouses for at least three years before being released from home consumption. The company had not proved as successful as hoped (Application for listing file, LSX archive, Guildhall Library).
3 Barker and Robbins, 1974, page 229; *Star*, 26 March 1928; *Motor Transport*, 2 April 1928; *Omnibus Magazine*, January 1930.
4 Reader, 1979, page 150.
5 This description of Hatry's exchanges with the town clerk of Wakefield is based on a memorandum prepared by Mr Allibone for use by the prosecuting team at Hatry's trial, and the transcript of the evidence given by Mr Allibone at the trial (TNA file DPP 1/91).
6 *The Times*, 13 March 1930, page 5.
7 McFerrin, 1969, page 14; Eichengreen, 2015, pages 124–129.
8 Memoranda dealing with the alleged irregularities (TNA file DPP 1/91).
9 The bank understood that Iron Industries had acquired a substantial holding of the shares of Allied Ironfounders Limited (memorandum dated 27 February 1929 to the board of directors, in support of the loan application, LBA file B1403/a/3). In practice, the shares were not formally acquired by Iron Industries. As for the related bank transfers, see letter dated 26 November 1929 from the DPP to the attorney general (TNA file DPP 1/91).
10 Reader, 1979, page 151.
11 M. Samuel & Company private office note dated 18 February 1929 (LBA file S/1/1/b/74). The directors of M. Samuel & Company recorded each of their meetings concerning transactions in which the bank was involved in 'private office notes' which appear then to have been circulated to all directors so that they shared knowledge of the state negotiations had reached. These notes were then bound in files now held in the LBA.
12 M. Samuel & Company private office note dated 8 April 1929 (LBA file S/1/1/b/75).
13 M. Samuel & Company private office note dated 17 April 1929 (LBA file S/1/1/b/75).
14 *The Economist*, 20 April 1929, page 862.
15 Connolly papers (NLA).
16 Boyle, 1967, page 211.
17 Montagu Norman's diary (Bank of England archive).

18 Letters from Montagu Norman to various bankers dated 1 June 1929 (Bank of England archive, file ADM 33/18).
19 Thomas and Morgan-Witts, 1979, page 181.
20 Thomas and Morgan-Witts, 1979, page 183.
21 As described by Arnold Bennett in a letter (cited in Woodhead, 2012, page 226).
22 Thomas and Morgan-Witts, 1979, pages 181–182.
23 Thomas and Morgan-Witts, 1979, pages 184–185.
24 Beddington-Behrens, 1963, page 141. Beddington-Behrens joined Myers & Company, a stockbroking firm specialising in new issues in 1929. He eventually established his own issuing house, Ocean Trust, in 1938. Ironically, on Hatry's death in 1965, Beddington-Behrens and Sir Henry d'Avigdor-Goldsmid, a bullion broker, were to criticise Hatry by suggesting that his actions to safeguard the steel scheme undermined the City's reputation for honouring promises (*Sunday Times*, 3 October 1965, page 31; 17 October 1965, page 29).
25 Entry for 18 June 1929, Montagu Norman's diary (Bank of England archive).
26 Thomas and Morgan-Witts, 1979, pages 201–202.
27 Trial transcript, day 5 (TNA file DPP 1/91, pages 38–39).
28 Greenfield, 1995, page 48.
29 Greenfield, 1995, page 48.
30 Trial transcript, day 5 (TNA file DPP 1/91, pages 44–45).
31 Trial transcript, day 5 (TNA file, DPP 1/91, page 49).
32 Meredith, 1931, page 309.
33 M. Samuel private office note, dated 21 June 1929 (LBA file S/1/1/b/76).
34 In evidence given at his trial in Milan, Gialdini claimed that 'never was any mention made in his presence of the criminal operations of Hatry and his accomplices' (*The Times*, 6 June 1931, page 11).
35 It was the normal practice for C&GS to be responsible for printing and controlling the blank documents without oversight from the authorities concerned (letter dated 1 October 1929 from the town clerk of Swindon to the DPP, TNA, file DPP 1/91).
36 Lloyds Bank internal reports on securities handling practices in the light of the Hatry collapse. There is a parallel between the fraudulent scheme adopted by the Pinners Hall team and the 'Salad Oil Swindle' in the USA in the 1960s. In that fraud, money was borrowed against salad oil that did not exist, ultimately against fake warehouse receipts for the oil. The banks which lent money failed to uncover the fraud because of poor checking of oil tanks and documents (Davies, 2018, pages 51–63; Miller, 1965).
37 Michie, 1987, page 89.
38 Michie, 1999, page 262.
39 Thomas and Morgan-Witts, 1979, pages 201–203; trial transcript, day 5, pages 34–36 (TNA file DPP 1/91).

References

Primary works: unpublished documents

Bank of England: Montagu Norman's diary.
Bank of England: Steel scheme papers.
Guildhall Library: LSX archive.
Lloyds Bank Archive: Lloyds Bank papers.
Lloyds Bank Archive: M Samuel & Company papers.
National Library of Australia: Connolly papers.
TNA: DPP papers

Primary works: newspapers and periodicals

Motor Transport.
Omnibus Magazine.
Star.
Sunday Times.
The Economist.
The Times.

Primary works: contemporary books and papers

Meredith, H. (1931), *The Drama of Money Making: Tragedy and Comedy of the London Stock Exchange.* (Sampson Low, London).

Secondary works

Barker, T.C. and Robbins, M. (1974), *A History of London Transport: Volume Two: The Twentieth Century to 1970.* (George Allen & Unwin. London).
Beddington-Behrens, E. (1963), *Look Back, Look Forward.* (Macmillan, London).
Boyle, A. (1967), *Montagu Norman: A Biography.* (Cassell, London).
Cressey, D.R. (1952), *Other People's Money.* (The Free Press, Glencoe).
Davies, D. (2018), *Lying for Money: How Legendary Frauds Reveal the Workings of Our World.* (Profile Books, London).
Eichengreen, B. (2015), *Hall of Mirrors: The Great Depression, the Great Recession, and the Uses – And Misuses – Of History.* (Oxford University Press, New York).
Greenfield, G. (1995), *A Smattering of Monsters: A Kind of Memoir.* (Little Brown, London).
McFerrin, J.B. (1969), *Caldwell and Company: A Southern Financial Empire.* (University of North Carolina Press, Nashville).
Michie, R.C. (1987), *The London and New York Stock Exchanges 1850–1914.* (Allen & Unwin, London).
Michie, R.C. (1999), *The London Stock Exchange: A History.* (Oxford University Press, Oxford).
Miller, N.C. (1965), *The Great Salad Oil Swindle.* (Coward McCann, New York).
Reader, W.J. (1979), *A House in the City: A Study of the City and the Stock Exchange Based on the Records of Foster & Braithwaite, 1825–1975.* (Batsford, London).
Thomas, G. and Morgan-Witts, M. (1979), *The Day the Bubble Burst: A Social History of the Wall Street Crash of 1929.* (Doubleday & Company, New York).
Woodhead, L., (2012), *Shopping, Seduction and Mr. Selfridge*, revised edition. (Profile Books, London).

11 The spinning plates crash

For many, Monday 24 June 1929 was important because it brought the opening of the Championships at Wimbledon. There was disappointment that the 1928 men's singles champion, Réné Lacoste, had decided not to defend his title, but excitement at the return of three former champions, not least Bill Tilden who had last won in 1921. In 1928, after he had lost to Lacoste in a gripping semi-final, it had been feared that he would never return. In the event, Centre Court was not full to see these former champions play, perhaps because members had heeded *The Times*' warning that they would not be hard pressed.[1]

After their agreement was reached a day earlier, Hatry and his associates had no time for tennis; they had meetings to arrange and preparations to make.

While Tabor was left to check that there were adequate stocks of blank loan receipts and to arrange for the printing of additional forms if needed, two key meetings took place with M. Samuel & Company and Lloyds Bank. It is a measure of Hatry's team's assessment of the relative difficulty of these two meetings that Hatry chose to meet M. Samuel & Company himself, while leaving Daniels to deal with Lloyds Bank.

Hatry's objective in meeting M. Samuel & Company was to confirm that the steel scheme was going ahead and to make sure that the bank's reduced participation in the scheme's financing was secure. Although Hatry had persuaded Bearsted to moderate his decision to withdraw from the scheme completely after the general election, the lack of enthusiasm was palpable and Hatry must have feared that even the smaller loan of £1 million might be withdrawn on any pretext.

The tone of the meeting was not encouraging – the bank's directors were not prepared to accept Hatry's assurances at face value. Where documentary evidence should have been available, they insisted on seeing it. In particular, they insisted on seeing the names of underwriters for the proposed steel company's share offer. The bank's loan offer was conditional upon the new share issue being underwritten. In other words, Hatry had to demonstrate that people with appropriate resources had guaranteed that they would buy the new holding company's shares if they were not bought by members of the public when offered for sale. From the bank's point of view, these guarantees served as a confirmation that the money raised by the sale of the new shares would be sufficient to repay the syndicate's loans, even if the offer failed to attract support from the public. Of course, for this confirmation to be worthwhile, it was important that the underwriters should be independent of Hatry and his companies. Otherwise, if the confirmations were merely provided by Hatry, they offered no more reassurance than a debtor's promise to pay – which M. Samuel & Company already had.[2]

Hatry would have had a better chance of satisfying the bank's directors if he had foreseen their insistence on written evidence that their conditions had been satisfied and had gone to the meeting armed with the necessary documents. Instead he promised to return a day later with a list of underwriters. On Tuesday 25 June, to the consternation of M. Samuel & Company's directors, Hatry's list of underwriters showed that the underwriting for a large proportion of the shares had been allocated to his own companies. In other words, the underwriters were not independent of Hatry and his companies. In the bank's increasingly sceptical eyes, he had failed to demonstrate enough independent support. He had not met the bank's condition. So perturbed were the bank's directors that they proceeded to check Hatry's list by, for example, seeking independent verification of Benenson's signature.[3]

By this stage, Hatry must have expected a negative reaction. When the bank's directors expressed their unease, he protested that his need for the loan was now urgent, implying that if the bank refused him the agreed loan, failure of the steel scheme would be their responsibility. Yet again, the bank refused to accept Hatry's protestations at face value and sought confirmation from National Provincial Bank that the need was as urgent as he had suggested. National Provincial Bank reported that the need was indeed urgent – shareholders were sending telegrams asking when they could expect to receive payment for the shares they had agreed to sell.

A few days later, on 4 July, Hatry provided a revised list of underwriters, pleading again that the money was needed urgently.[4] Eventually, M. Samuel & Company were persuaded that unless cash could be raised urgently, the deal would fall through, and agreed to release the cash in stages as the latest information from Hatry was digested.

M. Samuel & Company were not content to leave matters there; they required Hatry to return on a regular basis to report on the progress of the scheme. By this stage payment had been made for about two-thirds of the United Steel shares and the scheme appeared to be advancing satisfactorily.

Hatry then destroyed any chance that the bank might rely on his assurances. He asked that the smaller loan of £500,000 which was due for repayment on 9 July might be extended for three or four months. The bank was scandalised; what they had feared was coming to pass. It had been a clear condition of the additional steel scheme loan of £1 million that the smaller loan should be repaid on the due date, and Hatry had assured the bank that this would be done. In the bank's eyes, Hatry's request for an extension suggested that he was no longer in control of the situation and that his financial condition was parlous. The bank's directors replied that they needed time to consider this request and they would discuss its implications with Lord Bearsted.[5]

Hatry returned a day later on 5 July to learn the bank's considered response. On this occasion, the meeting was joined by Lord Bearsted, the bank's chairman, who, in the strongest terms, expressed his regret that Hatry had found it necessary to ask for the loan to be renewed. In the end, an extension of one month only was agreed, until 9 August. The bank's note of the meeting concluded: 'It was clearly understood that under no circumstances would this loan be further renewed'.[6]

On 25 July, three weeks later, Hatry returned to see Lord Bearsted and reported that he was 'short of the last £150,000' and asked whether the bank would make a further advance. Hatry must have known that this would seem a desperate request in view of the bank's earlier repeated refusals. Yet again he was refused but on this occasion with a suggestion that he might try the bank's stockbroker, Bourke Schiff, in the hope that a South African house might help. Bourke Schiff could not help, but Hatry managed to borrow £100,000 from one of his co-directors, the Marquess of Winchester. On 26 July, M. Samuel & Company agreed to advance £50,000.

Fatefully, Hatry returned to the bank just over a week later on 8 August and admitted that the £500,000 loan could not be repaid on 9 August. As explanation, he claimed that completion of a sale of his holding of Associated Automatic Machine Corporation Limited (AAMC) shares to an American company had been delayed. As the bank had lost its faith in Hatry's uncorroborated assurances, it was not prepared to accept at face value his story about a delayed share sale and demanded evidence of the sale. If the share sale had been documented but delayed, Hatry ought to have been able to produce the contract notes which could then be used as collateral for the loan. When the bank asked to see the documents, Hatry had nothing to show that this sale had been finally agreed. He would have been better advised not to mention the sale of AAMC shares. Reference to conclusion of a deal that he could not corroborate finally convinced the bank that he had become reckless and that it could no longer place any reliance on what he said.

The consequence for Hatry was severe. The bank refused to agree an extension of the £500,000 loan and told Hatry that the position would be discussed with Parent Trust & Finance which, at the bank's insistence, had guaranteed the loan. Hatry tried to turn aside this demand but the bank insisted. This was tantamount to Parent Trust & Finance being warned by M. Samuel & Company that the bank was relying on Parent Trust's guarantee for the recovery of the outstanding loan.[7]

In response to an urgent request from Lord Bearsted, John Guy, managing director of Parent Trust, attended a meeting at M. Samuel & Company's office a day later on 9 August – the date on which repayment of the loan was due – and then again on 10 August. Guy told the bank's directors 'that he was more worried about the present position than he ever had been before in his business life'. Not that he was worried about Hatry's solvency or the value of his collateral, rather Guy was concerned about liquidity and the due dates of liabilities which he was certain Hatry could not meet.

Before the steel scheme had been conceived, although Hatry's schemes had been regarded as adventurous, M. Samuel & Company had not seriously doubted his ability to bring them a successful conclusion or the credibility of his financial planning. By the end of the meeting Guy had confirmed what the bank had already sensed. He estimated that a year earlier Hatry's capital had been between £1,500,000 and £2,000,000 but that most of that capital had been taken up by Photomaton. He regarded Hatry's steel interests as potentially valuable but thought that they should be taken out of his hands as he was out of his depth. Hatry's cash crisis was serious.[8]

Guy's conclusions were powerful. They were consistent with the bank's own experience of Hatry's increasing recklessness – making promises that in the event he could not keep and making statements that on enquiry could not be substantiated. Finally, M. Samuel & Company must have been conscious that just as its scepticism about Hatry had been growing, more generally the City had become nervous of the similarities between Hatry's group and the Horne group.

M. Samuel & Company concluded that the £500,000 loan should not be extended. With effect from 9 August, Hatry remained in default and to reduce its exposure M. Samuel & Company began quietly to reduce the outstanding loans by selling the shares in Photomaton which had been deposited as security for Hatry's loans.

From that date, the bank declined to advance any more money, constantly demanded repayment of all outstanding loans and, when they could, continued to sell the shares which had been deposited as collateral. It was also made clear to Sir Arthur du Cros, the chairman of Parent Trust, that the bank was relying on the trust's guarantee of the loan to Hatry and it was looking to the trust to demonstrate that it had appropriate security to back the guarantee.[9]

These increasingly difficult exchanges between Hatry's group[10] and M. Samuel & Company were paralleled by exchanges with Lloyds Bank, Austin Friars Trust's principal clearing bank, and with its other supporters.

For Lloyds Bank, in common with most clearing bankers, Hatry's activities had offered attractive business. As the stock market had recovered from its depression in 1920–1921, Hatry had repeatedly applied for loans to finance new flotations. Not only had these flotations proved profitable for Hatry, but they had been profitable for the banks which supported him. When a loan was needed so that he could buy the shares of a company which was to be floated, the loan would only be required for a limited period and was repaid promptly from the proceeds of the flotation. It is not therefore surprising that the major clearing banks competed for his business. In accordance with the bank's normal procedures, when Hatry needed another significant loan from Lloyds Bank, James Gray, the manager of its Threadneedle Street branch, was required to obtain the approval of the bank's general managers and its board. During 1929, each of the memoranda which James Gray submitted for this purpose ended with the observation that the connection with Hatry was valuable to the bank and that Westminster Bank was attempting to take over the relationship.[11]

James Gray's diary shows frequent meetings with Hatry or one of his colleagues as they either sought new loans or changes in the investments deposited as security for existing loans.[12]

By the middle of June, Gray had begun to ask Hatry and his colleagues to explain how they would reduce their overdraft to comply with the agreed limit. He believed that at a meeting on 6 June he had been promised that by 25 June the balance on Corporation & General Securities' (C&GS) current account would be lower than the agreed limit. On 21 June, when the promised reduction had not yet been made, Gray refused to sanction a new loan to Porchester Trust, another company associated with Hatry. By 23 June, the date of Hatry's fateful meeting with his management team, the reduction of C&GS's balance which Hatry had promised would happen by 25 June had still not been made. On 24 June, Gray's day began with a meeting with Daniels to discuss the position at the same moment as Hatry was meeting the directors of M. Samuel & Company.

Although Hatry and Daniels might have expected that the Lloyds Bank meeting would be easier to manage, it proved more difficult than Daniels could handle. Gray asked how the Hatry group's overdraft was to be reduced as had been promised, but Daniels was yet again unable to explain how a reduction would be achieved or indeed confirm that a reduction would be achieved. Since Gray's question cannot have been a surprise, this suggests that Daniels had misread the position he faced. Failing to answer on previous occasions had not led to any serious consequences, so Daniels may have assumed that the meeting on 24 June would be no different. He was wrong. By failing yet again to answer requests for a reduction in the group's balances and by talking about rearranging the securities deposited as security, Daniels caused Gray to lose his patience and to face the risks that both the bank corporately and he personally were running.

Gray reported to the bank's chief general manager. The bank was no longer prepared to listen to Daniels, who had become discredited, so called Hatry to a meeting on 26 June with Gray and two of the bank's general managers. This was followed a day later by a meeting with the chairman of Lloyds Bank, J.W. Beaumont Pease, who had been regarded as one of Hatry's supporters.

For Hatry, the implication of these meetings was that management of his accounts had become a serious risk for the bank. In ordinary times, management of the relationship with a customer in good standing would be left in the hands of the branch manager. That Hatry's relationship was no longer to be left in the hands of the branch manager should have been a sign to him that he was no longer regarded as being in good standing. Although the general managers and the chairman were known to Hatry, they would not normally have been involved directly in meetings with him to manage his account. From time to time, his branch manager might require the approval of senior managers for actions he proposed to take but those approvals would be arranged privately out of the customer's sight. From 27 June, any requests for new loans, or extensions of old loans, required the approval of a general manager, not the branch manager, and had to be backed by valuable securities, excluding commercial securities which Hatry had floated himself (or 'shop' securities as Lloyds Bank referred to them). Compliance with these conditions and existing loan agreements was to be monitored by Gray at weekly meetings arranged with Edmund Daniels.

It was not an accident that Lloyds Bank changed its attitude towards Hatry's group at the same time as M. Samuel & Company was hardening its heart. M. Samuel & Company was also a customer of Lloyds Bank's Threadneedle Street branch, and its representatives met Gray frequently. They would have understood each other's attitude towards Hatry and his balances. Importantly, Lloyds Bank would have known when M. Samuel & Company began quietly selling the shares Hatry had deposited as security for his loans.

Similarly, James Gray maintained a relationship with Charles Lidbury, a general manager of Westminster Bank, another of Hatry's bankers, which often acted as a receiving agent for issues such as the Melbourne Board of Works issue in April 1929. Although initially the banks were not acting in concert, they were aware of each other's assessment of Hatry's financial position and reacted to him in that knowledge.[13]

It is difficult to believe that Hatry was not aware that he had lost the confidence of his bankers. The signs were clear to see. Yet, in practice, he continued to apply for new loans which he proposed to back with shares in companies he had floated. As Lloyds Bank had set its face against accepting these shares as good security, none of these applications succeeded. When eventually he realised that direct approaches would not work, Hatry arranged for applications to be made by friendly stockbrokers acting as surrogates. These approaches were also unsuccessful. Lloyds Bank had had its fill of Hatry's flotations. What Hatry was unable to do was to reduce his overdraft balances as required by the bank. Edmund Daniels was asked about this repeatedly at his weekly meetings with Gray, but between June and the end of August he was unable to point to any reductions or to make any proposals.

This process must have been profoundly worrying for Gray. He had been successful in his career, becoming manager of one of the bank's largest branches which handled the largest proportion of the bank's stock exchange-related business. Until the end of 1928, the relationship with Hatry had been one of the jewels in his branch's client portfolio, repeatedly producing opportunities for profitable loans. Within a few months, the relationship had become a nightmare, with a risk of losses that had concentrated the minds of the bank's general managers and its chairman.

Gray may have been conscious of a more sinister risk. S.J. Langton & Passmore, solicitors acting for Peterborough Trust in litigation with Lloyds Bank, were later to suggest that Gray knew or at least suspected that some of the documents tendered as security for the bank's loans were fraudulent.[14] There are, however, no contemporary documents which suggest that this was the case and there is no record that anyone thought this possibility merited investigation. The internal reports of the bank's inspectors only refer to poor clerical work rather than conspiracy.[15]

But another problem had arisen for Hatry's group: even with the benefit of the fraudulent scheme on which they had embarked at the end of June, they were unable to raise enough money. The gap was growing larger. In the aftermath of the problems of the Horne Group reported at the beginning of August, and with M. Samuel & Company's decision to sell the Photomaton shares it held as security, the market price of Photomaton shares began to fall, further exposing loans against which Hatry had deposited Photomaton shares as security. To deal with the further cash deficit this created, the collaborators attempted a second version of the fraudulent receipts trick which on this occasion took advantage of a short-cut procedure used by company registrars.

When an investor bought a company's shares from another investor, the purchaser would prepare a share transfer form which would then be sent to the vendor for completion. When the vendor had completed the form, it would be sent to the company's registrar with the vendor's share certificate so that the new shareholder's interest could be recorded in the register of shareholders and a new share certificate issued. When received by the registrar, the information would be noted and the share transfer form would be endorsed by the registrar to certify that a share certificate had been received and that a new one would be issued in due course, a process that might take some weeks. In the meantime, the certified share transfer form would be accepted by banks and others as the investor's document of title. Endorsement was a simple matter, usually involving no more than the impression of a rubber stamp and a hastily scribbled signature.[16]

It was Hatry's normal practice to recommend that one of his companies, Secretarial Services Limited, should act as the company secretary for any company he floated, so that his staff were well used to the procedure for certifying transfers and had the necessary rubber stamps. Blank share transfer forms were available at the shop of any commercial stationer in London, so the collaborators set about creating fraudulent certified share transfer forms as well as fraudulent loan stock receipts.

They knew that the deadline for redemption of the Wakefield receipts was drawing near,[17] that they were short of cash and were beset by demands for meetings from creditors and bankers.

When Wakefield Borough Council had raised money by an issue of stock in January 1929, most of the money had been left to earn interest in the hands of C&GS until the end of August 1929 when it would be required to redeem a retiring loan stock. It was agreed that there should be a meeting in August to agree precisely when the remaining cash should be paid to Wakefield.[18]

As planned, a meeting took place on 14 August and it was settled that £200,000 should be paid to Wakefield early in September and that the balance due of £124,000 would be invested by C&GS for a further six months. Any interest due to Wakefield was to be paid on 30 September.

On 1 September, Wakefield was obliged to make a large payment to redeem the old loan stock but had not received any further cash from C&GS. Concerned by this, the town clerk, Mr Allibone, wrote to C&GS on 3 September asking when the expected transfer of £200,000 could be expected. The reply was not encouraging. Mr Allibone was fobbed off. A junior member of C&GS's staff replied to the effect that the person responsible, the company secretary, John Dixon, was away from the office but on his return would be asked to reply indicating when the transfer would be made.

Understandably, this did not settle Mr Allibone's nerves for he still had no idea when C&GS's cash would be received. So he resolved to approach C&GS more directly and immediately. As he was in London on other business, he called at C&GS's offices on 6 September and saw Edmund Daniels. At this time of asking, Mr Allibone was told that arrangements had been made to remit £150,000 on 15 September and £50,000 on 17 September. Daniels apologised for the inconvenience but suggested that C&GS had not appreciated that the authority would require the money at the beginning of the month. He also promised that the dates of the planned remittances would be confirmed in writing by John Dixon on his return to the office. By 18 September, the expected cash had still not been received in Wakefield.

On 19 September, Mr Allibone was again in London on other business and again took the opportunity to visit C&GS's offices. When he called in the morning, he asked in turn for the people he had met before. He was told first that Edmund Daniels was at a meeting in the West End. He then asked for John Dixon and was told that he too was at the meeting in the West End. Finally he asked for Mr Bland, the assistant secretary, only to be told that he too was at the meeting in the West End. Mr Allibone was left with little choice but to leave without any answers to his questions. He did not give up, however. He returned that afternoon but was again told that the whole of the senior staff was still at the meeting in the West End. For a second time, Mr Allibone was obliged to leave without any answers. Later that afternoon, he called again at C&GS's offices for a third time with no better result. On this occasion, Mr Allibone returned to King's Cross and caught a train back to Wakefield where be briefed the council's Finance Committee on the situation which he found very disconcerting. Mr Allibone was only one of the creditors badgering Hatry's team.

In parallel, there were endless meetings between the Pinners Hall team and bankers wanting to know when loans would be repaid. When the promises had been given but could not be honoured, the team were faced with demands to explain their failure when they can have had no conviction that the banks would be anything but sceptical about their latest exculpations.

They were also hindered by the return of an old problem: Montagu Norman began again to lobby against Hatry to make sure that no banks gave way to his ever more urgent requests for money.

Ever since their first contact before 1914, Hatry, the inveterate networker, had not lost sight of Richard Norton who had borrowed money with Hatry's assistance. At the end of the war, his future father-in-law, Sir David Kinloch, refused to approve his daughter's engagement until Norton had paid off his debts, which he achieved but only by agreeing to give up his rights to an inheritance in return for his father clearing the slate. Thereafter, Norton had been obliged to earn a living, which he had done by becoming an investment banker with Kuhn Loeb.

The name of Kuhn Loeb appears among the members of Hatry's steel syndicate created in the early summer of 1929, although the participation was limited to 2,000 shares out of the syndicate's total participation of 1,813,980 shares. Kuhn Loeb had not been prepared to go beyond this and did not lend money to Hatry or his companies.

By chance, in September 1929 Norton was temporarily in charge of the London office as his partners were all abroad. One morning, early in the month, he took an unexpected phone call from Montagu Norman, the governor of the Bank of England, who merely said: 'Come and see me'. Presuming that the governor meant that he should go at once, Norton did not dare delay and went to the bank in some hurry. On arrival, he was shown into the governor's office and asked whether Kuhn Loeb had taken any part in private underwriting of a steel syndicate. When he confirmed that Kuhn Loeb was involved but only for a small amount, the governor replied: 'A nod is as good as a wink'. Montagu Norman had then rung a bell and Norton was shown out.

Norton recalled that he 'could not make out what on earth he meant' but assumed that whatever the governor's message might have been it must have been important. So he telephoned the other London partners, Gordon Leith, who was at that moment in Vienna, and Otto Kahn, who was in New York.[19] Gordon Leith understood the governor's message very well. In May, he had met Hatry at the offices of M. Samuel & Company and had been invited to lend a substantial amount of money to support Hatry's steel project. After this meeting he had visited the governor of the Bank of England to ask for advice on the scheme. Montagu Norman had answered with a vague and non-committal response. Norman's diary records that Leith had left saying: 'A nod is as good as a wink'.[20] In September 1929, Norman intended to ensure that his discouragement was remembered and that any further requests from Hatry for further loans were turned down. In any event, Kuhn Loeb followed the advice and resisted Hatry's requests for further assistance. They were not alone. Other City houses also declined Hatry's requests.

As the bankers' hearts hardened, and Lloyds Bank drew near to refusing to honour the group's cheques, Hatry and his colleagues turned to two final throws of the dice.

In an attempt to stem the fall in the market price of shares with which the group's reputation was associated, Hatry gave way to the temptation that afflicts many company promoters whose issues disappoint[21] – he mounted a price support operation. Various trust companies associated with Hatry's group of companies placed sell orders with London brokers for shares and stocks which Hatry had floated and separately placed buy orders for the same stocks and shares with country brokers. The aim was that reports of these transactions would create an impression that there was some demand for the shares which would in turn support their market price. In this, the operation failed, mainly because the team's second throw of the dice ended by bringing about a wave of selling.

Although the team had decided that they did not have the time to travel to New York to appeal to their contacts there,[22] they decided that there was time to travel to Paris. Daniels and Gialdini joined Hatry in travelling to Paris in the hope of persuading their contacts to lend the money that was still needed. The journey was uneventful save for Gialdini's behaviour. When the trip had first been mooted, Gialdini had suggested that after the visit to Paris, he and his wife would stay in Switzerland for a few days. Hatry readily agreed to this suggestion as he hoped that it would give Gialdini an opportunity to avoid a collapse by regaining his strength.

On setting out, both Hatry and Daniels had been surprised at the amount of luggage that Gialdini brought, which included an oddly bulging umbrella and a suitcase which he insisted on keeping with him in their compartment. When they saw him onto his train for Switzerland and wished him farewell, Daniels and Hatry wondered whether they might ever see him again. Their speculation was correct. Neither Hatry nor Daniels was to see Gialdini again. They were later to discover that Gialdini had prepared for the trip by realising his own assets and stealing a large amount from one of the group's companies. These were the contents of the case that he would not let out of his sight and the cause of the umbrella's weird bulges. He had also passed a message to his secretary asking her to destroy his papers in London. Gialdini found his way to Italy and stayed there. He knew that an 1873 treaty between Great Britain and Italy provided that alleged offenders should not be extradited but prosecuted in whichever country they were residing. He had escaped prosecution in England.[23]

Once he knew that the mission to Paris had failed, Hatry asked Daniels to reserve seats for the return journey to London. Sharing Hatry's depression, Daniels asked whether he should make second-class reservations. He was told to book a first-class compartment – there would be time enough later for compromising on their comfort.[24]

Not only had the visit failed to raise additional money, but it also had an unhelpful consequence. Throughout their struggle to find money, the team had feared that rumours of financial embarrassment would make their task impossible, so they had impressed on everyone the need for discretion and had largely succeeded in avoiding leaks and rumours. News of their visit and its failure leaked in Paris and brought about a wave of selling of Photomaton shares among French investors.

On their return to London, Hatry and Daniels were assailed not just by news of the selling of Photomaton shares, but also by evidence that the group's creditors were becoming desperately concerned about payment.

Two days after their return to London, they were again due to meet the general managers of Lloyds Bank to report on progress. They cannot have been surprised to be told that, with Westminster Bank, Lloyds Bank had decided to commission an investigation by Sir Gilbert Garnsey, a partner of Price, Waterhouse & Company and one of the most eminent Chartered Accountants of his day. He was known to Hatry and was familiar with the terms of the steel scheme as he had been appointed one of the trustees of the steel syndicate.

On returning to his office in Pinners Hall, Hatry reacted to this news by contacting Sir Gilbert's office to request an urgent meeting, which was arranged to take place at 3 Frederick's Place, the offices of Price, Waterhouse & Company, at 10 a.m. the next day, Thursday 19 September. Hatry had decided that he had no choice but to make a full disclosure. He explained that he believed the group was insolvent and that its liabilities probably exceeded its assets by £15 million, perhaps by as much as £20 million. It was plainly impossible to meet any remaining commitments to the shareholders of United Steel, and the team had only been able to meet commitments during the past few weeks by means of creating loan receipts fraudulently for about £900,000. As he was later to do at trial, Hatry took full responsibility for the fraud, suggesting that his colleagues had only gone through with the plot out of their personal loyalty to him.

Garnsey was appalled by these revelations of which there had been no warning and needed some persuasion that they should be taken seriously. If Hatry were to be believed, the amounts involved were shocking and if they fell to be borne by any one of the clearing banks standing alone would have threatened its stability. He told Hatry that before deciding what should be done, he would speak immediately to his instructing banks, Lloyds and Westminster, and seek their advice – not least because of the public reaction that might follow if fraud on such a scale were to be made public. Hatry and his colleagues were to return to Frederick's Place in the afternoon to find out what had been decided.

In the meantime, Hatry and his colleagues John Dixon and Edmund Daniels took lunch with Stanley Passmore, the company lawyer who had acted for Hatry in most of his flotations. By this stage, it was evident that Hatry would need legal advice on how to deal with the inevitable prosecution – a service outside Passmore's experience. Passmore may have been over-eager in declining to act as his standing back was later resented by both Hatry and Daniels. In his place, Passmore suggested that Hatry should contact Wontners, one of whose partners was a member of Passmore's masonic lodge. After lunch, Hatry, Daniels and Dixon returned to Frederick's Place to be told by Sir Gilbert that he had spoken to his two instructing banks and to Montagu Norman at the Bank of England, and that Hatry should make a full confession to Sir Archibald Bodkin, the director of public prosecutions, who would be expecting his call. Although the banks and the governor had made other arrangements to moderate the reactions of the stock exchange and others, these were not discussed with Hatry and his colleagues.[25]

At the end of the afternoon, Hatry returned to Great Stanhope Street where he told his wife that everything looked bleak. Fearing the disaster that might be unfolding, she asked whether it was like Gerard Lee Bevan's problems seven years earlier when he was arrested. Hatry nodded before going to pack a suitcase. He spent the night at the Cecil Hotel in the Strand.[26]

At 9 a.m. the next morning, Hatry and his colleagues presented themselves with Mr Knights, a partner in Wontners, at Sir Archibald's office in Richmond Terrace. On being escorted into Sir Archibald's room, they were not invited to sit but left standing in front of his desk. On being asked why they had come, Mr Knights suggested that they wanted to make a statement. Sir Archibald then asked whether this was their own decision and stressed that they must expect no privilege in return. Hatry then acted as spokesman and repeated what he had said to Sir Gilbert Garnsey on the previous day, explaining that there had been irregularities. At that point Sir Archibald pressed a buzzer on his desk and two detectives entered the room: Inspector George Stubbings and Inspector Ward from the fraud team of the City Police which took responsibility for investigating most City frauds. Sir Archibald told him that Hatry and his colleagues wished to make a statement. Hatry then repeated his story again at the end of which the policeman was told by Sir Archibald to take them away.

Outside the door to Sir Archibald's room, Inspector Stubbings thawed a little, suggesting that Hatry and his colleagues should repair to the Charing Cross Hotel to allow him to prepare a warrant for their arrest and to draft a statement. When Hatry pointed out that it was almost time for lunch, the policeman told him that he could by all means take lunch.

Then, as they were about to part, the policeman made a surprising suggestion. He told Hatry that until an arrest warrant had been issued, the police could not stop Hatry boarding a train and disappearing. While it may seem improbable that such a suggestion might come from the police, not least from the senior officer in the fraud squad, the same officer was to be dismissed from the service eight years later for colluding with fraudsters evading the law.[27]

Hatry declined, ate a good lunch at the Charing Cross Hotel, and went to Wontners' offices where, with Daniels, Tabor and Dixon, he was later arrested by Inspector Stubbings, taken to Moor Lane police station and charged with using false pretences to obtain £209,141 with intent to defraud. Hatry's only reaction to being charged was that there had been no intent to defraud. The four associates were then held in custody overnight in the cells of Moor Lane police station before appearing in the Justice Room, Guildhall, on the next morning before Alderman Sir George Truscott. After Inspector Stubbings had given evidence of the circumstance of the arrest, Mr Knights applied for bail, arguing that the case had only come to court at such an early stage because the accused men had confessed, eschewing the opportunity to escape from the jurisdiction, and it was most unlikely that they would take advantage of bail and the resources available to them to flee. Sir George was unmoved, saying that in view of the amount of money involved he was not prepared to grant bail. The four accused were remanded in custody and taken to Brixton prison.[28]

Hatry was never again to sleep in the house in Great Stanhope Street where his 40th birthday had been celebrated nine months earlier.

Clarence Hatry's experience was not unique. The collapse of Austin Friars Trust shared characteristics with every financial collapse. Anyone who has lived through or observed a similar crisis at close quarters will recognise the increasingly frenzied series of meetings as more and more unconventional avenues to salvation are explored, the search for ways to avoid embarrassing meetings with people who can be ignored, the increasing desperation of creditors as they realise they may not see the return of their money, the clusters of professional advisers seeking to fashion solutions for their clients' problems and the approach of the tipping point when the final disaster can no longer be deferred. The same pattern is reflected in Anthony Trollope's description of the last days of Augustus Melmotte in *The Way We Live Now*, down to his description of his clerk beginning to count the cost of loyalty to him as he resists a request to join Melmotte in forging signatures on a deed.[29]

Ironically, the steel scheme ultimately proved a success. Once it had been fully implemented, the finances of Steel Industries of Great Britain had been reconstructed as the directors desired. Although the broader rationalisation of which Hatry dreamed did not take place, the new company was able to trade profitably under the strategic management which in 1927 had conceived a plan to rescue United Steel.

Hatry's weakness was that in his vanity he too readily believed he would find a way out of any difficulty and could not accept that he was taking absurd risks.

The consequences of the risks taken by Hatry were most cruelly visited upon unsuspecting innocents. As Hatry and his colleagues were contemplating imminent prosecutions, Mr Allibone's world was falling apart. Having briefed his Finance Committee about his growing concerns during the previous evening, crude reality was brought into focus when the morning post brought a surprising number of requests for conversion of loan receipts into formal certificates. They were surprising because the number of receipts submitted exceeded the total value of the authorised loan. Surplus loan receipts could only be explained by a serious administrative failure or a fraud. As his heart sank, and he recalled how C&GS had been avoiding him, Mr Allibone had no choice but to return to London to find out what had been going on.

In 1929, even the fastest train took more than three hours to reach Kings Cross, so Mr Allibone and the assistant accountant of Wakefield who accompanied him had plenty of time to ponder newspaper reports and speculation about the parlous condition of Hatry's companies. On arrival, they went directly to Barclays Bank, who acted for the borough as London agent for the receipt of applications for loan certificates. There they were told for the first time that the stock exchange had suspended dealings in Wakefield's loan stock.

They then went to C&GS's offices in Pinners Hall. Yet again there were no directors who could meet them – only Sir Gilbert Garnsey's investigators from Price, Waterhouse & Company. It was from them that they learned that Wakefield was most unlikely to receive any of the expected money.

It took many decades for Wakefield's finances to recover from this debacle. It was necessary to issue another loan stock to find the money Wakefield needed desperately but it was still obliged to service the loan stock issued in January 1929 which had been the target of Hatry's fraud. A special rate was levied for many years to cover the cost of these duplicated issues. It was several decades before ratepayers could forget Hatry.

Mr Allibone had previously been regarded as a cautious, prudent man but his career and reputation did not recover.[30]

Mr Allibone and the Borough of Wakefield were not alone in suffering the effects of Hatry's collapse. Lloyds Bank, his principal bank, found that it was at the centre of rumours about the scale of the losses it was facing. There was even a suggestion that the losses might exceed the bank's issued share capital. To counter these rumours, the chief general manager wrote immediately to all Lloyds' correspondent banks worldwide, assuring them that good security had been taken for all of the loans to Hatry's companies and that as a result any losses would be limited.[31] To one of these letters, W.H. Taylor, a former vice president of American Trust in San Francisco, replied:

> American interest in this matter was undoubtedly heightened by reason of the fact of its occurrence coincident with the reaction on the Stock Exchange here and the rise in the £ sterling. In San Francisco large black boards ... exhibited the price of the chief counters which were altered + or – by men with receivers fixed to their ears and there were also shown brokers opinions in the form of typewritten expert advices from New York and this in all the chief hotels which were crowded by bankers from all over USA for this convention. There was great excitement ...
>
> There can be little doubt that yesterday's reaction is the aftermath of the Hatry failure catching the market in a top heavy condition of stalemate. It was gossiped on the floor of the House as due to British plungers. Most of the bankers have something to say about it and read with avidity all kinds of cuttings from the British Press bearing on it and in my opinion are more inquisitive than they would like to appear.[32]

With the wisdom of considered hindsight, Hatry's collapse is not seriously regarded as a prime cause of the Wall Street crash late in October 1929. But to contemporary observers in San Francisco, the failure had precipitated a collapse.

Notes

1 *The Times*, 24 and 25 June 1929.
2 M. Samuel private office note, 24 June 1929 (LBA file S/1/1/6/77).
3 M. Samuel private office note, 25 June 1929 (LBA file S/1/1/6/77).
4 M. Samuel private office note, 4 July 1929 (LBA file S/1/1/6/78).
5 M. Samuel private office note, 4 July 1929 (LBA file S/1/1/6/78).
6 M. Samuel private office note, 5 July 1929 (LBA file S/1/1/6/78).
7 M. Samuel private office note, 8 August 1929 (LBA file S/1/1/6/78).
8 M. Samuel private office note, 12 August 1929 (LBA file S/1/1/6/78).
9 This was done at a meeting with Sir Arthur on 15 August to which he had been urgently summoned from the south of France (M. Samuel private office note, 15 August 1929, LBA file S/1/1/6/78).
10 The record of the meeting with Sir Arthur du Cros on 15 August notes that he appeared to be 'somewhat angry' (M. Samuel private office note, 15 August 1929, LBA file S/1/1/6/78).
11 LBA file B 1403/a/3.
12 LBA file B 1403/a/8. The following paragraphs are largely based on the entries in Gray's diary.
13 Hatry and Daniels were probably unaware of this connection. In a conversation some years later, Daniels observed that: 'Lidbury of Westminsters and Gray were sort of competitors at that time for [Daniels'] favours, and that it was extremely unlikely that Gray would know of any of his dealings with Westminster Bank' (Prison Officer Rees's notes of a meeting on 7 June 1932, TNA file HO 144/21217).
14 Prison Officer Rees's notes of a meeting in prison on 7 June 1932 between the solicitors, Hatry and Daniels (TNA file HO 144/21217).
15 Letter dated 9 October 1929 to the chief inspector, head office (LBA file B 1403/1/13).
16 Internal report of the Lloyds Bank Special Committee on Market Securities, 1930 (LBA file B 1403/1/14).
17 There are suggestions that increasingly desperate attempts were necessary to delay matters. Hollow, 2015, page 59, citing Manley, 1976, page 56.
18 Memorandum prepared by Mr Allibone for the DPP (TNA file DPP 1/91, page 6). The following paragraphs are also based on the memorandum.
19 Wood and Wood, 1954, page 152.
20 Bank of England archive.
21 Eichengreen, 2015, page 113, citing three examples: (1) Bank of United States, the creation of Joseph Marcus, whose stock began falling in April 1929. Ultimately, the bank failed on 11 December 1929 (*New York Times*, 20 December 1930, page 1); (2) Banque Adam, the creation of Albert Oustric, whose shares also fell in the wake of the 1929 crash. Oustric was prosecuted on charges of fraud (Bonin, 1996); and (3) in 2008, when the shares of three Icelandic banks fell in the wake of a crisis the banks' owners responded by buying their own shares. Various directors were later prosecuted on fraud charges (Baldursson and Portes, 2013).
22 There had been negotiations over a sale of Hatry's interest in United Steel to a group which had obtained options to buy the share capital of two other steel

companies as a prelude to a wider reorganisation of the steel industry. That group understood that American finance was available to support such a proposal. This was confirmed by Sir Mark Webster Jenkinson, a director of Vickers, who indicated that J.P. Morgan would support such a scheme (memorandum dated 18 September 1929, Bank of England archive, file SMT 118/4).

23 The DPP later received evidence that Gialdini had for some time been preparing for flight. It was alleged that he had been accumulating French francs abroad 'by means of transactions in which his name would not appear' on 14 August, 3 September and 5 September (letter from Slaughter and May, solicitors acting for Crews and Company, stockbrokers, TNA file DPP 1/91). If this report was correct, it implies that at least one member of Hatry's team had concluded in mid-August 1929 that a collapse was probable, if not inevitable.

24 Thomas and Morgan-Witts, 1979, pages 289–290.

25 Thomas and Morgan-Witts, 1979, pages 291–292.

26 *Sunday Telegraph*, 8 August 1965, page 4.

27 Home secretary's answer to a parliamentary question (*The Times*, 26 February 1938, page 7).

28 Thomas and Morgan-Witts, 1979, pages 293–294.

29 Trollope, 1875, volume II, page 259.

30 The problems created in the 1920s for local authorities such as Wakefield when dealing with City markets with which they were not familiar were not unique. In 1988 it was found that, beguiled by the City, the London Borough of Hammersmith and Fulham was accounting for a half of 1% of the global market in derivatives (Campbell-Smith, 2008, page 192). Similar problems were to occur in the United States (Tickell, 1998, page 873).

31 Letters dated 25 September 1929 (LBA file HO/GM/Bea/25).

32 Letter dated 15 October 1929 (LBA file HO/GM/Bea/25).

References

Primary works: unpublished documents

Bank of England: Montagu Norman's diary.
Bank of England: Steel scheme papers.
Guildhall Library: LSX archive.
Lloyds Bank Archive: Lloyds Bank papers.
Lloyds Bank Archive: James Gray's diary.
Lloyds Bank Archive: M. Samuel & Company papers.
TNA: DPP papers.
TNA: Home Office papers.

Primary works: newspapers and periodicals

New York Times.
The Times.
Sunday Telegraph.

Primary works: contemporary books and papers

Trollope, A. (1875), *The Way We Live Now.* (Chapman, London).

Secondary works

Baldursson, F.M. and Portes, R. (2013), 'Gambling for Resurrection in Iceland: The Rise and Fall of the Banks'. CEPR Discussion Paper number 9664.

Bonin, H. (1996), 'Oustric, un financier prédateur (1914–1930)', *Revue historique*, volume 205, pages 429–448.

Campbell-Smith, D. (2008), *Follow the Money: The Audit Commission, Public Money and the Management of Public Services, 1983–2008*. (Allen Lane, London).

Eichengreen, B. (2015), *Hall of Mirrors: The Great Depression, the Great Recession, and the Uses – And Misuses – Of History*. (Oxford University Press, New York).

Hollow, M. (2015), *Rogue Banking: A History of Fraud in Interwar Britain*. (Palgrave MacMillan, Basingstoke).

Manley, P.S. (1976), 'Clarence Hatry', *Abacus*, volume 12(1), pages 49–60.

Thomas, G. and Morgan-Witts, M. (1979), *The Day the Bubble Burst: A Social History of the Wall Street Crash of 1929*. (Doubleday & Company, New York).

Tickell, A. (1998), 'Creative Finance and the Local State: The Hammersmith and Fulham Swaps Affair', *Political Geography*, volume 17(2), pages 865–881.

Wood, M. and Wood, A. (1954), *Silver Spoon: The Memoirs of Lord Grantly*. (Hutchinson, London).

12 The trial

As Hatry, Daniels, Tabor and Dixon sat in the Charing Cross Hotel eating their lunch, they reflected on Inspector Stubbings' suggestion that they had a chance to flee if they would only take it, following the examples of the fraudsters Jabez Balfour 35 years before and Gerard Lee Bevan seven years before. While flight might have seemed attractive to others who were not involved, to them it seemed desperate. After Gialdini had broken with his colleagues and decided to flee, they had made no plans so would have had to extemporise in choosing destinations and routes. Without ready-made plans, there would have been little time to organise their families. What was more, they reflected on the example of Gerard Lee Bevan.[1]

On 31 January 1922, a special manager had been appointed to City Equitable Fire Insurance, the reinsurance company that Bevan had bought from Hatry in 1915, and on 3 February the company applied to be wound up. Six days later, on 9 February, the partners of Ellis and Company, the stockbroking firm of which Bevan had been senior partner, issued a statement dissolving the partnership with Bevan. On the previous day, Wednesday 8 February, Bevan and his mistress Jeanne Petruisot had already left the country. At 8.30 a.m., leaving a tip for the doorman at the Carlton Hotel in Haymarket where for many years Bevan had retained a suite, they took a taxi to Croydon airport whence they departed by plane for Paris. Perhaps Bevan had noted the proud claim of Imperial Airways that its planes often flew when the steamers could not leave harbour. Their departure was not immediately noticed and was not acknowledged by the newspapers until, on 10 February, his wife Sophie told a reporter from *The Times* who had enquired about her husband's whereabouts that Gerard had been 'ordered abroad for an indefinite period'. When the departure was noticed, however, the newspapers questioned how it was that the chairman of a collapsed reinsurance company should have been able so easily to escape the law and its consequences.

Bevan only stayed in Paris for two days – long enough to secure an endorsement for his passport from the British passport office which enabled him to travel to Greece and Turkey, provided he could obtain the necessary visas. On 12 February, he took the overnight train to Marseilles where he obtained Greek and Italian visas and then headed east, entering Italy at Ventimiglia on

Tuesday 14 February. Bevan had left the British civil service to play catch up. An arrest warrant had still not been issued, but the British government requested other European countries not to issue new visas. By 22 February, Bevan was in Naples requesting a visa for Constantinople from the Spanish consul who was the local representative of the government of Turkey. In deference to the British government's request, the Spanish consul refused, telling Bevan that he must first obtain an appropriate passport stamp from the British consul general. When Bevan called at the British consulate his passport was confiscated but, in the absence of an arrest warrant, the consul could not detain him. When notification of an arrest warrant arrived at last on 25 April, Bevan had already left Naples, travelling with a second passport.

Neither the newspapers' special correspondents who had been sent to join the chase nor the police could discover where Bevan might have gone after leaving Naples, which led the Metropolitan Police to distribute a 'wanted' notice in several languages across the continent. Tiring of a fruitless chase, the newspapers diverted their attention to any members of Bevan's family whom they could find. The *Daily Express* tracked his wife Sophie to the Hotel Bristol in Paris, where her lawyers were attempting to recover assets said to have been hers that her husband had abstracted. Meanwhile, the *Daily Mail* had followed the same lead and published photographs of Bevan's wife and his mistress side by side, which encouraged disobliging comparisons of Mrs Bevan with Mlle Petruisot.

In March 1922, Bevan was in Austria using the name Léon Vernier which appeared on the passport he was now carrying. There are various stories about the way in which Bevan had obtained this passport. His own story was that it had come into his hands at Vicenza in northern Italy. As the police established that Léon Vernier was a real person, and the passport had been issued legitimately, it had presumably been stolen and then sold.

Bevan seems to have moved repeatedly between a number of Austrian towns, attracting the attention of the authorities in each before he decided to move on. He was finally arrested on Tuesday 13 June. When two detectives burst into his room, Bevan reached into a waistcoat pocket, took out a small bottle containing a white tablet and put it in his mouth. Assuming that this was a suicide pill, the detectives tried unsuccessfully to get the tablet out of his mouth. Bevan fought for several minutes with such ferocity that the two detectives had to call on reinforcements before he was dragged away to a first aid station where his stomach was pumped. In a fashion which recalls Conan Doyle's story, *The Man With the Twisted Lip*, for two days Bevan lay in the hospital attached to the criminal court where he steadfastly denied his identity. By the end of the two days, his beard had grown, showing at its roots that his hair's natural colour was lighter than the colour it had been dyed. Realising that the game was up, Bevan asked to be shaven, after which he resembled the photograph that had been circulated by the police in London.

It took some time for the formalities of extradition to take effect so that Bevan did not stand trial at the Old Bailey until the end of November. On

Tuesday 5 December 1922 he was found guilty and sentenced to seven years' imprisonment. In his sentencing remarks, the judge, Sir Horace Avory, commented: 'Your offence is further aggravated by your flight from this country, leaving your partners and your co-directors to bear the burden of the disgrace which you brought upon the firm and upon the company.[2]

For anyone contemplating flight, Bevan's experience was not propitious. Discovery would have been even more probable if the four colleagues had attempted flight together. Moreover, if Hatry had escaped on his own, he would have left his three colleagues to face the music, at risk of bearing the brunt of public dismay at Hatry's responsibility, and not simply their own. Bevan's escapade had also thrown insensitive and unwelcome attention upon his wife, Sophie, and their daughter, Christabel, who had drawn attention when she was at Southampton to witness her father's return. Moreover, all Bevan's subterfuges, using false passports and disguises, had failed. If flight had achieved anything, Mr Justice Avory's sentencing remarks suggested that it had lengthened Bevan's time in prison. Hatry may well have thought that he would be better advised to confess and assist the authorities as that might avoid aggravating the judge and lead to a shorter period of imprisonment.

This is what he did. Some have suggested that his confession was not as accurate or as helpful as it might have been and it is certainly the case that the overall numbers mentioned by Hatry somewhat exaggerated the group's deficiency of assets. It is, however, unlikely that any inaccuracies hindered Sir Gilbert's investigation as the trial took place in January 1930, barely three months after the group's collapse and materially faster than most other fraud prosecutions in the 1920s. Moreover, the speed of the confession may have had unfortunate consequences for Hatry personally.

On the afternoon of Friday 20 September, the police presented Hatry with a statement they prepared for him using their notes of his oral confession. This draft referred to the generation of forged documents and was eventually to become the foundation for a charge of forgery. Hatry signed the draft statement before it could be reviewed by his lawyers and so admitted that he was guilty of forgery. He later claimed that this was a mistake.[3] The surplus loan receipts that had been issued were false and fraudulent, but they were arguably not forged. Hatry's company, Corporation & General Securities Limited (C&GS), was authorised to issue such certificates and the correct forms were used. In this sense they were not forged, even if they were fraudulent. In view of Hatry's confession, there would have been little point in putting this technical argument to the jury, so there is no knowing what a jury would have made of it. Quite possibly if it were to be regarded as casuistical it would have hardened hearts against him rather than working in his favour. What is certain is that when he signed the confession, Hatry had not appreciated that the maximum sentence for forgery was 14 years, whereas the maximum sentence for fraud was only seven years.

When the trial began at the Old Bailey, the prosecution was led by the attorney general, Sir William Jowitt, indicating the government's view of the importance of the case. Before the 1929 general election, Jowitt had served as MP for Preston as a member of the Liberal Party. He had maintained a long-term friendship with Clement Attlee, whom he had first met at his preparatory school, and who was instrumental in Jowitt's appointment as attorney general when the new Labour government found that there were no Labour MPs with suitable qualifications. While this had avoided an embarrassment for the Labour government, for a while Jowitt was distrusted by back-bench Labour members.

All four defendants pleaded not guilty so that the prosecution was obliged to set out its full case, which took four days. At the beginning of the fifth day, after the prosecution case had been concluded and on the recommendation of their barristers, the defendants all changed their pleas to guilty.

At this stage, there was little to be done by the defendants' barristers other than to plead in mitigation of sentence, led by Hatry's barrister, Norman Birkett KC, later an appeal court judge and a judge at the Nuremberg war trials. To avoid any suggestion that Hatry belittled the crimes to which he had pleaded guilty, Birkett commenced his plea by admitting that:

> Mr Hatry realises that the foundations of security and of confidence in the City and in the commercial world generally have been gravely injured, that a blow has indeed been struck at the integrity of public credit and of private dealing and … Any man in the City of London who so conducts himself as to tarnish that reputation so as to make it more difficult for business men to take documents at their face value for what they appear to be, deals a severe blow to what I have described as the greatest asset left to this country.[4]

Having said that, Norman Birkett advanced four points in mitigation. The first was that when they met on 23 June 1929, and embarked on their fraud, Hatry and his associates knew that it would not have permanent effect. It would either be reversed quickly as money was received on completion of the steel scheme or it would be exposed by the end of September. As such, its purpose was to save a large number of people from losses that they might otherwise have suffered. Birkett characterised Hatry as saying:

> When I saw that matters were getting serious, I pledged every penny in the world that I possessed, my reputation, and it may be my liberty, to avert what I knew would otherwise have been a terrible crash. I took grave personal risks, whereas I could then so easily have let things go and have walked off a free man. The losses would have fallen on thousands of shareholders all over the country, instead, as now, upon a comparatively limited few; and, moreover, by having taken these risks I am now irretrievably and irreparably ruined, my name has become a by-word, and, if I am found guilty, when I leave prison, whenever that may be, my punishment will begin all over again.[5]

The second point advanced by Birkett was that the fraud had not benefited Hatry personally: 'just a word about a distinct matter, and that is the evidence of Sir Gilbert Garnsey that not one penny piece had gone into the pocket of Mr Hatry, or, indeed into the pockets of any of the Defendants'.[6] The third point was that Hatry had applied all of his personal resources in an attempt to avoid the collapse which had proved inevitable:

> when you find that not merely has a man not had a single penny but … on the testimony given in the witness box by the Prosecution that that man had depleted himself of all his possessions, his family settlements – everything he had in the world – and now faces bankruptcy, I am satisfied that your Lordship will regard that as most material in this matter of mitigation.[7]

The fourth point was that Hatry had assisted the police investigation: 'the criminal charges were formulated wholly and solely upon the information that Mr Hatry himself gave, and without it the Prosecution must have been very long delayed'.[8] Norman Birkett concluded by appealing to the judge to leave Hatry some hope by imposing a sentence that would:

> make it manifest that any interference with the integrity of credit cannot and will not be permitted – a sentence which, in its element of seasoning with mercy, should not crush, or break, or destroy, to give years of unrelieved gloom, but that it should be a sentence which would permit Mr Hatry to maintain, through the duration of the sentence, whatever it may be, hope – which is the last earthly thing he has – that one day he my live to redeem the career which had been so finally and tragically shattered.[9]

The other defendants' barristers then pleaded in mitigation on behalf of their clients, stressing that Hatry had been the leader and that they had contributed as functionaries.

Whatever Hatry may have thought before his trial, when Norman Birkett concluded his plea in mitigation there was little prospect of the judge being swayed. Birkett faced the dual disadvantage that Hatry and his associates had confessed their guilt and there was almost no foundation for the crime to be excused. Birkett's suggestion that Hatry had not benefited personally from the crime ignored the fact that Hatry was attempting to save his reputation and his fortune. Were these not potential benefits?

Birkett's chances of success in his plea of mitigation had already been limited by the choice of judge. Sir Horace Avory had a reputation. He was the senior King's Bench judge, having been appointed in 1910. He had been involved in all the major fraud cases since 1900 in one capacity or another and later admitted that he favoured officiating at fraud trials above all other cases.[10] He was not speaking carelessly when in sentencing Hatry he commented that his frauds were: 'far more serious than any of the great frauds upon the public which have been committed within the last 50 years'.[11] He was speaking from his personal experience. Doubtless that depth of experience had inured him to many of the arguments that could be advanced in mitigation of crimes of which defendants had been found guilty. It had also contributed to his reputation as the most dreaded 'hanging judge' of his age. He was called 'thin lipped, cold, utterly unemotional, silent, and humourless, and relentless towards lying witnesses and brutal criminals' and 'impervious to bluff and merciless to perjury'.[12] He was known for his 'acid drops', the name given by Old Bailey hacks to his caustic interjections, one of which was aimed at Norman Birkett's suggestion that Hatry's actions had ensured that members of the public had not suffered heavy losses: 'Are the banks not to be included in the general public?'.[13]

In a 'cruel and ice-cold voice',[14] Sir Horace effortlessly dismissed all of Birkett's pleas. That Hatry had confessed was no more than an acceptance of inevitable exposure:

> I do not think there is much if any merit in that confession, because you knew at the time that investigation was on foot, and you knew that the moment there was any investigation these frauds must inevitably be discovered, and the proof of those would have been comparatively simple, and therefore in making that confession you were merely succumbing to the inevitable.[15]

As for the suggestion that the fraud was intended only to be of short duration, the judge commented disparagingly:

> it is nothing more nor less than the threadbare plea of every clerk who robs his master and who says he hoped to repay the money before his crime was discovered by backing a winner. Except that yours is on a large scale there is no difference between that excuse which was put forward than the excuse which is daily made by the dishonest clerk or servant, and therefore I can give no effect to that plea.[16]

The upshot was that Sir Horace sentenced Hatry to the maximum sentence provided for forgery: 'I am unable to imagine any worse case than yours … and therefore … the sentence of the Court is that you be detained in penal servitude for 14 years'.[17] On the charges of conspiracy, Hatry was sentenced to two years imprisonment with hard labour, to run concurrently with the sentence of 14 years. At this point, Hatry turned to leave the dock, but was called back for the judge to complete his remarks.

The sentence was severe – it applied the maximum permitted by law in every respect and was the longest sentence handed down in 1930 by any court in England for a non-capital crime. It also equalled the longest sentence imposed for fraud by a company promoter: the sentence of 14 years composed of two consecutive sentences of seven years which was handed down to Jabez Balfour in 1896. This would have been well-known to Sir Horace as he had served as a junior barrister for the prosecution in that case. Observers recalled that Hatry looked surprised[18] and that his wife fainted and required medical attention.

By the time he reached Prisoner's Row, the stone corridor of 23 cells in which prisoners awaited the Black Maria which would take them to prison, Hatry must have recovered for when he was asked whether he wanted anything to eat he replied drily: 'Just a savoury'.[19]

It is difficult to imagine a more disastrous outcome from Hatry's point of view. He had already suffered the destruction of his business, but also now suffered the loss of his liberty and the consequential disgrace. He also now faced bankruptcy. To rub salt into the wound, on the very day that Hatry was sentenced, 25 January 1930, the *Illustrated London News* carried the announcement that his newly refurbished house at Stanhope Gate was to be auctioned on 6 March.[20]

In a striking repeat of previous events, his disgrace and bankruptcy were both the result of his own mistakes. By agreeing a course of action which was from the beginning known to be fraudulent, he had brought about his fate just as he had done before the 1914–1918 war when he somewhat naively accepted two bills of exchange. His position in 1930 was different as he had provided for his family's needs so that their financial position was protected from the consequences of his disgrace, but this must have been cold comfort.

For the City, the Hatry collapse was an embarrassment. For the Borough of Wakefield, it caused losses which were to embarrass the authority[21] and would cause added costs for ratepayers for many years. For others, it caused years of dispute about who should bear the losses. For example, it took some years before the litigation between Kleinwort Sons and Associated Automatic Machine Corporation over the treatment of false share transfers was determined by the House of Lords.

But, overall, the Hatry trial and its outcome were not an unmitigated disaster for the City. By commenting on what he plainly regarded as an egregious fraud, the judge was implying that no system, however robust, could be proof against the determined criminality of a fraudster such as Hatry. It was to be regretted that the crash had occurred but that alone should not be a reason for distrusting the system. Some newspapers even congratulated the authorities on the speed with which Hatry had been prosecuted, observing that in New York the authorities had been much slower to respond. This message was important because the City was feeling vulnerable to a newly elected Labour government which came to power with a promise to reform after years of campaigning against what was seen as anti-social financial chicanery. Behind the distraction provided by Hatry's trial, the City and more particularly the stock exchange were able to improve their rules and discipline incautious members without attracting undue attention.[22]

In his book on the crash in 1929, J.K. Galbraith described Hatry as 'one of those curiously un-English figures with whom the English periodically find themselves unable to cope'.[23] In using Hatry's degradation as a screen, at least the City showed that it could cope with figures such as Hatry. It had used his corporate transactions as an opportunity to make profit from risky deals without endangering the reputations of established houses. When the end came, his collapse was used as a welcome distraction. This distraction proved effective as was demonstrated a few years later by complimentary references to UK new issue practice in the debates over the 1933 Securities Act in the USA: 'except for a very unusual Hatry … the distribution of securities is a decorous, traditional business, offering its wares only to institutions and wary family solicitors'.[24]

As the stock exchange was painfully, aware, this distraction was belied by private reports of collusion between members and abusive street traders.[25]

Notes

1 The following paragraphs are based on the description in Vander Weyer, 2011.
2 Vander Weyer, 2011, page 243.
3 In a letter dated 30 March 1930 to the Marquess of Winchester who had served as chairman of Austin Friars Trust, Hatry wrote 'he Corporation stocks … had become irregular and were never forged …' (Marquess of Winchester, 1934, inset after page 272). Later, in a statement for use in the litigation concerning irregular Drapery Trust transfers, Hatry asserted: 'it is important to note that all scrip certificates issued in respect of stock issues sponsored by C&GS were their own documents of title issued by them at Pinners Hall and not by the Corporation' (TNA file HO 144/17846). The same point was also made in a booklet entitled *The Hatry Case: Eight Current Misconceptions* circulated in March 1938 by Hatry's son, Cecil. This booklet claimed that 'eminent counsel express opinion that charges of forgery would not have been substantiated if contested' but it has not been possible to trace copies of the formal opinions said to have been obtained (TNA file HO 144/21218). Later in 1938, Hatry's supporters arranged a meeting at the Houses of Parliament during which members of both houses were briefed by lawyers who had appeared at Hatry's trial on the case for his early release. None of the lawyers referred to the technical argument over whether Hatry had been guilty of forgery (transcript of meeting on 27 July 1938, TNA file HO 144/21218).
4 Trial transcript, day 5, page 14 (TNA file DPP 1/91).
5 Trial transcript, day 5, pages 18–19 (TNA file DPP 1/91).
6 Trial transcript, day 5, page 27 (TNA file DPP 1/91).
7 Trial transcript, day 5, page 28 (TNA file DPP 1/91).
8 Trial transcript, day 5, page 29 (TNA file DPP 1/91).
9 Trial transcript, day 5, pages 37–38 (TNA file DPP 1/91).
10 Sir Home Gordon recalled: 'he twice told me that of all the cases he tried, the one that interested him most was Hatry's. He really preferred the intricacies of a financial case to the human tragedy connected with murder trials' (*The Times*, 17 June 1935, page 21).
11 Trial transcript, day 5, page 55 (TNA file DPP 1/91).
12 Brewer's Dictionary (1970).
13 Trial transcript. TNA file DPP 1/91.
14 Hutchinson, 2015, page 362.

15 Trial transcript, day 5, page 55 (TNA file, DPP 1/91).
16 Trial transcript. TNA file DPP 1/91.
17 Trial transcript, day 5, page 55 (TNA file DPP 1/91).
18 Kinross, 1982, page 57.
19 *Sunday Telegraph*, 8 August 1965, page 4; Greenfield, 1995, page 50.
20 *Illustrated London News*, 25 January 1930, page 118.
21 An enquiry by a select committee of the House of Lords exposed mistakes made by the authority in agreeing to Hatry's terms (*The Times*, 13 March 1930, page 5).
22 Michie, 1999, pages 261–263. Adoption of this approach was not unique to the UK: 'Corporate America prefers being prosecuted to being regulated' (Buell, 2016, page 241). See also Calavita and Pontell, 1994, page 310.
23 Galbraith, 1954, page 113.
24 Flexner, 1934, cited in De Bedts, 1964, pages 47–48.
25 Committee minutes, August 1929. LSX archive Guildhall Library.

References

Primary works: unpublished documents

TNA: DPP papers.
TNA: Home Office papers.

Primary works: newspapers and periodicals

Illustrated London News.
Sunday Telegraph.
The Times.

Primary works: contemporary books and papers

Brewer's Dictionary. (1970) *Brewer's Dictionary of Phrase and Fable* (Centenary Edition). (Harper & Row, New York).
Marquess of Winchester. (1934), *Statesmen, Financiers and Felons.* (Privately published, London).

Secondary works

Buell, S.W. (2016), *Capital Offenses: Business Crime and Punishment in America's Corporate Age.* (W.W. Norton, New York, NY).
Calavita, K. and Pontell, H.N. (1994), 'The State and White Collar Crime: Saving the Savings and Loans', *Law & Society Review*, volume 28(2), pages 297–324.
De Bedts, R.F. (1964), *The New Deal's SEC: The Formative Years.* (Columbia University Press, New York).
Flexner, B. (1934), 'The Fight on the Securities Act', *Atlantic Monthly*, volume CLIII(2).
Galbraith, J.K. (1954), *The Great Crash 1929* (2009 reprint). (Penguin, London).
Greenfield, G. (1995), *A Smattering of Monsters: A Kind of Memoir.* (Little Brown, London).
Hutchinson, J. (2015), 'Postscript', in Grant, T. (ed.), *Jeremy Hutchinson's Case Histories.* (John Murray, London).

Kinross, J. (1982), *Fifty Years in the City: Financing Small Business.* (John Murray, London).
Michie, R.C. (1999), *The London Stock Exchange: A History.* (Oxford University Press, Oxford).
Vander Weyer, M. (2011), *Fortune's Spear: The Story of the Blue-Blooded Rogue behind the Most Notorious City Scandal of the 1920s.* (Elliott & Thompson, London).

13 The prison years

For those watching in court, sentencing marked the end of a process. For Hatry and his colleagues, it marked a beginning.

While the severity of the sentence was a surprise, imprisonment was not. Once Hatry and his associates had confessed, they knew that imprisonment was certain. They cannot have known, however, how they would bear the indignities which imprisonment would bring.

They may have tried to learn from the experiences of others they had known, such as the embittered Gerard Lee Bevan. They may have read the prison memoirs of another company promoter, Jabez Balfour. Like Hatry, he was sentenced to serve 14 years in prison after a trial at the Old Bailey which had also involved Horace Avory, although as a junior member of the prosecution team rather than as the judge. Balfour's memoirs record the gradual degradation he endured as he became an inmate: riding in a Black Maria shackled with other newly convicted prisoners, the first encounter with a prison barber, the removal of his private clothes and possessions, their replacement with shabby prison clothes, the denial of a mirror, the loss of access to books and newspapers, learning to sew mailbags, the constant sense of being watched, the loss of privacy.[1]

Hatry experienced all of these indignities as he was admitted to Wandsworth. For a man known to be so fastidious about his appearance that he polished the insteps of his shoes, the experience must have been shocking. Small wonder is it that his first prison photographs show a diminished figure, seemingly ill at ease with the unprepossessing clothes he had been given. He did not write memoirs of his life in prison, but his early petitions to the prison governor show how difficult he found life with most of the other inmates at Wandsworth who:

> had been in prison before and of these a large proportion consisted of hardened criminals, sexual perverts and men convicted of loathsome and despicable crimes in which they seemed to glorify … I do not think that anyone but a prisoner living among these individuals as I was compelled to do, can possibly visualise the appalling degradation … I have had to hear their disgusting conversation, the sordid details of the foulest of

> crimes, the blasphemous and obscene language day in and day out. The baseness of some of the men and the horrors of Wandsworth Gaol beggar description.[2]

Hatry's words suggest that he had yet to accept that many regarded his own crimes as 'loathsome and despicable'.

In Hatry's case, any depression caused by these privations was deepened by events outside the prison. His offices at Pinners Hall were being dismantled. Just before his trial began, his desk had been sold at auction for £29 – less than the £30 paid for Edmund Daniels' desk. As reported in the *Illustrated London News* in the week of the trial, the house at Great Stanhope Street had been emptied of furniture in preparation for an auction in March. When the auction took place, the house was bought in – the highest bid was far below the amount that had been spent on buying and refurbishing it.

Whatever emotions he may have felt as he left the dock in the Old Bailey, Hatry would not have been alone if he were apprehensive. There were others who were uneasy about his imprisonment. For the Home Office he presented a challenge. How could a normal prison regime cope with a man known for his skill in manipulating rules? Would he not treat the Prison Commission's rules in the way he had treated the rules of the stock exchange?

On remand in Brixton prison, Hatry had been helping accountants and lawyers trying to unravel the tortured mess that he had created. Sir Gilbert Garnsey was investigating the affairs of Austin Friars Trust and its involvement in the steel scheme. Barton Mayhew & Company was investigating the share registers of Associated Automatic Machine Corporation, another team from Price Waterhouse was investigating Photomaton and Lloyds Bank was investigating numerous allegations that it had mishandled share certificates which it had realised were not as they seemed. Many, many companies were trying to work out whether they had inadvertently become liable. Others were looking for someone who could be obliged to make good their losses. Of these, a large proportion saw Hatry as a source of information and explanations.

Hatry attempted to respond to all who sought his assistance, not least because this enabled his barrister, Norman Birkett, to make much at the trial of how cooperative his client had been. There was another benefit. Almost all of the meetings took place in the centre of London, away from Brixton prison. Barristers were reluctant to travel far from their chambers, and it was not easy in prison for Hatry to refer to the books and records in which companies had recorded their transactions. Consequently, these visits took the prisoner away from the prison environment and returned him, albeit only for a while, to the cultured, civilised life of the City and led to concerns in the Home Office that: 'These wealthy rogues have tried at every point and in every way to secure indulgences that would never be allowed to ordinary accused'.[3] As the meetings became known to the newspapers, the Home Office had been embarrassed by reports emphasising the privileges that Hatry and his associates were enjoying in apparent disregard for the public's desire for retribution against the fraudsters.

After lengthy discussion with Sir Archibald Bodkin, the director of public prosecutions (DPP), Sir Ernley Blackwell, the Home Office's principal legal adviser, and the secretary of state, a number of ground rules were agreed for the guidance of the governor of Brixton prison while the prisoners were held there on remand. It was accepted that Messrs Hatry, Daniels, Tabor and Dixon had to be made available for the preparation of their defence and that these meetings should take place at the Old Bailey for the convenience of counsel. The prisoners could be transported in taxicabs, at their own cost, but no more than two prisoners were to be allowed in a cab and two accompanying prison officers should be in each cab. Although smoking would be allowed in the meeting room (but not during the cab journeys), there was to be no 'ostentatious smoking' of cigars. Although lunch could be arranged by the prisoners' lawyers, champagne lunches were not to be provided and lunch should also be provided for the accompanying prison officers. While the Home Office accepted that the bare fact that such meetings had taken place could not be kept secret, the prisoners' lawyers were expected to accept that the meetings should not be given any undue publicity.[4]

When the prisoners were admitted to Wandsworth prison, after the trial, it was the Wandsworth governor's turn to ask for guidance. He was given the same instructions, together with the fervent hope that the meetings could be discouraged and might gradually come to a halt. Although the rules relieved the pressure on the prison for a time, they were to prove inadequate.[5]

The instincts of Home Office officials had been correct. As prisoners on remand, Hatry and his associates had tried to take advantage of every privilege that might be available to dilute the effect of the prison regime. This did not stop after the trial. Hatry began his term of imprisonment with a small number of objectives: to make his years in prison as bearable as possible, to continue his business activities and to seek every opportunity to shorten his sentence. He was determined to bend the prison rules to serve his objectives.

As Jabez Balfour had realised 20 years earlier, Hatry soon recognised that his years in prison would be more bearable if he conformed to the prison's regime and appeared to have accepted his fate. This had the advantage not only of making daily intercourse more pleasant but also of maximising the time which would be deducted from his sentence for good behaviour. At first achieving this outcome was not straightforward. Hatry's notoriety attracted attention from other prisoners who wanted to talk to him and put schemes to him – especially schemes for his escape. To dodge this unwelcome attention, Hatry and his associates kept themselves apart from other inmates and took care not to involve themselves in disputes. These efforts were successful in creating a good impression, which was reflected in the prison chaplain's report on the first four years that Hatry and Daniels served. Revd C. Seymour King observed of Daniels that 'He has settled down to things well and is not at all bitter. His chief concern is for his colleague

Hatry. A very decent sort of man'.[6] Revd King's report on Hatry was equally benign:

> He feels his position very keenly and the disgrace of the whole thing. Otherwise he has settled down to things and looks at his imprisonment philosophically. He feels very keenly what is said about him in the press. He is concerned about his family.[7]

Yet everything may not have been as it seemed. Although the chaplain detected no bitterness, there were signs that when talking between themselves both Hatry and Daniels behaved differently. By chance, a prison officer prepared exceptionally detailed notes of meetings between Hatry, Daniels and Atherton Powys, who was Hatry's personal solicitor and acted as his administrator during his years in prison. These notes show that both Hatry and Daniels were bitter about Gialdini, the 'rat', to the extent that Hatry enthusiastically suggested to the DPP how he could eliminate the weaknesses in the case against Gialdini.[8] They were both dismissive of Stanley Passmore, the solicitor who had dealt with most of Hatry's corporate transactions, accusing him of encouraging litigation for the sole purpose of increasing his firm's fees. They agreed that the borough treasurers of Swindon and Gloucester had committed perjury at the trial. Far from accepting his conviction, Hatry showed himself to be determined to disprove the charge of forgery on which he had been convicted.[9]

Prison Officer Rees's notes of these meetings were seen by Major Grew, the governor of Maidstone prison, who may have had them in mind when he added his report on Hatry to the chaplain's report already quoted, and echoed Lord Bearsted: 'Very well behaved. Good worker. Hatry is a sort of dual personality. I have seen both sides of his character since he has been here. I do not trust him'.[10]

Against the general impression of compliance with the prison regime, Hatry and his personal solicitor, Atherton Powys, tried to use every excuse to get him out of prison. There were frequent requests for Hatry to attend meetings and for these to take place in the centre of London for the convenience of others. Hatry's correspondence was voluminous and was often the cause of debates between the governor and the Home Office over whether Hatry should be allowed to receive particular letters or documents and the facilities he needed at the prison to review what he had been sent. At one stage, consideration was given to involving an independent person in censoring the documents sent to Hatry, rather than relying on hard-pressed prison officers. Decisions to return letters rather than pass them to Hatry led to extended exchanges between lawyers which on one occasion led Sir Ernley Blackwell to tell Powys that as Hatry's administrator he should act without reference to Hatry – as if he were the executor for a person who had been dead for five years.[11] This comment itself became the subject for debate. In practice, the Home Office was not able to restrict this activity which declined naturally as one by one the disputes which followed the crash were settled.

As far as pursuit of his business activities is concerned, Hatry achieved rather less success. In his meetings with solicitors dealing with disputes arising from the crash, Hatry often went beyond the provision of evidence by suggesting transactions by which the disputes could be resolved. In the case of Steel Industries of Great Britain, he became involved in a series of meetings with Russell Kettle, a Chartered Accountant, and Sir Arthur du Cros, which focused on Hatry's proposals for developing the holding company's capital structure and relieving the embarrassing position in which Parent Trust and Finance found itself.[12] None of these discussions came to anything, partly because of restrictions imposed by the Home Office which, before approving requests for meetings, required solicitors and others to undertake that they would only discuss past transactions and not proposed future transactions. More domestically, during his regular monthly visits, Hatry was able to advise his son, Cecil, to invest in steel shares using the funds raised by the eventual sale of 5 Great Stanhope Street. On his release in 1939, Hatry was to find that their ventures had been profitable.[13]

In parallel, Hatry's team began to develop a strategy for reducing his sentence. At first, an appeal on Hatry's behalf appeared to offer the best chance of shortening his sentence. This was to prove mistaken as when Norman Birkett argued for leave to appeal there was little that could be added to his pleading at trial, all of which had been dismissed by Sir Horace Avory whose great friend, Lord Hewart, the Lord Chief Justice, was the most senior of the judges who heard the appeal. On 18 March 1930, the Court of Appeal concluded that the sentence handed down by Sir Horace Avory had not been a day too long and refused leave to appeal. By seeking leave to appeal, Hatry had lengthened his sentence as the court directed that the sentence should be treated as having begun on the day of the appeal hearing, not the day of his conviction and sentencing.[14]

That left only one way of reducing the sentence beyond the normal arrangement by which time was deducted for good behaviour: a request to the home secretary for remission of a part of the sentence which might be granted if it came to be accepted that the sentence had been unduly vindictive. As feeling against Hatry was so great in 1930, an immediate application was out of the question and could not realistically be considered before 1935, by which time all of Hatry's associates would have served their shorter sentences. In preparation, Hatry's team needed to sustain the public's awareness of Hatry and the length of his sentence, so that in due time preparation of an application could be considered with some hope of success.

Hatry's regular visitors provided a channel of communications necessary to support the placement of newspaper articles to encourage public interest. Throughout his time in prison, Hatry received monthly visits from his son, Cecil, and slightly less frequent visits from his solicitor and administrator, Atherton Powys, whom he had known since 1915. In the early years, he saw his wife in the margins of meetings with lawyers in central London,[15] but when those meetings became less frequent she also visited Maidstone prison regularly with his daughter, Diana. These visits were supplemented by other more occasional visits by former collaborators such as Arthur Collins, with whom Hatry had developed his local authority loan stock issues operation.[16]

The first article to be placed in the newspapers did not help Hatry's cause. On the weekend after the end of the trial, the *Sunday Express* carried a long article which was described as the first of a series which would describe Hatry's career. There was an immediate reaction against this article which seemed too obviously to be inviting sympathy for a fraudster who many thought should be learning to accept the justified retribution that his sentence represented. Readers asked how a convicted fraudster could have been allowed to speak to the press about his life. Future editions of the newspaper did not carry any further articles, and Cecil Hatry was obliged to send apologetic letters to banks and other houses which had suffered losses in the crash, explaining that the article had not been based on interviews but on autobiographical notes that his father had prepared for the use of his barristers at the trial.[17]

On 16 December 1930, the *Evening News, Daily Mail* and *News Chronicle* reported that Hatry had been seen at the Law Courts where he had been expected to give evidence:

> At lunch time a [four] course lunch, including wine, was taken in the room, and Hatry was afterwards seen to be smoking a cigar.
>
> Late in the afternoon, Mrs Hatry, dressed in a long fur coat, walked quickly down the long corridor and was allowed to see her husband. The instant she entered the room, Hatry embraced her and Mrs Hatry burst into tears.
>
> They sat the end of a table near a fire talking in low tones, Hatry smoking innumerable cigarettes and his wife occasionally joining him. They had tea together.[18]

When asked for his comments, the prison governor expressed his disgust at the position in which his officers had been placed. Mrs Hatry had arrived unexpectedly when the lawyers left at the end of their meeting. As her arrival was witnessed by a small number of journalists who happened to be present, any attempt to deny her entry would have caused a scene which the journalists would have reported eagerly. The prison officer on duty had decided that it would be preferable to allow Mrs Hatry into the room, a decision which the governor commended. He also complained about the unfairness of the *News Chronicle* report which commented that Hatry was much more smartly dressed than his accompanying officers.

On 5 April 1931, *The People* reported that Hatry had been confirmed in the Anglican Church and that with his associates he had joined the prison chapel choir for which Dixon sang solos. Again the governor was asked to comment as complaints about the article were received from Hatry's family. In his response, the governor suggested that the report was inaccurate. While

Hatry had indeed been confirmed in the Anglican Church, neither he nor Daniels had joined the chapel choir. It was suggested that Dixon may once have sung a solo at the last harvest thanksgiving but did not do so regularly. The governor had no knowledge of how the information had reached the newspaper.

Newspaper reports such as these continued throughout Hatry's sentence; the Home Office could not find a way of stopping them.[19]

Against this background, Hatry's team began to polish the arguments they would use to undermine public disgust over the crimes he had committed and from time to time they took soundings to assess the chance that a public campaign to release Hatry would be successful.

The first of these soundings was taken in conjunction with C.O. Humphreys & Sons, the solicitors acting for Edmund Daniels who, with time off for good behaviour, was due to be released in April 1935. In May 1934, a letter was sent to the home secretary inviting him to consider remitting a part of Daniels' sentence on the grounds that his sentence had been unreasonably extended by the four months that he had spent on remand before the trial. The solicitors suggested that it was most unusual that bail should have been denied and that in view of Daniels' good behaviour and the assistance he had given to parties trying to resolve the problems caused by the crash, a remission of his sentence was justified at least to the extent of the time spent on bail. All of these arguments applied equally to Hatry's position.

They proved unpersuasive. There had been an appeal against the magistrate's decision to deny bail at which the issues had been fully argued before a judge, who was not persuaded that the prisoner's confessions had been as disinterested as they claimed. The secretary of state was advised to reject the application, which is what he did.[20]

Seven months later, in December 1934, a further, more sophisticated, application was sent on Daniels' behalf to the home secretary. On this occasion, the application was made by a member of parliament rather than a solicitor. His application was supported by further letters from others including three local magistrates, a personal approach to the home secretary by Sir Arthur du Cros and a printed memorandum analysing the Hatry crash.

The formal application again highlighted the bail argument, although on this occasion it was augmented by references to the trials of Lord Kylsant and Sir Arthur Wheeler, who had both been accused of fraud and had been allowed bail. As for the printed memorandum, which had been prepared under the supervision of Hatry's son, Cecil, and Sir John Crisp, one of Hatry's lawyers, it was hoped that the document would undermine popular misconceptions about the Hatry crash.[21]

Although Daniels' solicitors were able to show that their application for clemency had a measure of support within Daniels' community, the Home Office officials could find in it nothing to justify changing the decision which had been made in May 1934. The references to Lord Kylsant[22] and Sir Arthur Wheeler[23] were swiftly dismissed on the ground that, in the light of

Sir Horace Avory's comments at trial, their offences were not nearly as serious as those of Hatry and his associates.

The memorandum received much more detailed attention, however, for the officials recognised it as 'one prepared to obtain remission of Hatry's sentence' that was only being 'tried out' on Daniels' behalf. It advanced three main contentions which were closely related to the arguments used by Norman Birkett unsuccessfully in his plea of mitigation at Hatry's trial. The first was that the losses caused by the crash had been much exaggerated and had not affected the wider investing public, only professional financial interests. The second suggested that Hatry and his associates had not committed forgery in the sense of issuing false documents. The third was that it had been intended that the suspect documents created by Hatry and his associates were intended to be replaced quickly before anyone might suffer a loss.

The first contention was dismissed on the grounds that even if the alleged exaggerations of the losses caused by the crash were left out of account in any event, the remaining losses were still large and in any case the memorandum did not explain why the losses of 'professional interests' should not be regarded as losses. The second contention was dismissed as a technicality. Even if the documents uttered by Hatry had not been forged, they remained fraudulent. Finally, the third contention that the fraudulent documents were supposed to be replaced quickly involved an acceptance that a fraud had occurred – it was not an exculpation. It had been dismissed by Sir Horace Avory when sentencing Hatry and was again by the Home Office. The Home Office concluded: 'none of these considerations seem to afford any ground which would justify a reduction of Hatry's sentence'.[24]

Not only was Daniels' request for clemency rejected, but the conclusion with regard to Hatry's sentence was mentioned by the home secretary in a private meeting which had been requested by Sir Arthur du Cros with such force that Sir Arthur subsequently wrote to the home secretary stressing that he had not requested that Hatry's sentence should be reduced.[25]

Although this approach was unsuccessful, one possible impediment to a successful application was removed in the summer. Sir Horace Avory died in June 1935, still in harness at the age of 83. At the beginning of 1935 he had celebrated the 60th anniversary of his call to the bar and, had he lived, in the autumn would have celebrated the 25th anniversary of becoming a judge at a dinner being organised by the Old Bailey mess, of which he had been the first president. Before granting remission of a sentence, the home secretary would invite the comments of the trial judge who had handed down the sentence, which in Hatry's case would have been likely to elicit an objection from Sir Horace. Any potential embarrassment of this type was avoided by Sir Horace's death.

Another year was allowed to pass before another attempt was made to judge the possibility that an application to reduce Hatry's sentence would be successful. In March 1936, Commander Oliver Locker-Lampson asked a question about the sentence in the House of Commons, suggesting that it seemed 'very vindictive'. He received no encouragement from the home secretary. This should not have been a surprise. For some years, the *Daily Mail* had campaigned against share trading abuses and at the end of 1935 had faced a libel action by one of the share traders it had exposed. The newspaper had been completely vindicated by the court's acceptance of the truth of its reports. As a result, public antipathy against fraudulent share trading was again at a peak and it was unrealistic to expect that there would be sympathy for an application for clemency from a convicted share trading fraudster.[26]

Yet another year passed before the next approach was made to the Home Office. In April 1937, Norman Birkett KC, the barrister who had acted for Hatry at his trial, spoke to the deputy secretary at the Home Office, Sir Alexander Maxwell, suggesting that people in the City planned to make representations to the home secretary in favour of remission of part of Hatry's sentence. Birkett's approach to Maxwell was followed up by letters from Harry Clifford-Turner, the solicitor, and George Lansbury, the former leader of the Labour Party, among others. On this occasion, apart from telling Norman Birkett that the home secretary would not be prepared to receive a deputation, the Home Office procrastinated as the question of Hatry's sentence had become more complicated.[27]

There was no greater official sympathy for Hatry over his crimes and the length of his sentence. The arguments put forward in the memorandum that had been submitted early in 1935 were no more persuasive than they had ever been. But in one respect attitudes had changed: a new home secretary, Sir John Simon, was interested in penal reform and proposed to review the longest sentences being served by inmates. He had also undertaken that by the end of 1937 he would review the sentences of a group of prisoners who in 1932 had been involved in a major disturbance at Dartmoor Prison. The cause of the riots is generally attributed to the prison's food, but there had also been other instances of disobedience, such as a model prisoner attacking a popular guard with a razor blade and rough treatment of a prisoner being removed to solitary confinement. At the parade on the day of the riot, 50 prisoners refused orders and the rest were marched back to their cells but refused to enter. At this point, the prison governor and his staff fled to an unused part of the prison and secured themselves. The prisoners then rampaged through the prison, releasing prisoners who were held in solitary confinement. Eventually reinforcements for the prison staff arrived and the riot was quickly subdued.[28]

The victim of the serious assault which had occurred a day or two before the riot was Prison Officer Ernest Birch, a man with 29 years' service, whose injuries were later claimed to have been so severe that they ended his prison service career. Eventually, 33 convicts were prosecuted for their part in the riot and two for assaults that had occurred earlier. In November 1936, a campaign for a review of the additional sentences which had been imposed as a result of the prosecutions had led the home secretary to undertake that a review would take place before the end of 1937.

The difficulty for the Home Office was that prison officers at Dartmoor had suffered violence at the hands of the mutineers who had subsequently proved troublesome inmates. In contrast, however egregious his crimes may have been, Hatry had not been violent and had proved a model prisoner. Indeed, in his review of the eight years of imprisonment which Hatry completed in January 1938, the chaplain of Maidstone prison reported:

> A man of splendid and blazing intellect. Fed and enriched by constant study of the best thoughts of the great minds in the financial world. He has a radiant imagination and never-failing memory. He has faced up with good determination to his sentence always bearing an optimistic outlook and has been an influence for good in the place. Concerned to do well and atone for past mistakes.[29]

The point was not lost on Hatry's supporters. It cannot have been an accident that on 10 December 1937, the day after the home secretary announced that the sentences of the Dartmoor mutineers who remained in prison would be reduced by 25%, the *Daily Sketch* reported that Hatry had written to his wife stating that he hoped to be home for Christmas. The report continued:

> A prison officer told the 'Daily Sketch' last night: 'One thing is certain – if Hatry goes he will be greatly missed by both prisoners and officers of the prison, all regard him not only as a model prisoner but as a friend and a gentleman'.[30]

This report was 'authoritatively denied' but the tide had turned. At the beginning of 1938, the Home Office began to give thought to how a reduction of Hatry's sentence might be justified rather than whether it should be reviewed. Only one ground could be found on which a mitigation of sentence might be suggested: that since his conviction Hatry had given much information and assistance to those engaged in straightening out the financial tangle that resulted from the crash.[31]

Whether they sensed this turning of the tide is not clear, but Hatry's team chose this moment to circulate yet another version of the memorandum on the Hatry cash. On this occasion the document concentrated on what were termed 'Eight Misconceptions'. Slowly, circulation of the memorandum led to supportive articles appearing in such periodicals as *Truth*.[32]

Within the Home Office, the issue was left in the hands of Sir Alexander Maxwell, shortly to become the permanent secretary. After receiving advice on how remission of Hatry's sentence might be justified, Sir Alexander waited for four months before recommending to the secretary of state that Hatry might be released on licence in February 1939 rather than in August 1940. In justifying his recommendation, Sir Alexander distinguished between two motives for imprisonment: retribution and deterrence. He argued that although at the time of Hatry's conviction, soon after the crash had occurred, many had thought that his crimes justified the maximum sentence, it was to be expected that with the passing of time this almost instinctive reaction would wane. He also argued that whether Hatry were released in 1939 or in 1940, the deterrent effect of the sentence would be the same. Sir Alexander went on to acknowledge that similar considerations would apply to many long sentences and that there should be a specific reason for reducing Hatry's sentence which might be provided by Hatry's assistance for the investigations into the crash.[33]

Whatever Sir Alexander wrote formally in his recommendation to the home secretary, there was a further consideration. The Home Office cannot have been convinced that Hatry's sentence would have any deterrent effect whatever. Throughout his time in prison, there had been a constant fear that he would somehow be able to continue his business activities from within the prison and that if this were to be exposed, the prison service would be roundly condemned for having permitted him to do this at the risk of another crash. It had been difficult enough for the Home Office to control Hatry while he was in prison, and the government had no power to control his share trading if he were released. After all, this had been the message of the *Daily Mail*'s campaign against fraudulent share trading. During 1936, in the aftermath of the *Daily Mail*'s successful defence of a libel action, consensus support had grown for a requirement that all share traders should be licensed and registered as a means of excluding undesirable traders. Proposals for a licensing scheme had been developed by a committee under the chairmanship of Sir Archibald Bodkin, the former DPP, and legislation to enact the proposals was being drafted during the first half of 1938.[34] Once the legislation was in force, it would be possible to exclude Hatry from share trading and once that was possible any reduction in the deterrent effect of his sentence would not matter.

It cannot have been a coincidence that it was only two days after he had attended the Cabinet meeting that approved the proposed share pushing legislation that Sir Samuel Hoare, by this time the home secretary, approved the steps which led to Hatry's release and wrote to the Lord Chief Justice to ask whether he would object. Nor can it have been a coincidence that the projected date for Hatry's release was February 1939, which was close to the date on which it was expected that the new legislation would receive the Royal Assent.[35]

While these developments were taking place within the privacy of the Home Office, Hatry's supporters continued to apply pressure. A month after the home secretary had written to the Lord Chief Justice, Sir Thomas Moore convened a meeting of MPs and peers in Committee Room 7 at the House of Commons. Although neither Norman Birkett nor the former Attorney General Sir William Jowitt attended, in their absence the meeting was addressed by barristers who had taken part in Hatry's trial as members of the prosecution and defence teams. The mood of the meeting can be judged from the words of St John Hutchinson, who had supported Norman Birkett at the trial:

> fourteen years is a shattering sentence, a really shattering sentence; had it been ten years, we should not have thought it a light sentence, but it would not have been a very heavy sentence. I do not want to be sentimental about it, but I had an opportunity of seeing Mr Hatry after he first went in, and it was terrible, frankly, the shattering effect it had had upon him, and so the Governor told me even after a year … it could do no possible harm if he was let out now – no possible harm.[36]

From the Home Office's point of view, such meetings created a risk that by releasing Hatry it would be seen to have given in to political pressure – an impression it wanted to avoid. To this end, it was decided that Hatry's release would not be announced formally but would instead be communicated to the press informally once Hatry himself had been told. This is what was done, although, as an added precaution, the day chosen for the informal communication was overshadowed by the crisis in relations between Germany and Great Britain. As a former foreign secretary, Sir Samuel was one of the small number of Cabinet members who had spent the previous few days in discussions about the crisis. Hitler was expected to speak at Nuremberg on that evening, and the week was to end with Neville Chamberlain flying to Munich. Monday 12 September 1938 was archetypically what would in later years be known as a 'bad news day'. While Hatry's planned release was noted by all the newspapers, it did not receive the over-heated attention that the Home Office feared.[37]

In the weeks which followed, the decision was accepted without demur or comment – an outcome which was encouraged by the Home Secretary who quietly persuaded MPs who had supported Hatry that there should be no celebrations, let alone the dinner at the House of Commons which they had planned to mark his release.

Hatry was eventually released just before the end of January 1939, to be met at the gates of Maidstone prison by his son, Cecil, who had been his most consistent supporter while in prison and the most active campaigner for his release.

While he had achieved the early release for which he had hoped, it was to prove a disappointment. Although freed from prison, Hatry could not expect to return to his previous activities; the new Prevention of Fraud (Investments) Act 1939 put paid to that. Moreover, although he had aimed at persuading the authorities that he had not committed forgery, he had also failed in this. At no point during the efforts made to secure his release was there any acceptance of what he regarded as the merits of his case. He was freed early not because anyone thought he had not been guilty as charged but because some had begun to wonder whether he had been made to bear too much responsibility for weaknesses in the City's systems. Some were embarrassed that he had been scapegoated.

There were aspects of his prison experience for which Hatry could be grateful, however. His cause had been supported by a group of friends and former associates who had proved loyal and constant. Before his release from prison, the closest colleague, Edmund Daniels, not only cooperated with Hatry's efforts to secure an early release, but went on to manage Hatry's investment company, Stanhope Estates, thereafter. Among other associates, Hatry was consistently supported by Sir John Crisp whose father, Sir Frank, Hatry had first met in 1914; Atherton Powys, who had been acting as the solicitor of the Earl of March when Hatry first met him in 1915; and Arthur Collins, the local authority loan expert whom Hatry had first met in 1924. Beyond this small group, there were many people in business and politics who assisted Hatry's cause, perhaps because the severity of Hatry's sentence, and the stinging words with which Sir Horace Avory handed it down, had been counterproductive. Gradually it came to be realised that the stock exchange's systems had not been as sound as they might have been and that many others had conspired with gangs of abusive share-pushers to exploit naive investors. If there had even been doubt on that score, it was scotched by the *Daily Mail*'s vindication in a libel action brought by a share-pusher who claimed to have been traduced by the newspaper.[38]

Hatry was still able to inspire loyalty – a gift which would stand him in good stead in facing the challenges of his constrained freedom.

Notes

1 Balfour, 1907, page 34 et seq.
2 Petition dated 9 March 1931 (TNA file HO 144/21217).
3 Minute, 4 December 1929 (TNA file HO 144/21217).
4 Memorandum, 18 December 1929 (TNA file HO 144 144/21217).
5 Minute, 1 February 1930 and subsequent exchanges (TNA file HO 144/21217).
6 Reports prepared in January 1934 (TNA file HO 144/20643).
7 Reports prepared in February 1934 (TNA file HO 144/21218).
8 Letter dated 4 February 1931 from Atherton Powys to the solicitor to the DPP enclosing a letter from Hatry suggesting how the case against Gialdini might be strengthened. He explained his interest by suggesting that if Gialdini were to be acquitted: 'it cannot but reflect upon my evidence and that of my former colleagues, besides which Gialdini throughout was the prime instigator and mover in all these wrongful transactions' (TNA files HO 144/17845 and 17846).
9 Notes of a meeting on 7 June 1932 (TNA file HO 144/21217).
10 Reports prepared in February 1934 (TNA file HO 144/21218).
11 Minute, 11 March 1930 (TNA file HO 144/21217).
12 For example, Mr Kettle wrote to Hatry at length in a letter dated 22 August 1934, which followed and preceded an extensive correspondence (TNA file HO 144/21217).
13 United Steel 'emerged from reorganisation in a stronger financial position' (Eichengreen, 2015, page 115, citing Chandler, 1990, page 329).
14 *Daily Mail*, 18 March 1930.
15 *Daily Mail*, 16 December 1930.
16 References to prison visitors are all based on the register of Hatry's visitors in prison held in his prison file (TNA file HO 144/21217).
17 *Sunday Express*, 26 January 1930; letter dated 1 February 1930 (LBA HO/GM/Bea/25).

18 *Evening News, Daily Mail, News Chronicle*, 16 December 1930; statement by Prison Officer S.R. Smith dated 17 December 1930, statement by Prison Governor C. Rich (TNA file HO 144/21217).
19 *The People*, 5 April 1931, page 1; memorandum by Prison Governor B.D. Grew dated 10 April 1931 (TNA file HO 144/21217).
20 Letter dated 3 May 1985 and subsequent exchanges (TNA file HO 144/20643).
21 Letter dated 11 December 1934 (TNA file HO 144/20643).
22 Lord Kylsant, the former chairman of the Royal Mail Steamship Group, was found guilty in 1931 of having uttered a fraudulent prospectus (Kynaston, 1999, pages 231–232).
23 Sir Arthur Wheeler was found guilty of fraudulent conversion in 1931. Earlier that year he had been declared bankrupt when falling share prices had reduced the value of shares which he had pledged as security for bank loans (Dennett, 1979, pages 33–34).
24 Minute, 31 January 1935 (TNA file HO 144/210643).
25 Letter dated 20 February 1935 (TNA file HO 144/210643).
26 *The Times*, 9 March 1937, page 8.
27 Minute, 21 April 1937 (TNA file HO 144/21218).
28 Du Parcq report, 1932.
29 Report dated 25 January 1938 (TNA file HO 144/21218).
30 *Daily Sketch*, 10 December 1937. Similar reports had already appeared in *Evening News*, 8 December 1937 and *Daily Herald*, 8 December 1937.
31 Minute, 5 February 1938 (TNA file HO 122/21218).
32 Letter from Cecil Hatry dated 16 March 1938 (TNA file HO 144/21218; *Truth*, 3 August 1938, page 146).
33 Memorandum from Maxwell to the secretary of state dated 24 June 1938 (TNA file HO 144/21218).
34 The Bodkin Report, 1937.
35 Letter dated 27 June 1938 (TNA file HO 144/21218).
36 Transcript of meeting on 27 July 1938, page 7 (TNA file HO 144/21218).
37 Advice on the manner of an announcement accepted by the secretary of state on 3 September 1938 (*The Times, Manchester Guardian, Daily Telegraph, Daily Mail, Daily Herald*, 13 September 1938).
38 'What the jury had to consider was whether Mr Singer was a swindling share pusher and whether the Bank of London was a swindling bucket-shop. That was the real sting of the libel'. In short order, the jury found that Mr Singer was a 'swindling share pusher' and that the Bank of London was a 'swindling bucket-shop'. The *Daily Mail* was acquitted of the alleged libel and awarded costs. The judgment in the libel action was reinforced a month later when Jacob Factor, who had stood behind Mr Singer, had agreed to transfer £360,000 to the liquidator of Bank of London Limited (*The Times*, 19 December 1935, page 5; 25 January 1936, page 4; evidence of E.R. Dew to the Bodkin Committee, 20 January 1937, TNA file BT 55/107; Swinson, 2017, pages 180–181).

References

Primary works: unpublished documents

TNA: Home Office papers.
TNA: Prisons Commission papers.
TNA: Board of Trade papers: Bodkin Committee.

Primary works: newspapers and periodicals

Daily Herald.
Daily Mail.
Daily Sketch.
Daily Telegraph.
Evening News.
Illustrated London News.
Manchester Guardian.
News Chronicle.
Sunday Express.
Sunday Telegraph.
The People.
The Times.
Truth.

Primary works: government and parliamentary reports

Bodkin Report. (1937), *Share Pushing: Report of the Departmental Committee Appointed by the Board of Trade 1936–1937.* (Cmd 5539). (HMSO, London).

Primary works: contemporary books and papers

Balfour, J.S. (1907), *My Prison Life.* (Chapman and Hall, London).

Secondary works

Chandler, A. (1990), *Scale and Scope: The Dynamics of Industrial Capitalism.* (Belknap Press for Harvard University Press, Cambridge).

Dennett, L. (1979), *The Charterhouse Group 1925–1979: A History.* (Gentry Books, London).

Eichengreen, B. (2015), *Hall of Mirrors: The Great Depression, the Great Recession, and the Uses – And Misuses – Of History.* (Oxford University Press, New York).

Kynaston, D. (1999), *The City of London: Volume III: Illusions of Gold 1914–1945.* (Chatto & Windus, London).

Swinson, C. (2017), *Regulation of the London Stock Exchange: Share Trading, Fraud and Reform 1914–1945.* (Routledge, London).

14 Hatchards

Hatry had a brief period in which to make plans for his release. He first petitioned the home secretary to be relieved of the normal requirement that prisoners released on licence should report regularly to the police – a requirement that constrained freedom of movement. This was readily granted. He then applied for a passport, which was granted in December 1938, a month before the planned release. So it was that after a short period living in the flat his wife had been occupying in London, Hatry was able to travel for a holiday in the southern French town of St Raphael, in a villa that his wife had rented.[1] When they returned, Hatry and his wife took up residence in the Dorchester Hotel, accepting an introduction by Sir Francis Towle who had led the development of the hotel[2] and had served as a director of several of Hatry's companies in 1919.

The Home Office was hoping for a period of silence. Its plans had successfully avoided unwelcome publicity for the decision to release Hatry, and again proved successful in limiting newspaper attention for his release. Only a single photographer appears to have been present to record Hatry's emergence from prison and newspapers only noted the release some days after it had occurred. In welcoming his release, Hatry's political and business friends were discreet. For a while Hatry received no further public attention.

The silence came to an end in July 1939 with the publication of Hatry's latest project: a book entitled *Light Out of Darkness*.

In his introduction to the book, Hatry explained that he had spent his years in prison studying the causes of depression and war, problems which he suggested had defeated the greatest brains. As support, he quoted a speech in 1932 by his nemesis, Montagu Norman: 'the difficulties are so vast, the forces so unlimited, so novel, and precedents so lacking that I approach this whole subject not only in ignorance, but in humility. It is too great for me'.[3] The implicit message was that while the challenge may have been too great for the governor of the Bank of England, it had not been too great for Hatry, not least because imprisonment had permitted him to devote all of his attention to the study. He claimed that in preparation of his ideas, he had digested 'over a thousand carefully selected works, reading deeply into history, economics, foreign and Empire affairs'. The outcome was a proposal that the problems of depression and war could be mitigated, if not eliminated, by large-scale emigration programmes. His book suggested that the causes of political and economic instability could be found in the maldistribution of population and in the interdependence of nations. Some had been led to claim that they must acquire new territory even at other people's expense, while others had resources that were imperfectly developed through lack of manpower.

Hatry proposed that the world should be divided into a few large and, so far as possible, self-contained economic units – a process that would involve big transfers which he suggested could be achieved by consent rather than by war. In his view this could be done by the single-minded application of the techniques of propaganda which had proved so successful in gathering support for warlike purposes. He acknowledged that there were examples of emigration programmes that had proved unsuccessful and suggested that this had resulted from the narrowness of the groups that had moved. It had taken a long time for groups that had sought land for agricultural use alone to develop into rounded communities supported by the wealth of skills and experience to be found in well-established communities. He suggested that new programmes of emigration should aim to move whole communities but to be successful would need comprehensive support. Much of the book was devoted to an analysis of how this might be organised and financed. While acknowledging that the cost would be great, he argued that the money could be achieved if the thousands of millions of pounds being spent on armaments could be diverted to works of peace. Hatry suggested that people would find that the diversion of funds in this way would be no bad investment.

As demonstrations of how his proposal would avert problems that might otherwise lead to war, Hatry cited the challenges of East Prussia and the Sudetenland. At the time, East Prussia was divided from Germany by the Danzig corridor, a problem which might be resolved by replacing the Danzig corridor with a new corridor to the east of East Prussia. German ambitions of finding *lebensraum* could be satisfied by moving the Czech population overseas. None of this could be achieved quickly and, according to Hatry, might require 50 years.

To a twenty-first-century sensibility, these ideas are chilling and seem ill-suited to sit in the mouth of someone with Hatry's Jewish background.

Hatry claimed that his book had been written in the aftermath of and in response to the invasion of Albania by Italy in April 1939. While this claim seems improbable as it would have left little time for the book to be written and then produced before its publication in July 1939, it would support an interpretation of his position as a perhaps naive acceptance that appeasement of others' objectives through mass migration might be more acceptable than war. In effect, he accepted that pressures created by economic differences between states created the risk of conflict and was prepared to consider any non-warlike means by which the pressures could be alleviated without resort to conflict. After all, Hatry had experience of the practical problems of migration from his involvement with the migrations from Eastern Europe before the 1914–1918 war and his own family had escaped the background anti-Semitism of Zweibrücken in Germany by emigrating largely for commercial reasons. By taking over the family silk trading on his father's death, Hatry had developed relationships with the members of the family who were managing the silk mill in Sarreguemines and would have been affected by the destruction of the Zweibrücken synagogue in the anti-Semitic riots on Kristallnacht in November 1938. The synagogue had been a close neighbour of the family dyeworks. The family's experience was that emigration had served as a form of deliverance.

In the context of the summer of 1939, when the world was preparing for war, Hatry's ideas did not attract a large following, although it was later reported that 30,000 copies of his book were sold and it led to exchanges of correspondence in the press, which mostly concentrated on the impracticality of his ideas.[4] Interest soon petered out.

Hatry's attention was attracted to another project.

He renewed his acquaintance with Piccadilly, the location of his office as an insurance broker before the 1914–1918 war and of the Cavendish Hotel frequented by so many of his clients and his associates. In 1939, he was also drawn back to the area by the chronic insomnia which he suffered after his imprisonment as the Turkish baths in Jermyn Street next to the Cavendish Hotel were open throughout the night.[5]

There was a bookshop, Hatchards, within 50 yards of his former office. For bookselling, 187 Piccadilly was a fine location:

> the perfect address for a shop catering to the 'carriage trade', almost opposite Albany, a mere stroll from the clubs of St James's and Pall Mall, and a neighbour of Fortnum & Mason. A gentleman could – and still can – spend a happy morning visiting his shoemaker, his hatter and his wine merchant in Lower St James's Street and his shirt-maker in Jermyn Street, rounded off with some gentle browsing in Hatchards before enjoying a leisurely lunch at White's or Boodles.[6]

However good Hatchards' location may have been in theory, in 1939 the shop was in financial difficulty; it could not maintain the extensive stock which customers expected and sales were falling.

Its financial problems stemmed from the fact that the owners who were in awe of their many titled customers allowed most of their purchases to be charged to accounts rather than requiring them to be settled at the point of sale in cash. As account balances were allowed to run for years without settlement and no charge was made for this extended credit, the shop was short of cash, owed back wages to staff, could not afford to settle publishers' bills and thus could not replenish its stock. In effect, a large proportion of its customers were treating Hatchards like a lending library but without paying an annual subscription.[7]

Hatry became aware that the owners, the Shepherd brothers, could see no way out of the predicament and would be prepared to sell.[8] Borrowing £500 from his wife, Hatry offered to buy the shop, handing over the £500 there and then as a 10% deposit and suggesting that the Shepherd brothers could stay until their retirement. The offer was accepted immediately.[9]

Hatry then set to work sorting out the shop's financial problems. He wrote to every debtor, stating that in one week's time he would remove all of the books from the shop's windows. As a sign of pride in the shop's clientele, the shop would display in its window a typed list of the customers showing how much each owed and for how long each balance had been outstanding. One can imagine the storm of complaints which greeted this announcement, but, for Hatry, tolerating the abuse was worthwhile. Most customers paid their debts rather than risk publicity. Within a fortnight, enough money had been received to pay the back wages owed to staff and to settle the balance of the purchase consideration Hatry had agreed to pay for Hatchards.

That left the task of settling outstanding accounts with publishers. Hatry visited each of the major publishers who were owed money and presented them with a choice. They could demand payment instantly which would lead to closure of the shop, the loss of a potentially lucrative sales outlet and the recovery only of a small proportion of the outstanding debts. Alternatively, he asked them to continue supplying books, giving him six months for the business to recover. He promised that he would then begin to pay the debts which would be fully paid off within a further six months. They agreed.

In honouring these promises, Hatry was assisted by an ill wind that brought him good fortune. War broke out. People were kept indoors by the blackout and later by the Blitz. Apart from listening to the wireless, reading was the most obvious way to pass the time. Book sales boomed and, with them, Hatchards' profits.[10]

In achieving this happy outcome, Hatry was assisted by Cyril Edgley, who was general manager of Argosy and Sundial Libraries, a company which provided services to private and public lending libraries.[11] They were introduced to each other by J.R. Crane, who was a director of Rich & Cowan, who had published *Light Out of Darkness*.[12] Hatry invited Edgley to become general manager of Hatchards, an offer which he initially declined but was eventually persuaded to accept on a part-time basis as he continued to manage Argosy's book purchasing. After moving into Hatchards premises when the Argosy building was bombed in September 1940, Edgley was appointed general manager of Hatchards in January 1941, but found he had insufficient time for both companies and resigned towards the end of 1941, becoming a director of Hatchards soon afterwards.[13] His professional contribution to the management of Hatchards had been critical to its recovery. The shop's stock was rebuilt and its rare books business was reorganised. A room was created in which lecture meetings could be held and a programme of public lectures by authors was organised and advertised.[14] After Edgley's resignation, he was replaced by Albert Tabor, who had been a member of Hatry's management team at Pinners Hall in the 1920s and had been a co-defendant at Hatry's trial in January 1930 but had no experience of managing a bookshop – a weakness that was partially made good by Edgley's availability as a director and occasional consultant. Hatchards' sales grew steadily throughout the war from about £42,000 in 1939 to about £119,000 in 1944. At the end of 1945, Edgeley was reported by *The Bookseller* to be claiming that sales were 'better than any wartime year'.[15]

The connection with Cyril Edgley presented another opportunity which in 1943 led to Hatry acquiring a controlling interest in Argosy & Sundial Libraries. Although the war years found many bookshops thriving, there was some pressure for small shops, including bookshops, to amalgamate to reduce the costs of distribution and financing stocks. There was also a nervousness among many smaller booksellers that with the levels of discounts demanded by libraries and schools and the difficulty of finding adequately qualified staff at acceptable wage rates, traditional bookselling would not prove profitable after the end of the war. Here was an opening for Hatry to do what he had done before his imprisonment: form a new combine by acquiring bookshops. By 1945, he had formed a network of 19 bookshops around the original shop in Piccadilly through acquiring F.&E. Stoneham's chain of shops in the City and the Burnside Bookshops in north-west London, among others. He had also acquired book wholesaling businesses supplying public and private lending libraries, and in 1940, after a catastrophic fire at the premises of the premier wholesaler, Simpkin Marshall, he had acquired that business's remainders department. Cyril Edgley took a leading role in managing this group, becoming a member of the committee of management and general manager of the group's shops other than the Hatchards shops in Piccadilly and Wolverhampton.

So far, Hatry's development of Hatchards had been a success. A shop that had been in difficulty had become the centre of a chain of booksellers with professional management whose sales had proved buoyant. Unfortunately, he did not stop there. Whereas up to this point Hatry had concentrated on acquiring bookshops and wholesalers who were all involved in closely related businesses which could jointly take advantage of economies of scale, Hatry had begun to acquire other businesses which did not share a close relationship with retail bookselling such as Crosby Lockwood, a printing company, and T. Werner Laurie, a publisher.

Hatry seems to have believed that the group would benefit from owning a publishing company whose products would be sold by the group's bookshops, and a printing company which would print the books commissioned by the publisher. In time, Hatry was to carry this further by buying companies that produced printing and binding machinery which would be used by the printing company to manufacture books. In practice, there was little synergy between the elements of this exercise in 'vertical integration'. Bookshops exist to sell to customers the books which interest them, whichever publisher is responsible for them. In normal circumstances, a bookseller could not hope to derive a benefit from concentrating on the sales of a single publisher. To make a profit, publishers need their books to be printed at the least cost commensurate with the quality of product they desire. Forcing a publisher to use one printer for all books may not be (and in the case of Hatchards was not) a good way of achieving a competitive price. Similarly, publishers need their books to be bound at the least cost commensurate with the outcome desired, whatever the merits or demerits of the equipment produced by an in-group manufacturer. On top of all of this, the acquisition of disparate companies in different trades caused consternation within the group's management team, leading to the resignation of Cyril Edgley, and stretched its management resources, as the example of T. Werner Laurie shows.[16]

At first, on acquisition, the publishing company was overseen by Hatry's daughter, Diana, who had no particular qualification or experience relevant to publishing but was available in part because of the failure of her marriage to Miles de Orellane Tollemache, a naval officer who was the son of the headmaster of the Imperial Service College until its closure in March 1942. This was intended to be only a stopgap measure while Hatry looked for someone else. The need was met as a result of a chance meeting between Hatry's son, Cecil, and George Greenfield who recalled that on a bright summer day in 1946 he found himself outside Hatchards after being 'demobbed' from the army at the end of the war. Having served continuously for more than four years overseas, he was entitled to six months' leave on full pay and was enjoying the experience of being paid for doing nothing. By chance, as he was looking at Hatchards' window, Cecil, Hatry's son, came out of the shop and recognised him. In 1944, they had both been serving in the Rifle Brigade in what is now called Iraq and had not seen each other for two years. Over lunch, Cecil asked George Greenfield what he planned to do when his leave was over and suggested that he might run Werner Laurie. Greenfield was initially reluctant. Although he had recently had a war novel published, he felt ignorant of the book trade and thought it a rather speculative business. However, lulled by good wine and Cecil's enthusiasm he eventually agreed to meet Cecil's father. By the end of that first meeting, George Greenfield had agreed that from 1 January 1947, the end of his extended leave, he would manage the publishing house at a salary of £1,000 per year and that in the meantime he would gain some experience by acting as an outside reader of manuscripts submitted to Werner Laurie in the intervening months.[17]

Soon after he started at Werner Laurie, George Greenfield asked Hatry for a briefing. Hatry responded by asking what he meant. On being told that Greenfield wanted to know what books he was supposed to publish, Hatry replied it was up to Greenfield: 'You're the publisher, not me'.[18] On seeing that the inexperienced Greenfield was nonplussed by this, Hatry expanded his guidance by saying:

> You go ahead and publish what you like for a full year. At the end of the year, we'll look at the balance sheet. If it ends up in black ink, fine – you go on for another year. If it ends up in red ink, I'll give you the

> gypsy's warning but you'll still go for another year. But if at the end of the second year, there's still red ink on the balance sheet, you're fired. You understand? Right, that's my briefing for you.[19]

That was the basis on which they operated for the next five and a half years.

In practice, the group was dependent on Hatry. Although there was a board of directors, day-to-day management decisions, especially decisions on finance, were not always reported comprehensively to the directors so that decisions were frequently taken without the benefit of discussion and challenge.[20] Unfortunately, his management style was hit and miss. In the case of George Greenfield, he happened to find a man who had great aptitude for the book trade and was to become highly successful, although not as a publisher but as a literary agent. In later years, Greenfield represented a number of very well-regarded authors such as David Niven, Rex Harrison, Sir Edmund Hillary, Sir Vivian Fuchs and Enid Blyton. Under his leadership, Werner Laurie was to prove successful.

But there were also notorious failures both of selection and supervision. In 1950, Hatry was approached by a consultant who pointed to the chance to buy a patent from the Custodian of Enemy Property at a bargain price. The Brehmer machine allegedly transformed the process for stitching together groups of a book's pages or 'signatures' before covers were attached, and had proved its efficacy in Germany during the war. Hatry acquired the patent and hired the consultant to manage British Brehmer Limited, the company formed to exploit the patent. This decision was a mistake. The machine, which Hatry had not evaluated, did not function properly and the consultant used his position to defraud Hatry's companies of £30,000 to £40,000.

Even some of the more promising appointees such as George Greenfield could not avoid making some mistakes as they were learning 'on the job' and without helpful guidance.

Avoidable mistakes such as the acquisition of the Brehmer patent depressed the group's earnings, which were not maximised by the recruitment of people who had talent but no experience and others such as Albert Tabor who were appointed out of loyalty to old associates who lacked employment. Someone had to bear the cost of their inevitable mistakes while learning on the job.

As a consequence, the Hatchards group's finances became troublesome as profits stumbled and the cost of financing the group grew.

At first, Hatry's acquisitions were financed by private borrowing. When Hatchards was first bought, Hatry's wife loaned him money to serve as a deposit for the Shepherd brothers' equity in the shop, while Sir Thomas Moore, the Earl of Jersey and others lent the money required to buy the shop's stock (about £12,000). Subsequent purchases, such as the remainders department of Simpkin Marshall, had been financed partly by further private loans and partly from the profits earned by the Piccadilly shop. By 1945, these sources of cash were no longer adequate to finance Hatry's ambitions. A draft offer for sale was prepared by Ashurst Morris Crisp but this proposal did not proceed.[21] In June 1944, the government had brought into force the Prevention of Fraud (Investments) Act 1939, on which Sir Samuel Hoare had relied in approving Hatry's early release from prison, and which prevented Hatry's direct involvement in share offers of this kind.

To fill the gap, Hatry took advantage of what would now be described as an 'aggressive tax avoidance' scheme. Taxpayers wishing to shelter income from high rates of income tax were invited to buy shares in the holding company of the Hatchards group. The initial purchase was matched by an undertaking to buy back the shares at a future date. On repurchase the price payable was to be higher than the original purchase price and calculated to produce a gain which would equate to the interest that would have been earned on a loan. Although loan interest would have created an income tax liability, the gain on repurchase of the shares would be treated as a capital gain which did not attract a tax liability. Initially, this scheme proved attractive to taxpayers with sufficient income to be interested in avoiding the highest rates of tax, but it became burdensome for Hatry's group. As the initial agreements expired and the shares had to be repurchased, the group's need for financial support had to be faced again. When this happened, the easiest answer was to repeat the process but this had the undesirable result that the starting point would be the higher price at which the shares had been repurchased. In other words, the group's financing liabilities grew by compounding the quasi-interest that was payable because it could not easily be treated as a charge to the group's profit and loss account.

By 1947, the compounding effect was proving such an embarrassment that the company was driven to realise the value of the lease of Hatchards' premises at 187 and 188 Piccadilly by a sale and lease-back. Subsequently, Hatry engineered the sale and lease-back of the Park Royal premises of Argosy. Although this relieved the pressure on capital, the higher rental charges that followed worsened the group's trading results. Eventually, the group was forced to sell assets to realise cash to reduce its liabilities. In 1950, Godfrey & Company, which owned 13 shops selling 'everything musical' was sold to Isaac Wolfson. Later one of the group's printing companies was sold to Iliffe Press. Then Argosy & Sundial Library Services was sold, as was the group's head office in Tudor Street, just off Fleet Street. Finally, in January 1952, it was announced that Wyman and Sons Limited were to buy 23 shops, including the F.&E. Stoneham group in the City of London and the Burnside group in the suburbs. The Hatchards group was being dismantled.

The sale to Wyman & Sons exhausted the patience of the directors of Hatchards Limited, the subsidiary which still owned and managed the Piccadilly shop. They became concerned that the proceeds of the sale of the group's assets were not being recycled to repay the advances that Hatchards had made to the holding company to buy those assets and realised that they might have been too trusting in allowing Hatry to manage the group without thoroughly reporting all his plans and actions to them. Moreover, it was obvious to them that the holding company had been selling the most profitable companies which left it with the least successful, such as British Brehmer, which could not be relied upon to secure repayment to Hatchards of its advances to the holding company. Facing the seriousness of their position, the directors began to demand explanations from Hatry. Notably, Sir Thomas Moore, who had been instrumental in securing Hatry's early release from prison and in his original acquisition of the Piccadilly bookshop threatened that if adequate explanations were not provided, they would report to the police that they suspected that Hatchards had been the target of a fraud organised by Hatry.

The directors of Hatchards were not the only group to be concerned. A small number of high-worth individuals who were shareholders in Hatchards Associated Interests, as a result of Hatry's tax-based scheme, began to fear that their holdings would not be recoverable. For them, the attraction of the scheme depended on being able to resell their interests under their agreements with Hatry. But a number of events suggested that recovering their money might be in doubt. They realised that the rapid sale of the group's most profitable subsidiaries suggested that the group was in difficulty. They did not know how great that difficulty might be and whether the company sales had led to profits or losses, as in January 1952 the group's accounts for the year ended 31 March 1951 had still not been published. Finally, at the beginning of 1952, the group decided not to pay an annual dividend. Two of these shareholders, M.A. Hassid and Ian Henderson, began to lobby the Board of Trade to appoint an inspector to investigate Hatchards Associated Interests to discover whether there was evidence of fraud.

Throughout the spring and early summer of 1952, the pressure on Hatry from these two groups grew, until it came to a head at the beginning of July when the Annual General Meeting of shareholders was imminent. On 5 July 1952, it was announced that Hatry had resigned all of his directorships and had gone into a nursing home following a complete nervous breakdown. The newspapers reported an unnamed colleague saying that 'He has been unwell for some time. An unlimited power of attorney which he gave to his attorney has now been exercised on his behalf with the result that he is no longer a director of any company'.[22]

From this point, Hatry took no further part in the management of the group; his treatment prevented it. He later recalled that he underwent a 'course of brain shock treatment for chronic insomnia'.[23] It was left to the remaining directors to clear up.[24]

At the shareholders' meeting which was held soon after Hatry's resignation, the directors were at a disadvantage. Although they knew that the group's financial position was unsatisfactory, they were not able to explain to the shareholders how this had come about. Audited accounts for the year ended 31 March 1951 were still not available and would not be circulated for another two or three months, a delay that was difficult to understand since the principal subsidiaries' accounts had all been published and approved by their shareholders.[25]

When the audited 1951 accounts were finally published, the location of the problem became clear: the auditors' report was qualified because the holding company's account with Hatry was still being investigated.[26] At the shareholders' meeting to consider the annual report and accounts, shareholders became frustrated that the directors were still unable to answer questions on the transactions engineered, not least a loan of £10,000 that had been made to Hatry's brother, Eric.[27]

Matters were eased soon after the meeting when the company's name was changed from Hatchards Associated Interests to Printing and Allied Holdings Limited so that the subsidiary Hatchards Limited[28] could be sold to William Collins and Sons with an uncontested right to use the name 'Hatchards'. As the interest in Hatchards was the principal remaining asset of the holding company, this sale clarified the financial state of the holding company and the shareholders' irritation over what had led to its demise gradually subsided.

Notes

1 *Sunday Telegraph*, 8 August 1965, page 4.
2 This was a considerable gift as the Dorchester became known as one of the safest bomb shelters during the war (Sweet, 2011, pages 89–90; Towle, undated, page 27).
3 Hatry, 1939, page xv.
4 Review notice: *The Times*, 4 August 1939, page 17; Letters: *The Times*, 7 August 1939, page 6; 11 August 1939, page 11.
5 *Sunday Times*, 1 January 1967, pages 10–11 (supplement).
6 Greenfield, 1995, page 51.
7 Description of trading difficulties in draft application to the stock exchange for permission to deal in the company's shares (particulars of companies, page 1, TNA file MEPO file 2/610084).
8 Statement of Sir Thomas Moore (page 2, TNA file MEPO 2/610084).
9 Greenfield, 1995, page 52.
10 Greenfield, 1995, pages 52–53.
11 *The Bookseller*, 12 February 1942, page 100.
12 Statement of C.R. Edgley (page 1, TNA file MEPO 2/610084).
13 *The Bookseller*, 5 February 1942, page 88.
14 Description of trading difficulties in draft application to the stock exchange for permission to deal in the company's shares (particulars of companies, pages 1–2, TNA file MEPO file 2/610084).
15 Greenfield, 1995, page 62; *The Bookseller*, 20 December 1945, page 869.
16 Greenfield, 1995, page 68.
17 Greenfield, 1995, pages 43–45; Greenfield, 1998, page 171.
18 Greenfield, 1995, pages 43–45.
19 Greenfield, 1995, pages 43–45.
20 Statement by Sir Thomas Moore (page 1, TNA file MEPO 2/610084).
21 The document does not explain the circumstances in which it might have been used. As Hatry was not licensed under the Prevention of Fraud (Investments) Act 1939, it could not have been used as a public offer. It might have been intended for use in raising money privately.
22 Greenfield, 1995, pages 43–45.
23 Statement based on interviews with S.M. Duncan on 11 August, 15 and 27 October and 1 November 1954 (TNA file MEPO 2/610084).

24 *Daily Mail*, 16 July 1952, page 3.
25 *Daily Mail*, 16 July 1952, page 3; 17 July 1952, page 4.
26 *Daily Mail*, 28 October 1952, page 2.
27 *Daily Mail*, 15 November 1952, page 2.
28 *Daily Mail*, 6 December 1952.

References

Primary works: unpublished documents

TNA: Metropolitan police force papers.

Primary works: newspapers and periodicals

Daily Mail.
Sunday Telegraph.
Sunday Times.
The Bookseller.
The Times.

Primary works: contemporary books and papers

Hatry, C.C. (1939), *Light Out of Darkness.* (Rich and Cowan, London).
Towle, F.T. (undated), 'A Brief History of a New Enterprise', in Bound with Arlen, M. *A Young Man Comes to London: An Original Short Story.* (Privately published, London).

Secondary works

Greenfield, G. (1995), *A Smattering of Monsters: A Kind of Memoir.* (Little Brown, London).
Greenfield, G. (1998), *Chasing the Beast: One Man's War.* (Richard Cohen Books, London).
Sweet, M. (2011), *The West End Front: The Wartime Secrets of London's Grand Hotels.* (Faber and Faber, London).

15 After Hatchards

News of the Hatchards group's financial difficulties and the disposal of its shops had spread and had led to speculation in the newspapers in Bulawayo in Southern Rhodesia that Hatry was contemplating joining his son, Cecil, who had moved there some years before and had taken an interest in a hotel. This led to the Commander of Bulawayo CID writing to New Scotland Yard to ask for information about Clarence Hatry's offences. In response, the Metropolitan Police supplied a six-page report of Hatry's activities which ended: 'Exhaustive enquiries have been made in financial and trade circles with the result that no person has voiced any suspicions against Hatry's business methods since his release from prison'.[1] The Metropolitan Police's report did not recommend whether the Bulawayo police should permit Hatry to enter Southern Rhodesia and the concluding paragraph of the report might suggest that there should be no objection. However, any possibility that emigration to Southern Rhodesia might have been an acceptable way to escape from his problems must have been scotched by the suspicions surrounding his part in the demise of the group in July 1952. In any event, he stayed in London to recover his health and disentangle himself from the Hatchards group.

Recovery from his nervous breakdown proved problematic. His stay in a nursing home was prolonged and he later recalled that he was given electric shock treatment. Although he had emerged from his treatment by the summer of 1953, he suffered a road accident in the autumn in which his pelvis was fractured and he was yet again immobilised. These successive adversities left him frail, often hampered by angina.[2]

Meanwhile, an unsatisfactory shareholders' meeting in November 1952, at which the holding company's directors had still not been able to answer shareholders' questions, had led the Metropolitan Police to commence an investigation. In parallel, and in response to representations from two of the largest shareholders, M.A. Hassid and I. Henderson, the Board of Trade appointed an inspector under the Companies Acts. The police investigation rapidly concluded that the evidence immediately available was insufficient to support fraud charges and it was resolved to wait for the conclusion of the Board of Trade inspection.[3]

Ironically, the person appointed as inspector by the Board of Trade was Stanley Duncan, a partner in Price, Waterhouse & Company, who had worked with

Sir Gilbert Garnsey, and who, after Sir Gilbert's death, had taken on the preparation of updated editions of Sir Gilbert's book on consolidated accounting.

Duncan found that the group had become embroiled in a convoluted series of transactions which it was presumed had been devised to resolve the group's financial difficulty. In principle, the scheme which Hatry attempted to implement was designed to place Hatchards Limited, the company which owned the Piccadilly shop, at the head of the group of companies in place of Hatchards Associated Interests. By doing this, the transfer to Hatchards Limited of the holding company's interests could be set against the advances by Hatchards Limited to the holding company, so restoring the health of the shop company's balance sheet. In practice, achievement of this desirable objective had proved problematic, partly because the amounts realised by sale of the holding company's assets had proved disappointing and because of difficulties in unwinding commitments to repay individuals who had been inveigled into holding shares by Hatry's tax-based scheme. What had been a simple scheme in principle had become submerged in a bewildering and complicated series of transactions. Duncan's five 'interim' reports attempted to disentangle these transactions but failed to find any evidence of fraudulent intent.

By the time that the fifth 'interim' report had been submitted, shareholders' agitation for action by the Board of Trade had subsided and it was decided that the Board of Trade inspection should be discontinued.[4]

For a while, the Metropolitan Police investigation continued. But the police's own enquiries produced no more evidence of fraud than Stanley Duncan's investigation, and further enquiry was discouraged by the disinclination of key shareholders to provide evidence. M.A. Hassid, Ian Henderson and the Countess of Seafield, through her solicitor, all indicated that they would prefer not to give evidence in a prosecution. Although all of them were suspicious of the role which Hatry had played, they all feared they might be vulnerable to prosecution if they could be shown to have acted illegally as unlicensed moneylenders in advancing money under the tax-based financing scheme Hatry had devised. Although the police were led by Hatry's background to be suspicious of the part he had played in the demise of Hatchards, the police enquiry did not proceed. The police's final gambit was to suggest to the Board of Trade that bankrupting Hatry should be considered, but the board decided that sleeping dogs should be left to lie.[5]

Ultimately, Sir Samuel Hoare had won. His agreement to Hatry's early release from prison had been delayed until he could be reasonably sure that Hatry could not return to his former activities. Although Hatry had been able to create a new group of companies around Hatchards, the financing scheme that he had been obliged to devise to circumvent the law's restrictions on his share trading activities had failed and he had been forced to dismantle the group. Hatry was fortunate in escaping from this debacle without further humiliation in the form either of a prosecution or civil actions for damages. The shareholders who might have sued him, such as the Countess of Seafield, were discouraged from such actions by their own vulnerability. He was, however, left to share with Captain Robert Maxwell the unenviable distinction of having been the subject of two Board of Trade inspections.

Some parties did not escape so lightly, however. It was discovered that his solicitor, Philip Game of Ashurst Morris Crisp, who had taken on the connection with Hatry on the retirement of Sir John Crisp, had misapplied a fund of which he acted as trustee, to support the shares of one of the companies in the Hatchards group. His firm was obliged to make good the loss and Philip Game's career as a City solicitor was over.[6]

Game was not alone. In November 1955, Atherton Powys, whom Hatry had first met in 1915 and who had managed Hatry's personal affairs during the prison years, was obliged to terminate his practice with effect from March 1954 and was struck off the Roll of Solicitors in November 1955. At the Law Society's Disciplinary Committee hearing, Powys explained that the greater part of his time had been occupied by the Hatchards group and that this retainer had been terminated suddenly, doubtless following Hatry's resignation. This had destroyed his income 'at one blow'. Under pressure from Hatchards group companies to pay sums due from him, he had misapplied funds which he held on behalf of other clients.[7]

Emerging from this long drawn out and, for him, depressing process, Hatry could begin to rebuild his fortune. Yet again he had lost heavily – he had been the largest shareholder in Hatchards Associated Interests so had suffered with others as the value of his investment had depreciated. Yet again he had lost a home, as he sold 'The Hermitage', a cliff-top house at St Margaret's Bay near Dover which Hatry had bought from Colonel J.J. Astor in 1946.[8] Yet again, his reputation had been diminished.

Hatry's next step was unexpected. In the 1950s, Charles Forte was building a chain of milk bars and coffee shops. Hatry seems to have copied Forte's initiative by taking over interests in two coffee bars: the Gondola in Wigmore Street and the Cavalier which he opened in Dover Street, not far from 180 Piccadilly, the location of his insurance broking office before 1914. Both were described as having air conditioning and heated terraces. Hatry was reported to visit the Cavalier on a daily basis and his wife was reported to be helping with the organisation in the kitchen and on the services floor. Hatry told a journalist: 'It is true that I am back in business and happy to be there. I have been very sick, but I am quite active again now and working very hard. My interests in the Espresso business are very small'.[9]

The coffee venture did not prosper as Forte's had done. Charles Forte proved to be an inspired manager of coffee shops and, eventually, of entertainment venues and hotels. Hatry was not an accomplished manager – his talents lay elsewhere.

Hatry next acquired an interest in a small private printer, Claridge, Lewis & Jordan, which in 1960 was absorbed into a Scottish agricultural engineering company, John Wallace & Sons, which had a stock market quotation.[10] Although it was intended to use John Wallace & Sons as a platform for transactions devised by Hatry, his involvement was not acknowledged publicly for fear that this would encounter a negative reaction. Hatry was careful to act as a private undisclosed adviser. With his guidance and encouragement, the company embarked on a programme of acquisitions in a fashion that would have seemed familiar to anyone aware of Hatry's former activities. In 1957, the group's trading profits had been running at about £50,000 per year. By 1962, they exceeded £500,000. The group's activities were extended beyond engineering to include kitchen furniture, outdoor clothing and jewellery manufacture.[11]

Although Hatry's involvement in the acquisition programme had not been acknowledged publicly, rumours began to circulate, encouraged by the fact that Clarence's son, Cecil, had returned from Southern Rhodesia and was a director of most of the subsidiaries of John Wallace. In July 1962, the rumours were confirmed by Nigel Lawson, then City editor of the *Sunday Telegraph*, in an article under the headline 'Clarence Hatry, at 73, tries again'.[12] This article produced the reaction which Hatry had feared: the company came under pressure to sever its relationship with him. In March 1963, Hugh Stenhouse, the chairman of Stenhouse Holdings, an insurance broking group, acquired the shares of Hatry and his associates and Hatry's involvement with John Wallace & Sons came to a premature end.[13]

Hatry was left with two groups of interests: London United Laundries and a group of knitwear companies.

The name of London United Laundries was changed twice: to Associated Cleaning Companies and then again to Affiliated Cleaning Companies to avoid confusion with the name of another company.[14] In mid-March 1963, the company announced that it had acquired controlling interests in four cleaning firms: Acme Industrial Cleaners, All England Cleaning, Express Window Cleaning and General Cleaning contractors.[15] As a result of these acquisitions, the group was able to claim to be the largest cleaning contractor in the country.[16] Although Hatry advised on these various acquisitions, he told Nigel Lawson that he did not intend to take any part in the management of the company and its subsidiaries, nor to have a long-term arrangement with the group.[17]

Hatry was as good as his word. Two months later, when Sidney Roberts, the new managing director of Affiliated Cleaning Companies, gave an interview to the *Daily Mail*, he stated that Hatry no longer had any connection with the group – he had sold out.[18] After his departure, the company proved successful and continued to trade profitably until it was acquired by the Pritchards Cleaners group in 1968.[19]

That left Hatry still working on plans for the knitwear companies. A new holding company, formed in 1964, was called Associated Knitwear and acquired interests in four companies: Joh Currie & Son, Cumroch Knitwear, Hill Jones and Channells Hi-bulk Knitwear. Its chairman was Cecil Hatry, Clarence's son.[20] Hatry was still working on this project in the year of his death, but early in 1966 the company received an offer for all of its share capital from Bond Street Fabrics.[21] That offer was accepted so another Hatry project yielded its independence. In this case, the merger was not successful. Bond Street Fabrics specialised in knitting fashion fabrics for others to make up, whereas Associated Knitwear's companies were involved in making garments. It took some years for the enlarged group to recover from the difficulty of merging these different activities.[22]

In the meantime, Hatry's life had come to an end. After his experience of rheumatic fever before 1910, his health had never been robust. He had walked with a limp and had suffered a series of health problems at times of peak stress. His nervous breakdown in 1952 was merely the latest incident of this type but had left him even more frail than before. After that he had suffered from angina and a police memorandum in 1962 reported that although he was still attending his companies' offices several days each week, he was very frail physically and was rarely allowed to move about without someone accompanying him.[23] In the months before his death, he suffered a series of heart attacks[24] before dying of cardiac failure in the Westminster Hospital on 10 June 1965 at the age of 76.[25]

Two months later his will was published. The net value of his estate was nil. As the *Daily Mail* proclaimed, the man who had been the millionaire tycoon of the 1920s and had once controlled companies worth £30,500,000 died penniless.[26]

Notes

1 Letter dated February 1952 (National Archives, file MEPO 2/610084).
2 Greenfield, 1995, page 72.
3 Report of DI Kennedy dated 5 December 1952 (TNA, file MEPO 2/610084).
4 TNA file MEPO 2/610084.
5 Report of Superintendent Bliss dated 16 January 1956 (National Archives, file MEPO 2/610084).
6 *Law Society Gazette*, August 1952, page 320.
7 *Law Society Gazette*, December 1955, page 379; January 1956, page 37; order dated 18 November 1955 (Solicitors' Disciplinary Tribunal Archive).
8 *News Chronicle*, 15 July 1952.
9 *Daily Mail*, 5 August 1955, page 3.
10 *The Times*, 30 October 1961, page 18.
11 *The Times*, 30 October 1961, page 2; 21 November 1962, page 4; 25 September 1963, page 9.
12 *Sunday Telegraph*, 15 July 1962, page 2.
13 *Sunday Times*, 7 April 1963, page 9.
14 *Financial Times*, 2 April 1963, page 18.
15 *The Times*, 16 March 1963, page 15.
16 *The Times*, 24 May 1963, page 21.
17 *Sunday Telegraph*, 15 July 1962, page 2; 3 March 1963, page 11; 17 March 1963, page 8.
18 *Daily Mail*, 24 May 1963, page 17.
19 *The Times*, 24.
20 *Daily Mail*, 18 October 1965, page 17.
21 *Daily Telegraph*, 9 April 1966, page 3.
22 *Sunday Telegraph*, 21 March 1971, page 24.
23 Memorandum dated 13 August 1962 (TNA file MEPO 2/610084).
24 *Sunday Telegraph*, 8 August 1965, page 4.

25 Death certificate. The certified causes of death were: (1a) Cardiac failure. (1b) Bronchopneumonia. (1c) Carcinoma of the bronchus. (2) Previous history of recurrent myocardial infarction.
26 *Daily Mail*, 25 August 1965, page 1.

References

Primary works: unpublished documents

Solicitors' Disciplinary Tribunal Archive.
TNA: Metropolitan police force papers.

Primary works: newspapers and periodicals

Daily Mail.
Financial Times.
Law Society Gazette.
News Chronicle.
Sunday Telegraph.
Sunday Times.
The Times.

Secondary works

Greenfield, G. (1995), *A Smattering of Monsters: A Kind of Memoir.* (Little Brown, London).

16 Reflections

In the years immediately before the 1914–1918 war, London was arguably the most significant financial market place in the world. Its position was not unchallenged. New York in particular was growing in importance, but London remained the market in which major international issues would be launched and in which issuers could be confident that financial risks of all types could be traded.[1]

Remarkably, in contrast to other European centres, to a large extent London operated without detailed constraint from public law. The London Stock Exchange was a private organisation which was managed by trustees and members, set its own rules and obliged its members to settle disputes within the exchange without resort to public law. To maximise its members' business, the exchange encouraged all manner of companies and organisations to seek finance by arranging for their shares and bonds to be dealt on the exchange. The effect had been to develop a marketplace which some have likened to the Wild West.

What there was by way of public regulation consisted largely of requirements for public disclosure of corporate information. Although these requirements had been reviewed repeatedly and from time to time had been improved, they remained limited and were not supported by consistent efforts to discourage and punish non-compliance. A period of aggressive investigation during the 1890s had been followed by a retreat from active governmental oversight.

Rather than rely upon public law regulation, members of the stock exchange and other financial markets depended on their private rules and conventions to defend reputations from the riskiness of their markets. They were dependent upon networks of trust built within frameworks of these private rules for confidence in the good character and financial standing of fellow members.

Achieving membership of the exchange did not require candidates to demonstrate financial skills, knowledge or commercial acumen. Rather they were expected to provide affirmations by existing members of good character and financial standing.[2] On becoming members, they were required not only to accept unlimited personal liability for their debts, but also to undertake that they and their immediate families would not become involved with trades that might conflict with their activities as members. They were also obliged to accept that membership would have to be renewed annually so that any shortcomings could lead to rapid expulsion without a formal disciplinary process through a simple decision by the committee against renewal of membership.

This is the world which at some point before 1914 Clarence Hatry committed himself to join, perhaps thinking that by his experience of loan broking and immigrant insurance he had demonstrated an aptitude for financial wizardry. For him commercial success alone was not the objective – acceptance and integration were both at least as important. During his childhood, Hatry had visited Zweibrücken whence his father Julius had emigrated to London in 1871, and, as a result, was aware of the sense of separateness and anti-Semitism which had contributed to the family's decision to send Julius, his father, to London. He understood the efforts that his father had made to integrate with English society and his own role in imperilling his father's achievement and causing his mother's bankruptcy.

However, acceptance as an equal member of the City community was problematic. His personal bankruptcy would long linger in the mind to justify doubts about his good standing. Although Julius had become a British subject by naturalisation, so that Clarence was born British, his recent German ancestry attracted comment during wartime. Although it was possible for Jews to gain acceptance, as Frederick Szarvasy was able to do, Hatry lacked a respected and influential sponsor who could ease his path. Against these drawbacks, financial skill alone was powerless.

The effects of these drawbacks can be seen in the opportunities that Hatry was to seize both during and immediately after the 1914–1918 war. When he began to reorganise and to float companies, he was to take on work that other people would not undertake. His association with Sperling & Company in 1917 and 1918 involved him in selling shares off-market directly to investors at a time when such issues were frowned upon because they exploited limitations in the government's wartime regulation of share issues. In so doing he attracted the resentment of members of the exchange for undertaking work that was denied to them by the temporary wartime regulations. Although Hatry was able to float a series of companies during the post-war boom, his flotations were of a different quality from those of more acceptable operators. When the partners of Clare & Company and Frederick Szarvasy began their company promotions again in 1919, they found openings to float substantial businesses with good prospects. These flotations were uncontroversial. Many of Hatry's flotations, in contrast, were suspect.

Whether hiding cash extraction and tax planning in the case of Leyland Motors Limited, hiding a restrictive governance structure in the case of Agricultural Industries Limited or obscuring weak commercial prospects in the case of Jute Industries Limited, Hatry's promotions involved misleading investors. In this, Hatry's function was to achieve on behalf of the vendors, his clients, commercial objectives which were problematic and which many City houses would not touch, although they were prepared to support the transactions covertly by participation in underwriting.

In adopting this approach, Hatry's clients were taking a risk, but Hatry was taking a similar risk by accepting their instructions. His approach created a series of safeguards against that risk. If proceedings were initiated against them on the grounds of fraud, his clients would presumably have argued that they had taken the best advice they could and been advised that the drafting of the prospectus or offer document had complied with both the law and current practice. Hatry would then doubtless have demonstrated that the public documents had indeed complied with all the necessary disclosure requirements. However, quite apart from a list of detailed disclosure requirements provided in Section 81 of the 1908 Act, Section 84 provided that directors and promoters would be held liable for untrue statements. As the court had found that the phrase 'untrue statement' would encompass a misleading statement and that the omission of a material fact might render a prospectus fraudulent, it might have been difficult for Hatry to demonstrate on every occasion that in this respect the law's requirements had been observed.[3]

Hatry must have been aware of this risk and considered how it might be mitigated. One curious feature of his business may explain how he regarded the risk that his promotions might be found to be fraudulent. He used to say that no one should lose money by investing in his promotions. Such claims were frequently made by company promoters, but Hatry alone acted on his assertions. Between 1923 and 1925, he not only disbursed his personal fortune buying up shares which he had promoted but whose price had fallen disastrously, but also distributed shares in his new company, Aylesbury Trust Limited (later renamed Austin Friars Trust Limited) to shareholders in Commercial Bank of London (which had been renamed Commercial Corporation of London). In 1928, he repeated the exercise, buying up the shares of Glasgow Bonding Company Limited. Much later, in the 1940s, Hatry bought back George Greenfield's shares in Hatchards Associated Interests when Greenfield reminded him of his promise. There are a number of reasons for Hatry acting in this way. He may have wanted to honour commitments to members of his syndicates or to maintain share prices to preserve the value of shares deposited as collateral for loans. But he may also have wanted to demonstrate that he had not intended that anyone should lose money as without demonstrable intent, he could not be found guilty of fraud. After all, this is how his barrister, Norman Birkett, presented the point during Hatry's trial. Even if the argument would not serve as a defence, Hatry may well have convinced himself his efforts absolved him of moral responsibility for what others may have regarded as fraud.

Whatever Hatry's private thoughts may have been, a prosecution for fraud would have brought to a close his activity as a company promoter. Even so, accomplishing improbable promotions on behalf of knowing clients did little to bring closer Hatry's acceptance and integration within the financial community of London. Superficially, making a personal fortune and acquiring the traditional symbols of wealth such as the racing yacht *Westward* may have appeared an achievement, as may joining the board of London Assurance and the council of the British Empire Union. But as the curious incident of Hatry's application for a baronetcy suggested, the City still regarded Hatry as an outsider who could not be trusted unreservedly. That Hatry had set himself the target of securing an honour at this stage suggests that he had not understood this and betrayed an outsider's insensitivity.

As the market recovered from the chastening depression of 1920–1921, its character and the type of new issues changed. With these changes, Hatry's activities also changed. There remained a large number of new issues seeking finance for the exploitation of new technologies such as artificial silk and of new consumer tastes such as cinema and greyhound racing. But in place of the 1919 issues which sought finance to enable businesses recovering from war to seize the opportunities which people confidently expected peace to bring, there was recognition that many industries and market structures required reorganisation, which led to a series of proposals and schemes for rationalisation.

Although Hatry continued to promote a number of new issues which capitalised on new technologies and public tastes, in the latter half of the 1920s his principal activities centred on amalgamations for which he had demonstrated an aptitude in the formation of Jute Industries Limited. He was able to enter this field as a result of two pieces of good fortune which spoke to his undoubted strengths and neutralised his weaknesses.

The first piece of good fortune was his introduction to Arthur Collins and the world of local authority finance. The challenge posed to Hatry by Collins was to reduce the cost of issuing local authority bonds. This did not require Hatry to advise authorities on how much money they should raise. Hatry did not have to structure an authority's balance sheet. He was to have no responsibility for managing the authorities' affairs. He merely had to use his knowledge of the marketplace to find the cheapest way of raising the money an authority required. Even in this he was to be assisted by Collins who was an active participant in Hatry's salesmanship. Hatry was able to rise to this challenge by applying his experience of company promotions to the issue of local authority loan stock and his experience of market trading to face down opposition from stock jobbers who had profited from the dominance of three broking firms who dominated the market for local authority and Empire loan stocks.

The second piece of good fortune was Ronald Gaze's insight that a combine of department stores could realise economies of scale which would transform the economic position of the large number of independent department stores. In this project, Hatry's role was again to be limited as it had been in local authority issues. Gaze was able to identify stores which would be good candidates for absorption into what became Drapery Trust. Gaze would then be responsible for managing the combine and realising the economies of scale.

Hatry's chief skills were his ability to devise schemes and to read the market so that he could implement his schemes. But his brilliant scheming was undermined by his weaknesses. His commercial judgement was suspect as he repeatedly ignored the risks faced by a business, perhaps believing that he would always be able to devise a new scheme to avoid any difficulty. He was a poor judge of people, surrounding himself with a team comprised of inexperienced sycophants disinclined to challenge his judgements. He was not interested in the detailed work involved in supervising organisations, people and transactions.

His greatest successes sprang from relationships with strong managers who were competent to make the key commercial judgements and who absolved him from playing a part in continuing management. This was well demonstrated by his achievements in local authority finance and in creating Drapery Trust.

While he was successful in reducing the costs of issuing local authority loan stocks, the project was ultimately to prove an embarrassment. Although Hatry had no role in managing the affairs of the local authorities concerned, their treasurers proved unable to assess the risks that his approach involved. In particular, they failed to appreciate and guard against the risk that was created by using one of Hatry's companies as the receiving agent for investors' subscriptions rather than a clearing bank. They proved unequal to the task of controlling Hatry's poor judgement of risk.

Contrastingly, when Drapery Trust reached its apotheosis in its acquisition by Debenhams, Hatry's suspect commercial judgement was neutralised. Although Hatry devised the transactions by which the acquisition was effected, the amount of new capital raised and the structure of the new group's balance sheet were both controlled by Maurice Wright, filling the role of the new group's finance director.

All of Hatry's schemes of amalgamation in the late 1920s display similar characteristics. London Public Omnibus Limited was built on the back of the technologically innovative Admiral Line whose management controlled the absorption of independent London bus companies.[4] Associated Automatic Machine Corporation Limited was built on an experienced management team. Allied Ironfounders was built around the management of a Scottish foundry. Even the ill-starred United Steel Companies project was to be based on a muscular management team which had convinced the company's bankers of their competence. The catastrophic failure of that scheme arose not from any weakness in the commercial proposition or the management team but in Hatry's foolhardy and ultimately criminal mismanagement of the transaction.

As he must have known, by adopting a course that was explicitly fraudulent, Hatry was endangering his long-term ambition of achieving acceptance within the City community. His descent into blatant criminality is one of the key mysteries of his career.

The first step was taken at the beginning of June 1929, in response to Hatry's meeting with Lord Bearsted following the general election. As far as is known, Hatry first worked with Lord Bearsted in the public offer of preference shares for Debenhams at the beginning of 1928. This was the final stage of establishing the new group after Debenhams' acquisition of Drapery Trust and was structured as an offer for sale. Although the transaction had been planned by Hatry, M. Samuel & Company was the offeror, showing that Bearsted was content with the terms of the offer as agreed by Hatry with Maurice Wright of Debenhams.

This association continued as M. Samuel & Company had lent money to Hatry to support his transactions.[5] In January 1929, the bank was among the first to lend money to support the formation of Allied Ironfounders[6] and in the initial stages of the steel scheme it was widely understood that Hatry and M. Samuel & Company were cooperating in their exploration of the project. Although the steel scheme was larger than many of Hatry's projects, the records of his discussions with M. Samuel & Company suggest that he approached the negotiations in the way he had approached previous transactions. In other words, there were extensive discussions of the terms of various parties' participation which proceeded on the basis of oral commitments later to be confirmed in formal agreements when all parties had formally agreed the terms. On this basis, Hatry believed he had the support of M. Samuel & Company, as the bank's records confirm:

> Hatry wished to know whether he had our approval to make an offer on the lines discussed, it being understood that when he sees what acceptances he has received he will come to us with a clear proposition, and with a knowledge of the amount of money actually required. In view of the fact that the offer stipulates for 95% of acceptances, there appears no risk, and we agreed to the course proposed.[7]

Reliance on oral commitments in this way was not only typical of the way in which Hatry worked, but also in keeping with the traditions of the City with its proud boast: '*pactum meum dictum*'.[8]

In this light, Bearsted's repudiation of his bank's commitment to the steel scheme cannot have been expected by Hatry; it would have seemed a devastating social comment. Hatry himself had nervously anticipated that the steel scheme's chances of success would be undermined if the Conservative Party did not win the election – a nervousness that Hatry would have guessed that Bearsted shared. Bearsted's attitude at least suggested that for some time he had considered repudiation as a means of avoiding the bank's exposure.[9] There had been no warning to Hatry.

Hatry would have treated the repudiation as a personal slight – a sign that he was not regarded as an equal who would reasonably expect that oral commitments would be honoured.[10] He reacted as he did in 1920 over a baronetcy. Out of vanity he determined to prove his denigrators wrong.

The initial decision to find funds to replace Bearsted's contribution did not make insolvency inevitable. After all, by 23 June, the team had managed to obtain a large proportion of the funds that were required to honour the offer to buy United Steel's shares. But it increased the cost of failure because the team was obliged to confirm to financial supporters that all of the required funding was in place. Subsequent withdrawal would have led to claims from parties they had been misled.[11] By 23 June the financial cost of bringing the scheme to a close had grown unpalatably. This does not justify the decision to resort to faking receipts and certificates but it helps to explain why Hatry's team chose this desperate ploy.

Once the decision was implemented events led inexorably to collapse and the eventual trial. Hatry's confession and the extensive documentary evidence rendered conviction inevitable, but not the severity of the judgment. By sentencing Hatry to the maximum term of imprisonment for forgery (14 years compared with seven years for fraud) and by adding his own stinging words of condemnation, Sir Horace Avory awoke public sympathy.[12] There was a growing realisation that certain stock exchange practices and the off-market activities of abusive share pushers such as Jacob Factor were at least as anti-social as Hatry's. This public sympathy, coupled with the loyalty shown by a small number of close friends to Hatry, sustained the campaign for his early release.

His activities after release at the beginning of 1939 showed that he had not grown any more adept in building on his strengths and shielding his weaknesses. Seeing the commercial opportunity represented by the run-down Hatchards and finding a way to finance the initial purchase of a controlling interest may suggest that he had not lost his financial skills. At first, he avoided the mistake of managing the bookshop himself by relying on Cyril Edgley, which left Hatry free to build a chain of bookshops to capitalise upon the wartime demand for books. However, when Edgley withdrew from managing the bookshop, Hatry filled his place, which exposed again his weaknesses as a manager, not least through his decision to embark upon vertical integration through a number of ill-judged acquisitions. As before, the unavoidable result was that the Hatchards group could not continue and it was dismantled.

When, a few years later, he acquired interests in two coffee shops, he showed again that he had not understood his limitations. It should not have been a surprise that with his poor approach to management Hatry was not able to emulate Charles Forte, who at the same time was showing how a fortune could be built by managing chains of coffee shops. It was only on forging a connection with Wallace & Sons that Hatry was again to find himself in an environment where his skills in structuring and negotiating transactions could be applied successfully, although on this occasion it was fear of negative public reactions to news of his involvement that kept the nascent group free of his management weaknesses.

Perhaps, therefore, it is not surprising that in death, as in life, Hatry was a controversial figure.

Hatry's funeral in a South Kensington church on an overcast morning in June 1965 was an opportunity for loyal friends and his family to contemplate his life.

Few committed their thoughts to print[13] but their views may have reflected the conclusions of the memorandum which Hatry's son, Cecil, and his family solicitor, Sir John Crisp, had prepared and distributed to support the campaign for an early release from prison:

> We know that Mr Hatry … erred, and in seeking to retrieve his error did much that should not have been done. But he was never a reckless adventurer of the vulgar legend. He was a man of high quality and notable achievement who was caught in a world of depression and hoped, by taking certain risks, to win through, not for himself, but for his enterprises. By the narrowest of margins he failed. He has taken harsh punishment.[14]

There were many who could not share these views. Hatry's public reputation would forever be defined by Sir Horace Avory's view that Hatry's frauds were 'far more serious than any of the great frauds upon the public which have been committed within the last 50 years'. Sir Horace was 'unable to imagine any worse case.[15]

Within two months of Hatry's death, the *Sunday Telegraph* published two articles under the headline 'The Tragic Tycoon' in which Michael Pearson, who was said to have known Hatry well, tried to 'set the record straight'.[16] His second article concluded:

> To many City people, his crash and the trial that followed meant merely that he was a crook. To my mind, this is harsh – for a crook, with his brain, would have retained his personal fortune under cover of his companies' limited liability. I suspect that many upright, honest men would have been tempted to do as Hatry did in the same circumstances.
>
> The saddest aspect is that his undoubted brilliance, that could have achieved so much more than it did, was limited by other features of his character. He should perhaps have spent all his career as he spent his last years – as the architect of companies that other men controlled. As it was, his successes were not so dramatic as his failures, but there were many more of them.[17]

Two months later, a rejoinder came in the form of an article in the *Sunday Times* by Sir Edward Beddington-Behrens who before the 1939–1945 war was a partner in the issuing house Myers & Company, and who had set up his own issuing house, Ocean Trust. Under the headline 'The Impartial Swindler' his article began:

> There has been considerable recent apologetic publicity about the late Mr Clarence Hatry: that he was really honest at heart and was only overwhelmed by circumstances beyond his control. I often met Hatry in the period prior to the 'Hatry Crash' and I consider this view to be entirely erroneous.[18]

Two weeks later, after further articles by Pearson and Beddington-Behrens, the *Sunday Times* published an article by Sir Henry d'Avigdor-Goldsmid, a banker and bullion dealer, under the headline 'The Bogus Tycoon' which concluded with:

> one last anecdote which I have always thought rather typical of the whole affair: When the Austin Friars Trust premises were sold up a friend of mine bought a box of the very imposing cigars specially made for Hatry himself. He gave me one and I shared his disappointment when I realised that though very large they tasted of nothing at all. They were just a part of the bogus tycoon set-up that Hatry so much enjoyed.[19]

Hatry may not have deserved the sneering tone of this article, but it is undoubtedly true that he failed to achieve his great ambition: acceptance as a commercial and social equal by the City in which he operated for the whole of his career. It is also true that many lost much as a result of his activities and some such as Philip Game and Atherton Powys saw their careers ended as a result of their close association.

More kindly, his friends such as George Greenfield attested to his endearing personal qualities:

> At his funeral service, a line of poetry kept running through my mind. 'After life's fitful fever, he sleeps well.' CCH's buccaneering forays through the City made him many enemies but he paid with ten good years for his failings. He had a generous heart and a sense of fun. I owe him a lot.[20]

Notes

1 Michie, 1987, page 35; Michie, 1999, pages 135–138.
2 'There can be no doubt that an enormous amount of harm is done to the prestige of the Stock Exchange by people who are allowed to join as full Members … without any training whatsoever for their profession' (views of William Tapp, a member of the Exchange, in 1938, cited by Kynaston, 1999, page 296).
3 Spafford, 1921, page 59 et seq.
4 Admiral Line was one of the first to be equipped with Leyland Motors' new six-wheeled buses which could carry more passengers with a minimal increase in cost per mile.
5 Private office notes dated 26 June, 22 and 23 November, 6 December 1928 (M. Samuel & Company records, LBA files S/1/1/b/60 and 61).
6 Private office notes dated 4, 7 and 8 January 1929 (M. Samuel & Company records, LBA file S/1/1/b/70).
7 The meeting was not attended by Lord Bearsted but by four other directors of the bank including Colonel Abel Smith and C.B. Leatham who took a leading role throughout the negotiations (private note dated 8 April 1929, M. Samuel & Company records, LBA file S/1/1/b/74).
8 'Every man's word is his bond'. See a comparison of City practice with New York practice in this respect in Beddington-Behrens, 1963, pages 140–141.
9 It was indeed in the bank's mind as evidenced by an exchange between Frederick Szarvasy, Colonel Abel Smith and C.B. Leatham (private office note dated 22 May 1929, M. Samuel & Company records, LBA file S/1/1/b/76).
10 This interpretation was correct. A few days later, Bearsted visited Montagu Norman, the governor of the Bank of England, and told him that he 'entirely

mistrusts' Hatry (entry for 18 June 1929 in Montagu Norman's diary, Bank of England archive).

11 Assertion by Sir Arthur Du Cros at a meeting with M. Samuel & Company (private office note dated 15 August 1929, M. Samuel & Company records, LBA file S/1/1/b/78).

12 See comment under the headline 'The Bogus Tycoon' (*Sunday Times*, 17 October 1965, page 29).

13 Michael Pearson was one of those who did (*Sunday Telegraph*, 1 August 1965, page 4; 8 August 1965, page 4).

14 Anonymous, 1938.

15 Trial transcript, day 5 (TNA file DPP 1/91).

16 Michael Pearson (1961) wrote a book entitled *The Millionaire Mentality* featuring descriptions of a number of millionaires including Hatry. He claimed that his description of Hatry was based on a series of long interviews in which Hatry had described the main turning points of his career.

17 *Sunday Telegraph*, 1 August 1965, page 4; 8 August 1965, page 4.

18 *Sunday Times*, 3 October 1965, page 31.

19 *Sunday Times*, 17 October 1965, page 29.

20 Greenfield, 1995, page 72.

References

Primary works: unpublished documents

Bank of England: Montagu Norman's diary.

TNA: DPP papers.

Primary works: newspapers and periodicals

Sunday Telegraph.

Sunday Times.

Primary works: contemporary books and papers

Anonymous. (1938), *The Hatry Case: Eight Current Misconceptions*. (Privately published, London).

Spafford, C.H. (1921), *The Law of Misrepresentation in Prospectus*. (Butterworth, London).

Secondary works

Beddington-Behrens, E. (1963), *Look Back, Look Forward*. (Macmillan, London).

Greenfield, G. (1995), *A Smattering of Monsters: A Kind of Memoir*. (Little Brown, London).

Kynaston, D. (1999), *The City of London: Volume III: Illusions of Gold 1914–1945*. (Chatto & Windus, London).

Michie, R.C. (1987), *The London and New York Stock Exchanges 1850–1914*. (Allen & Unwin, London).

Michie, R.C. (1999), *The London Stock Exchange: A History*. (Oxford University Press, Oxford).

Pearson, M. (1961), *The Millionaire Mentality*. (Secker & Warburg, London).

Index